Praise for *Butterfly in the Typewriter*

"[A] highly readable biography. . . . It does an impressive job filling in the gaps and helping readers better understand this complex writer."

—*BookPage*

"Along with its portrait of a complicated, conflicted, and flawed young writer, *Butterfly in the Typewriter* provides a comprehensive look at Toole's childhood, college years, his army posting in Puerto Rico, and his lifelong love affair with New Orleans." —*Atlanta Journal Constitution*

"A complete telling of the sad but triumphant story. . . . The life that unfolds here is full of contrasts: laughter and pain, popularity and isolation, failure and success." —*San Diego Union Tribune*

"It's an exhaustively researched chronicle of the remarkable life of John Kennedy Toole. . . . MacLauchlin's story . . . is heartbreaking. . . . I implore you to read the novel and *Butterfly in the Typewriter* now, to meet the man and Ignatius yourself before it's too late." —*VanityFair.com*

"[An] exhaustive biography. . . . Required reading for anyone interested in this enigmatic literary figure; indeed, in Southern literature in general."

—*Washington Times*

"For anybody who has faced rejection (and who hasn't?), this book contains a lifetime worth of wisdom." —*Cleveland Plain Dealer*

"This is a sad story well-told." —*Buffalo News*

"*Butterfly in the Typewriter* is as close to unraveling the enigma of the often-mysterious John Kennedy Toole as we are ever likely to read, and his story makes for an engrossing read." —*New City*

"A fascinating account of Toole's short, intense life. . . . For anyone carrying more than a passing interest in *A Confederacy of Dunces*, this bio is, of course, a must-read." —*Shepherd Express*

"MacLauchlin has created a book that is literary, erudite, and accessible all at the same time. He has married scholarship with storytelling, which is not an easy feat." —*Deep South Magazine*

"MacLauchlin does this tragic story justice, producing a gripping biography worth reading." —*The Advocate*

"[MacLauchlin] cleanly lays out the brief life of his subject and his work's unlikely afterlife. . . . A valuable biography." —*Kirkus Reviews*

"[A] thoughtful and thorough biography. . . . MacLauchlin does an admirable job distinguishing facts from speculation." —*Publishers Weekly*

Butterfly in the Typewriter

The Tragic Life of John Kennedy Toole and the Remarkable Story of *A Confederacy of Dunces*

Cory MacLauchlin

DA CAPO PRESS
A Member of the Perseus Books Group

For information, address Da Capo Press, 44 Farnsworth Street,
3rd Floor, Boston, MA 02210.
Editorial production by Lori Hobkirk at the Book Factory.
Designed in Garamond by Cynthia Young at Sagecraft.

Library of Congress Cataloging-in-Publication Data

MacLauchlin, Cory.
Butterfly in the typewriter : the tragic life of John Kennedy Toole and the
remarkable story of A confederacy of dunces / Cory MacLauchlin.
p. cm.
ISBN 978-0-306-82040-3 (hardcover)—ISBN 978-0-306-82104-2 (e-book)
1. Toole, John Kennedy, 1937–1969. Confederacy of dunces.
2. Novelists, American—20th century—Biography. I. Title.
PS3570.O54C666 2012
813'.54—dc23
2012000259

ISBN 978-0-306-82191-2 (paperback)

First Da Capo Press edition 2012
First Da Capo Press paperback edition 2013

Published by Da Capo Press
A Member of the Perseus Books Group
www.dacapopress.com

Da Capo Press books are available at special discounts for bulk purchases
in the U.S. by corporations, institutions, and other organizations. For more
information, please contact the Special Markets Department at the Perseus
Books Group, 2300 Chestnut Street, Suite 200, Philadelphia, PA 19103, or call
(800) 810-4145, ext. 5000, or e-mail special.markets@perseusbooks.com.

For Danievie, Elliott, and Liam

The book sold well, we understand,
Although the cover itself would command
A buyer's attention: a large, abstract bee
Crushing a butterfly with a typewriter key.

—John Kennedy Toole, from
"The Arbiter" (unpublished)

Contents

Contents

Introduction

The life and death of John Kennedy Toole is one of the most compelling stories of American literary biography. After writing *A Confederacy of Dunces*, Toole corresponded with Robert Gottlieb of Simon and Schuster for two years, exchanging edits and commentary. Unable to gain Gottlieb's approval, Toole gave up on the novel, determining it a failure. Years later, he suffered a mental breakdown, took a two-month journey across the United States, and finally committed suicide on an inconspicuous road outside Biloxi, Mississippi. Years later, his mother found his manuscript in a shoebox and submitted it to various publishers. After many rejections, she cornered author Walker Percy, who found it a brilliant novel and facilitated its publication. It became an immediate sensation, winning the Pulitzer Prize in 1981, twelve years after Toole's death.

Since then, *A Confederacy of Dunces* has been hailed as the quintessential New Orleans novel. As many New Orleanians attest, no other writer has captured the essence of the city more accurately than Toole. And to this day the city celebrates its honored author. A statue of the protagonist, Ignatius Reilly, stands outside the old D. H. Holmes Department Store. Characters from the book make Mardi Gras appearances. And any reader of the novel who visits the French Quarter will certainly smile at the ubiquitous sight of a Lucky Dog cart.

But the novel exceeds the confines of regionalism. While Toole roots the characters and the plot in New Orleans, his narrative approach reflects influences from British novelists Evelyn Waugh, Kingsley Amis, and Charles Dickens. Within American literature Toole is closer to Joseph Heller and Bruce Jay Friedman than he is to iconic Southern writers Flannery O'Connor and William Faulkner. In the scope of Southern literature, *Confederacy* seems an aberration. But within the scope of the modern novel, it is at home in its dark humor and acerbic wit.

Its continued success offers the most powerful testimony to its ability to reach past the bounds of that swath of land between Lake Pontchartrain and the Mississippi River. To this day, it continues to garner readers. It has been translated into more than twenty-two languages and remains in print all over the world. Teachers and professors use the novel in their classes, from high school lessons on satire to graduate courses in creative writing. Plans for a film version of the book have been in development since its publication. And it recurrently appears on the "best of" lists periodically published in popular media. Notably, author Anthony Burgess places *A Confederacy of Dunces* alongside *For Whom the Bell Tolls* and *The Catcher in the Rye* in his *New York Times* article "Modern Novels; the 99 Best." Clearly, *A Confederacy of Dunces* is more than a humorous romp through a Southern city; it is a classic of modern literature.

And its place is rightly earned. In the foreword to the novel, Walker Percy describes it as a compilation of Western thought and culture, from Thomas Aquinas to Don Quixote to Oliver Hardy. He considers the menagerie of characters a crowning achievement. And he recognizes it as a comedy that exceeds mere humor and ascends to the highest form of *commedia*. But as Percy celebrates the great accomplishments of the novel, he grapples with the detectable sadness in the book, one that is rooted in the biography of Toole. Percy writes, "The tragedy of the book is the tragedy of the author—his suicide in 1969 at the age of thirty two." Henceforth, readers of *Confederacy* have negotiated this intriguing paradox of the tragicomedy; the reader's laughter is never far from the tinge of sadness in remembering Toole's tragic end. More so than most novels, *A Confederacy of Dunces* prompts the reader to ponder the life and death of the author. And while his suicide is well known, his personality, his struggles, and his triumphs, in essence, his life has hitherto remained an obscure entry within the collection of biographies of twentieth-century novelists.

Some critics may defend Toole's marginal place within the canon of American literature. Having only one novel of merit, he is easily dismissible as a one hit wonder. While talented, he does not provide scholars with a breadth of novels to dissect. But such criticism has rarely quelled biographical interest in Harper Lee, Emily Brontë, or Margaret Mitchell. And if we base our measure on quality, then the prolific writer has no more value within the literary canon than the individual who composes a single masterpiece.

In fact, interest in Toole has never waned since the publication of *Confederacy*. As early as 1981, writers and scholars recognized the remarkable story of his life and its place within literary history. Until her death in 1984, Toole's mother, Thelma Toole, received many requests of permission to write a biography of her son, and she patently declined them. But in her reply to the request of James Allsup, an acquaintance of Toole from his army days in Puerto Rico who had since become a professor of English, Thelma outlined the essential rigors required of any Toole biographer:

> Dear Mr. Allsup:
>
> Your qualifications to write a biography of my son are excellent, but, if I granted your request this is what it would imply: you would have to live in my home for several months, perhaps, a year, perhaps, more; then, you would have to read carefully a wealth of material, pertaining to my son; then, you and I would decide what to use, what not to use; then, we would begin collaboration.

After listing these stipulations, she politely declined his request.

To any established professor, Thelma's hypothetical expectations would be absurd. But she accurately portrays the difficult grounds a Toole biographer must navigate. Even for his mother, who usually appeared quite omniscient in regard to her son, composing the narrative of Toole's life was a daunting task. She attempted on one occasion but got no further than a few pages.

Such challenges became painfully evident in the first biography of Toole, *Ignatius Rising: The Life of John Kennedy Toole*, written by René Pol Nevils and Deborah George Hardy. While Nevils and Hardy provide readers with an unprecedented resource in that they published the correspondence between Gottlieb and Toole, albeit without Gottlieb's permission, they also depict Toole as a man suffering from an Oedipal complex, suppressed homosexuality, alcoholism, madness, and an appetite for promiscuity. Toole becomes a caricature of the fatal artist. While some reviewers forgave Nevils and Hardy for their indiscretion, many friends of Toole found the book insidious. Toole's friend Joel Fletcher angrily observed, "The authors have so carelessly written half-truths and untruths about a friend who is not here to defend himself."

Troubled by the sensationalism in *Ignatius Rising*, Fletcher authored *Ken and Thelma*, in which he offered a balanced biographical sketch of Toole, grounded in interviews and his own memories. But as Fletcher admits, his book "is a memoir, not a biography." In *Ken and Thelma*, Fletcher writes, "A good biography of Toole is yet to be written. I hope that a future biographer of Toole will find this account a useful and accurate document." Indeed, he has offered the most credible work on Toole to date, and he has given me indispensible guidance for this book.

In my pursuit to understand Toole, I neither aimed to diagnose him, nor cast him in the mold of the tortured artist. In reading his letters, his unpublished poems and stories, and the same novels on his bookshelf at the time of his death, in interviewing his friends, family, and acquaintances, I have sought to understand Toole on his own terms. I have sought to compose a biographical narrative in which Toole would recognize himself if he were alive to read it.

Through this exploration, one sees Toole in his complexity. At times, the abnormal circumstances of his rearing and his social marginalization elicit sympathy. At other times, his sense of superiority and his curt comments make him deplorable. And yet, his friends, even those he offended, clearly enjoyed his stories and his wit. All the while, he struggled to define himself as either a scholar or a fiction writer, as either a son bound by filial duty or an independent man. In the end, his life exhibits a single case of a man full of humor and laughter, who strived for greatness but could not find a way to cope with his demons.

Of course, despite my best efforts, his mother, Thelma, will always be the primary hand that has shaped the way we understand his life. It was at her choosing which documents survived and which ones were discarded. While she saved miscellanea from his school days—blue books and math homework—she destroyed his suicide note. In interviews, she offered a nostalgic vision of her son, an emphatic, one-dimensional portrayal of her unrecognized genius, from birth to death. But she rarely discussed his mental illness. While she proclaims his mind a "Mt. Parnassus," she withholds insight into the earthquake that reduced him to rubble.

Avoiding such discomfiting moments in the life of her son, Thelma preferred to recall the moments she idealized, usually moments from his childhood. Reminiscing over the hours she spent gazing at her baby, she said, "Those eyes. Those magnificent eyes. Not only beautiful, but luminant. A light in them." Of course, there was no way for his mother to foresee the tragic end thirty-one years later. There was no way for her to foresee her grown son sitting in that car on a country road outside Biloxi, a garden hose channeling exhaust fumes into the cabin, extinguishing the light from his eyes.

But what mother, holding her newborn child, could imagine such horror at a time of such bliss? No, the shadow of his suicide did not loom over him as he slept in his cradle, as he swam with friends in the pool at Audubon Park, as he ventured to New York to attend Columbia University, as he taught English to Puerto Rican recruits, or as he composed his literary masterpiece. Only in retrospect does his suicide become the dark backdrop to his brilliance. In his lifetime he touched the lives of his family, his friends, and his students with his tenderness and humor. And through his singular novel he continues to touch the lives of readers all over the world with his ability to illustrate the most ridiculous, yet oddly realistic characteristics of humanity. And so, while his demise came at his own hand, his life story deserves the understanding and the celebration that we offer any writer who has left an enduring contribution to our world.

Chapter 1

Roots

O n a Sunday afternoon in 1963 in a small barracks room at Fort Buchanan, Puerto Rico, Sergeant John Kennedy Toole rested his fingers on the keyboard of a borrowed typewriter and stared into the emptiness of a blank page. For years he had dreamt of becoming a writer, but his attempts were fraught with disappointment. The novel he wrote at sixteen failed to win a writing contest and now sat in a box under his bed in New Orleans collecting dust. He deemed the poems and short stories he wrote in graduate school unworthy. And his summer before boot camp, which he dedicated to writing, yielded nothing substantial. Still, dozens, maybe hundreds of colorful characters populated his imagination, all developed from his observations of people. Weaving these characters into a narrative proved the great challenge.

So, once again, he approached the defining line where his story would either take flight or crash into obscurity. But this time his circumstances were different. His station in Puerto Rico offered him relief from the financial and familial pressures of his civilian life. And living one thousand miles away from home, he could ponder the unique ways of his city, New Orleans. Distanced and unburdened, Toole seized the moment. He recalled a character he had been developing for years, a behemoth of contradictions, a mustached man of refined intellect and grotesque manners, a highbrow buffoon with mismatched eyes, offering the perfect distorted lens through which to examine his city.

He broke the silence of the room with the first few keystrokes, sending forth the fat medievalist Ignatius Reilly into the carnival of New

1

Orleans life. The language started to pour out. Pent up energies of a decade flowed, filling page after page as he conjured the characters of his past and spun a tale of absurdity and hilarity. And over the next few months, a thrilling sense emerged in him that he was writing something readable, something publishable. His future success, the rave reviews, the devoted readers, the accolades and awards that would come, were entirely unknown to him. Nonetheless, as he cranked away at the typewriter in his small private room, as that fluttering music of the novelist danced out of the open windows, borne aloft in the Caribbean breeze, he ascended to his pinnacle moment. He crafted his masterpiece, *A Confederacy of Dunces*. And all the while he dreamt of his beloved New Orleans, that ark of culture, clinging to the banks of the Mississippi River. "The Paris of the South," "the birthplace of jazz," and "America's most interesting city," his hometown moved to its own rhythm, beckoning all the varieties and colors of humanity into the streets, where together they stirred the traditions of Europe, the Caribbean, Africa, and America, to create sounds and flavors all their own, making a world unto itself.

It is from this cultural complexity that the life and artistic vision of John Kennedy Toole came into being. As his friend Joel Fletcher once observed, Toole "was indigenous New Orleans. It was part of the fabric of who he was." Indeed, Toole spent much of his life discerning the unique people of his city, from flamboyant French Quarter drifters to elderly downtown women who yacked away over department store counters. He developed a sensitive ear and a sharp eye for the subtle quirks in a personality, even in a city brimming with eccentrics. But the foundations of his uncanny insights into a place that has fascinated and eluded writers for centuries actually began long before his birth. For New Orleans was far more than the place where he had grown up. He was a native son of the city, hailing from the European lines that merged in the expanding neighborhoods of the antebellum metropolis. His ancestors came from France, Spain, and Ireland, and all became New Orleanians, planting family roots in the wet soil of southern Louisiana.

Toole's earliest ancestor to the New World was his mother's great-grandfather, Jean François Ducoing, who came to the city from France near the turn of the nineteenth century. Ducoing gained local fame after "skillfully [handling] the solitary mortar" under the command of

Andrew Jackson at the Battle of New Orleans. Toole's mother proudly documented this deed in a baby book she kept for her son, but she seemed to overlook other historical accounts. For example, Ducoing was an associate of the legendary pirate Jean Lafitte. Both a romanticized outlaw and a fellow hero at the Battle of New Orleans, Lafitte led a gang of Baratarians who smuggled slaves and other goods taken from Spanish ships that eventually ended up in the markets of New Orleans. Toole's honored ancestor had some involvement in such exploits, ranging from insurance fraud of a marine vessel to the founding of Lafitte's sham government in Galveston. But such intrigue was not lost on Toole. Perhaps stretching the truth of his lineage, he once declared to one of his friends that he was not only the descendent of the celebrated Jean Ducoing, but he was also related to the famed corsair Jean Lafitte.

In addition to his French ancestor, Toole's grandmother on his father's side, Mary Orfila, was the daughter of a Spanish commission merchant, who came to New Orleans in the mid-nineteenth century. And thus Toole had the two primary pillars of New Orleans European heritage: the French, who founded the city in 1718, and the Spanish, who governed it over forty years. Their descendants were dignified by the classification of "Creole" and traditionally honored as "pure" New Orleanians.

But Toole's privileged ancestry was tempered by the earthy influx of the Irish. Both his mother and his father had ancestors from Ireland that had come to New Orleans during the potato famine of the mid-nineteenth century. Initially seen as a source of cheap labor, many Irish immigrants ended up digging canals waist deep in the swamps behind the city, a job determined too hazardous for valuable slaves. The Irish settled south of the old city, along the Mississippi River in an area that became known as the Irish Channel. Surviving great hardships, they eventually thrived, and they made a lasting impact on the unique downtown accent called Yat, which is resonant of dialects heard in the boroughs of New York City.

Toole's mixed lineage tells part of the story of New Orleans—how it grew by waves of immigration and how ethnicities established their own neighborhoods in which they kept their traditions alive. In this way New Orleans mirrors some of the great port cities of Baltimore, New York, and Boston. But eventually, as families merged and moved, ethnic lines blurred. While his mother's side proudly carried the Creole heritage of the French name Ducoing and his father's side carried the Irish name Toole, in the late 1800s the Ducoings and the Tooles ended up neighbors in an area of the city called the Faubourg Marigny, just outside the old city. The fact that a Creole and the son of an Irish immigrant were neighbors, signifies, on one hand, the decline of the Creole stature in the economy of New Orleans, but on the other hand speaks to the ability of the working class to carve a respectable place for themselves in the city, despite the old social order. And each of these families had a child born to them near the turn of the century: the Toole boy and the Ducoing girl grew up one block away from each other on Elysian Fields Avenue, the same "raffish" street that Tennessee Williams set his ill-fated romance *A Streetcar Named Desire*.

Toole's mother, Thelma Agnes Ducoing, was born in 1901. From her earliest days she aspired to theatrical stardom through acting, dancing, and singing. Later in life, she proudly boasted her early entrance into performance art. "I began my stage training at the age of three," she would say, rolling her R's with all the flourish of a Shakespearean actor. A proud Creole, her father instilled in her an appreciation of the arts and "culture," which she passed on to her son. Unfortunately, her father also had a proclivity for other women. As an unremitting adulterer throughout Thelma's childhood, he came and went as he pleased. Only later in life did it strike Thelma as odd that he would openly take another woman on a leisure trip to Cuba, leaving his wife and family behind. He was the first of many men that disappointed Thelma. But such pain caused by her father likely fueled her fiery spirit. In 1920 she graduated from The Normal School of New Orleans with a certificate to teach kindergarten. And in that same year she earned a degree from the Southern College of Music. For a time she entertained dreams of going to New York City, but she could never abandon the place for which her ancestor, Jean François, fought to protect. She decided to stay in her hometown and teach music and theater at the public schools.

As she began her career as a teacher, she started her courtship with John Dewey Toole Jr., a man vastly different from her father. Quiet and subdued, his focus and his talents must have signaled to her a promising future. She remembered him in his early days as, "A handsome man . . . with legal ability, oratorical ability, and mathematical ability."

Born in 1899, John Toole Jr. was always a bright student. When he was eight years old his father died, bringing great hardship to the family, but John maintained his dedication to academics with the encouragement of his older brother. At the newly opened Warren Easton High School on Canal Street he earned top grades, showing strength in mathematics. In 1917 he took first honor in a debate contest and was awarded a full scholarship to Louisiana State University. But he turned it down, deciding to stay in New Orleans. He served in the army at the end of World War I, although he never left the country. And while he attended a few courses at Tulane University—one final attempt at higher education—in 1919 he settled into a job managing a parts department at a car dealership. Holding a position of "great responsibility" and a "high salary," he began courting his outgoing young neighbor Thelma Agnes Ducoing.

Although John and Thelma were gainfully employed, they never fulfilled the aspirations of their youth. He never achieved a college degree, and she never stood in the limelight of a Broadway show. But they were both in their mid-twenties, nearing the age when marital prospects would become limited. So with their grandest dreams deferred, the would-be scholar and the would-be actress wedded on December 29, 1926, at Saint Peter and Paul Church around the corner from their homes. They began their life as husband and wife at the height of the Roaring Twenties. They moved to a house on Bayou St. John, next to the expansive City Park, where they enjoyed throwing parties and entertaining guests.

Thelma fondly remembered those early days, but she never forgot how she suffered the sexist policies of the time. The New Orleans public schools would not allow a married woman to hold a full-time position. Forced to give up her job as a teacher, but never content to be a homemaker, she continued to teach as a self-employed instructor, director, and piano player, offering lessons in music, charm, and elocution. Around the time they were married, John left his managerial position in the parts department to sell Oldsmobiles and Cadillacs. It must have been a potentially lucrative prospect in 1926. They moved to the edge of the affluent Uptown neighborhood for a time, just a few blocks from Tulane University. The Great Depression sparked by the economic crash of 1929 hit John and Thelma hard, since John's salary was dependent on commission. John lost his job; they lost their furniture, and they lost their home. In 1932, much to Thelma's disappointment, they were forced to move back to the Marigny and live with John's mother.

With the honeymoon glow of their nuptials having long extinguished, the couple found themselves in the same neighborhood in which they started. Six years passed as the old Marigny fell into further disrepair, like many areas of the city. John and Thelma crept into their thirties, and it appeared Thelma was unable to conceive. They had spent a decade together in a childless marriage, each year their happier days receding further into the shadow of memory.

But in 1937 the Fates spun an unexpected thread. As their son would later tell his friends, one day at a party, which is never without libations in New Orleans, Thelma Toole tripped on some steps and tumbled to the ground. The fall must have jostled her insides enough to remove whatever stood in the way of her and motherhood, because shortly thereafter, she got pregnant. And her son, telling the story of his mother's fortunate fall, seemed to relish the accidental nature of his origin.

As was expected, the pregnancy changed everything. John secured a new salesman job at Ponchartrain Motors in the Central Business District. Car sales increased as the country emerged from the Great Depression. And the Tooles moved to a house in the heart of Uptown, an ideal place to raise children in New Orleans. It was home to palatial suburban estates along St. Charles Avenue, two private universities, two all-girl colleges, the best primary and secondary schools in the city, a lush park that spanned 190 acres, including fountains, palm tree–lined promenades, and a zoo—all shaded from the hot Louisiana sun under vast canopies of evergreen, live oaks. It is no wonder that the Tooles, once established in Uptown, remained so dedicated to staying in that neighborhood, even when they could barely afford it.

With all the preparations for a new baby in place, the Christmas season began, heightening their anticipation. And on Friday, December 17, 1937, at Touro Infirmary in the Garden District of New Orleans, John and Thelma welcomed their one and only child into this world, giving him the first name of John, and the name of Thelma's grandmother, Kennedy, as his middle name. For short, they would call him Kenny.

After the successful delivery, John Toole handed the attending physician a five-dollar tip. Remembering the awkward transaction between her husband and the doctor, Thelma would sneer, "He didn't even give me a bottle of perfume." Even the tender moments after the birth of their son could not soften some of the bitterness that had developed between John and Thelma over the years. But nonetheless, they cooed and awed over their little Kenny who had, as Thelma recalled, the most enchanting eyes.

And outside the hospital walls, the old Crescent City carried on its weekend merriment under a full moon of a clear, cool night. Like any Friday night in New Orleans, people wandered the streets and alleyways of the French Quarter. Brassy songs of jazz played everywhere from the "Negro night clubs" to the Blue Room at the upscale Roosevelt Hotel. Patrons dined on oysters Rockefeller at Antoine's, while on the streets laborers devoured oyster po'boys. And in view of Jackson Square and the Saint Louis Cathedral, French Market vendors prepared for the late-night revelers and the early risers, both craving *café au lait* and hot beignets. New Orleans was alive with the celebration of music and food. And our artist, John Kennedy Toole, newly born and cradled in his mother's arms, was heir to it all.

Chapter 2

Early Days in Uptown

Rising out of a strip of land below sea level and positioned between a flood prone river and the second largest estuary in the United States, New Orleans has always been a city of deep contradictions. In 1930 Herbert Hoover visualized a futuristic New Orleans with a soaring skyline, declaring it "a city of Destiny." And he echoed the sentiments of French explorer Sieur de Bienville who tried desperately to make his vision of *Nouvelle Orleans* come true after he founded the settlement in 1718. Surely he had doubts a few years later when the Great Hurricane of 1722 swept the settlement away, although he stubbornly rebuilt it. And Hoover must have also paused before uttering his words so soon after the devastating flood of 1927. Indeed, New Orleans has never done well conforming to an idea or a particular vision. But somehow it lives on as an impossible city, fighting the sinking earth beneath its feet, the waters that want to fill its streets, and the people that have undermined its enterprise from poorly constructed levees to corruption at every level, from mob bosses to mayors.

And Toole was born at a time when New Orleans was making great strides in its efforts to reinvent itself. Neither Hoover nor Bienville would have anticipated that this city of destiny would bet its economic future on a reflection of its past. While cities across the country strived to present the newest and most modern innovations, New Orleans went the opposite direction. Prominent businessmen harnessed the city's unique cultural heritage, repackaged it for tourists, and marketed it throughout the country. By 1938 Mardi Gras had expanded from a local celebration of social elites to "a national holiday celebrated in the unique city of New Orleans." The rundown French Quarter or *Vieux Carré*, once considered a blight on the city, was well on its way toward revitalization through preservation and restoration of its European charm. Strip clubs began setting up on Bourbon Street, echoing the indulgent past of the famous red light district, Storyville. And in February 1938, New Orleans celebrated, with great fanfare, the release of *The Buccaneer*, Cecil B. DeMille's film based on Jean Lafitte and the Battle of New Orleans. A year later, the battlefield where Toole's ancestor had fought so valiantly became a national park. With a gilded mirror positioned toward the city's past, and its deep-seeded sense of isolation, New Orleans began its love affair with itself.

But the visitor beheld only an intended version of the city. A tourist in the late 1930s was presented a kaleidoscopic parade of decadent fare and subservient African Americans, a mask that glossed over the city's intricate texture. The New Orleanians of Toole's generation grew up with a unique awareness of the many layers of the city, an awareness that the true city lies underneath the surface where one finds a complex patchwork, a city of cultural divisions carved out of the various neighborhoods, distinguished through accent, mannerisms, and worldviews. Bobby Byrne, a friend of Toole's, described the genesis of modern New Orleans as "a whole set of little places that eventually coalesced. And you have different attitudes" in each of these places. Of course, only the native would be sensitive to the characteristic differences.

So while John and Thelma had come from the Faubourg Marigny to settle in Uptown, from the Uptown perspective they would always be "downtown people." And downtown people, Bobby Byrne explained, are "all a little mad . . . some of them are really downtown mad . . . intensely private and intensely nosey." Thelma would, of course, contest. She always maintained that while she grew up among the "hot-blooded Italians" and "lowlifes" she never mingled with them. Citing her father's position as a clerk of court, she distinguished her family with its proud cultural heritage. While she observed and impersonated the "dagos yelling at each other" in their raspy voices, she always considered herself superior to them. "We had wicker rockers . . . two pianos in the house . . . and we always had maids!" she declared. According to Byrne, no matter how cultured or dignified she presented herself, the mores of

New Orleans took precedence. At least her son would have all the benefits of high society, and she would share with him the stories of the characters of the old neighborhood. Indeed, Kenny's upbringing in Uptown sophistication with the inescapable dose of "downtown madness" likely propelled him to seek out the unique neighborhoods, looking to observe and understand New Orleanians. He would discover his city behind the mask, delving into all its complexity by way of observing its people. And while he would roam about the town and eventually throughout the country, Uptown was always his home.

So in the final days of 1937, John and Thelma brought their precious Kenny home. They enjoyed the wonderment of their newborn child in their house at 1128 Webster Street next to Audubon Park. They celebrated a memorable first Christmas, with a huge tree and newly purchased European ornaments. A few weeks later he was baptized in the Catholic Church at Loyola University. In the late spring of 1938, the extended Toole family spent an afternoon together at the park. There his father, aged but proud, held his smiling Kenny boy high in the air, up to the sun. It appears the child had entered into a warm family embrace.

But neither the new home nor the joyful celebrations could merge the rift that had formed between John and Thelma. For reasons unclear, she took issue with the entire Toole family. Publicly, she never questioned the talents of her husband, claiming him the best of the Tooles, but privately she judged that he had never lived up to his potential. "He could have been a professor," she remarked. And his decision to leave his steady job of managing a parts department in order to sell automobiles, shortly after they were married, always bewildered her. While he enjoyed some loyal clients at the car dealership, Thelma lamented that he was a fool with money, always claiming herself the main breadwinner in the home. But where Thelma saw foolishness, other people saw integrity. At times, John worked against his own interests as a salesman to follow his moral compass. Before selling an automobile to a walk-in customer, he would often make sure the person could afford it. If a family came into the dealership, and he noticed the children's shoes were worn through, he would dissuade the head of the family from purchasing the vehicle, suggesting they wait a few months to get the new model.

His nephew, Harold Toole Jr., fondly recollects the success of his uncle. From what he saw, John Toole provided well for his family. Harold recalls,

> He was the top salesman at the only top-end car dealership in New Orleans and the surrounding area at the time. . . . His entire clientele were the who's who of the then "upper crust" of New Orleans society.

According to Harold, John's clients simply requested a car. Knowing his clients' tastes, John "would choose the style, color, motor, and accessories." The car was delivered, and with no discussion of price, the client paid for the vehicle and usually offered John "a very handsome tip."

Thelma recalled different anecdotes of his salesmanship. While he certainly had high-end clients, he was not the shrewdest of businessmen. Perhaps eager for one of those generous tips, on one occasion he took out a personal loan of three hundred dollars to cover the initial down payment on a car for a judge. Days later, Thelma had to go retrieve the money from the judge. To put himself at such financial risk for an affluent client while Thelma raced around town teaching music lessons and tracking down loan obligations, struck her as thoughtless. Of course, her issues with John in regards to money or his career choices may have been indicators of deeper marital problems. In a heated moment at the end of her life, she claimed her husband "never honorably supported his multitalented wife and multitalented son."

Fortunately for John, children often remain blissfully unaware of the ways of work and money. Regardless of the ebb and flow of his income, John and his son shared a mutual interest in automobiles. From an early age, Toole became infatuated with these works of industrial art—an appreciation that lasted his entire life. Before he was two, he was propped in the driver's seat of the family car for a picture. His hands on the wheel, he turned his head toward the camera, ready to hit the road. On his first trip out of New Orleans, he accompanied his father to Lansing, Michigan, the home of the Oldsmobile factory. At the age of two years, he could identify different makes of motorcars as they drove by: "Cadillac, Oldsmobile, Packard, La Salle, Ford, Chevrolet, Dodge, Plymouth, Studebaker, Buick, Pontiac"—he could name them all. And when he was only five years old, in either an over-eager or oddly oblivious moment, John allowed him to drive around the block in the family car. When Thelma spotted her angel rounding the corner, his eyes just above the steering wheel, peering out of the windshield, she was furious. But her reprimands did not quell the shared love of automobiles between father and son.

And, yet, aside from their interest in cars, John and his Kenny boy never seemed to form a close bond. "Thelma wouldn't allow it," claimed Harold. But Thelma once cryptically mused in an interview, John "had other interests." For the formative years of Toole's life, his father often sought escape away from the home. And while Toole never lost his affection for automobiles, perhaps an aspect of his father he could appreciate, in his early years his mother was his guide and his mentor.

Thelma cherished her son. After his birth she decided to work only three days a week in order to spend as much time as possible with him. On the days she worked, a nanny named Beulah Mathews would look after the young boy, until Thelma, eagerly returning home from work, arrived at the door. On her days off, Thelma and Kenny would spend hours strolling through Audubon Park. She was the only white woman, as she recalled, pushing her child in his stroller; the Uptown women, she commented, would never be seen doing the job of a domestic. And, after a full day out at the park, he still pleaded for Thelma to read to him, often staying up until 11 p.m., immersed in a world of stories. He required at least two hours of reading every night. Most nights, Thelma entertained his demands, but when exhausted from miles of walking in the park, she handed the responsibility over to his father. And even as she found many faults in John, she warmly recollected his poor, dramatic interpretation of fictional voices and how patiently he responded to their son's curiosity.

Thelma also exposed Kenny to the cultural riches of their city, the aspects of New Orleans he did not see in Uptown. "What he didn't know about New Orleans," she claimed, "I told him—Santa Battaglia—the brawls and that hot Italian blood. I told him of that colorful neighborhood where I grew up, the magnificence of my culture, which I gave to him." Thelma also exposed him to the refined aspects of New Orleans culture. He attended his first Mardi Gras Ball at the Roosevelt Hotel when he was two years old. He had an annual portrait taken of him in his Mardi Gras costume. And at the age of five when he came home one day from school "humming the first four measures of 'Habanera,'" a song his teacher had played in class, Thelma recognized his "keen ear." She told him the aria was from *Carmen* and a few days later took him to see Bizet's famous opera of Spanish romance at the Municipal Auditorium. From hearing the stories of New Orleanians yelling from the stoops of shotgun homes in the Marigny to attending operas and participating in a royal Mardi Gras court in one of the finest hotels in the South, Toole was introduced to culture as a vast spectrum of class, race, and experience.

He also exhibited a remarkable speed of intellectual development. From an early age, he showed exceptional ability in observation and expression. He once described the voice of a little girl he met at a party as "silver clanging." And one night when his mother shut off the light to his room he commented, "This darkness is darker than garden soil." Such remarks charmed his mother. Entering kindergarten at the age of four, he declared he would please his teacher. And he did so throughout his education.

However, at the end of his first year he had not met the required age of five, so he was not recommended to the first grade. The idea of him repeating kindergarten when he had demonstrated the intellectual ability to progress unsettled Thelma. She appealed to the superintendent, citing her son's talents, and he was finally allowed to continue to the first grade at McDonogh 14 School. After one month, he came home complaining that he "wasn't learning anything." The curriculum was too simplistic for him. So his mother made an appointment with the school psychologist to have him tested.

In preparation for the test, Kenny's father spent hours every day working with him on math. Finally, the day of the test came. He went into a closed room with a psychologist, while Thelma waited outside. She had presumed his strength would be in language arts, but to her surprise he showed exceptional strength in math. And he had scored 133 on the IQ test, with a 160 being the category of genius. But the psychologist, Thelma claimed, said his score "would have been higher" except he became bored with the test and he stopped talking. "I'll tell you why he stopped talking to you," Thelma replied. "He was observing you." His mother often explained how his "great asset" was "studying people and observing everything keenly." The young boy found people far more intriguing than any tests of the intellect. The psychologist recognized him as an unusually bright and perceptive child, although he was not classified as a genius. However, the request for advancement was approved. And at the age of five, when most children are still in kindergarten learning to read and count, Toole entered the second grade.

The accomplishment of skipping two grades so early in his schooling served as proof to Thelma that she had a genius for a son. She certainly deserves credit for nurturing his imagination and intellect. But it seems her son had little choice in being so successful. From the moment he was born, his mother deemed he was destined for greatness. He was "a rarity in the category of newborn," she explained, "because there was an aura of distinction." The nurses at the hospital had never seen a baby with such lively facial expressions, she reported. And Thelma was convinced her child was a natural born leader of sorts: when he cried in the nursery, "everyone cried." In her remembrances of him as a child, his mother always emphasized his maturity. In a keepsake baby book, Thelma chronicled his early years but races past his infancy, seemingly eager to showcase the development of his mind, his awareness, and his wit. He had "the charm of a six-month-old baby" from the day he was born. It seemed to her he was "ready to get going and achieve" from his first moments of life. And when she told him that he was going to go to school at the age of three, the same age at which she started school, he rebelled. "He had the mentality of a six-year-old," she explained. From his intellect to his looks, his mother was convinced he was a prodigy. She even thought he shared a "striking resemblance" to the son of World War II hero General Douglas MacArthur. And, of course, at the heart of Kenny's talents was a devotion to his mother. "I want to please you, Mother," he said to her, frustrated, one day, "but I don't know how."

A nurturing guidance eventually turned to eager encouragement that chased prestige and success. Thelma celebrated how he was "always two years younger than his classmates," and yet they still looked up to him. She emphasized how he could stand in judgment of them. "Those children thought I was Shakespeare," he bragged to her after a class presentation. He often referred to his classmates as "those children" when speaking to his mother. In that phrase she heard his earned sense of superiority. But certainly such posturing would have social consequences as well, even among children. If the young Kenny distinguished himself from his classmates with disdain, one wonders how he would cultivate relationships.

Yet, classmates of Toole do not recall him having a superiority complex. They do remember, however, the immediate attention he gained as a student. Jane Stickney Gwyn, one of Toole's former classmates, recalls how he was "a bright star from the moment he entered McDonogh 14." One day their teacher wrote "arctic" on the board, and each student had to pronounce the word. They all lazily dropped the middle "c," pronouncing it "artic." Only Toole stood up and pronounced it correctly. Of course, having a mother who was an elocutionist gave him an advantage.

Any sense of superiority Toole held above his classmates was tested when he started putting on weight. For a time in his youth, Toole became quite plump, and unfortunately he suffered teasing from other children. He quickly identified his wit as his best defense. As Thelma reported, one day he endured the taunts of one of the sons of the owners of the Leidenheimer baking company, makers of "Zip Bread," a brand widely used for po'boy sandwiches throughout New Orleans. When the Leidenheimer boy called Toole fat, he quickly retorted, "Doesn't your daddy make *Jip* bread?" The response delighted Thelma, although she always maintained he was never chubby; she preferred the term "brawny." Nonetheless, Toole remained self-conscious about his weight his entire life.

In addition to his sharpening wit, he impressed his neighbor and fellow student John Geiser with his intuition. On the first day of school and months thereafter, Geiser walked with Toole the seven blocks to McDonogh 14. One of the lasting memories that Geiser has of Toole is a rather off-handed remark in 1942. The United States had been involved in World War II for almost a year and Roosevelt still gave his fireside chats on the radio, but television was an emerging medium. One day Toole described television to Geiser as "a mixture of movies and radio" and then predicted, "After the war, TV will be as popular as the radio." Considering this prediction became quite true, Geiser remembers it as an astoundingly prescient comment to make at the time. Toole was always sensitive to his surroundings, and it was clear, even to him at five years old, the world was quickly changing.

During his early schooling, the social climate of World War II and the following afterglow of the victory dominated the tenor of the time, especially in New Orleans, which served as a final stop for many servicemen before heading abroad. The war unified the country, and schools made it their responsibility to indoctrinate students with ardent patriotism. As evident in some of Thelma's sheet music titled *Songs for Schools at War*, children sang about the poorest of Americans giving up their "tebacker" and "smelly beer" in order to purchase war bonds. "Uncle Sam sure gets our bet," they sang. The mentality of sacrifice and investment in the war effort proliferated through every aspect of American culture.

And as the war came to an end, Toole grew into his boyhood years and no longer posed doll-like in pictures with Mardi Gras costumes. For a time he enjoyed typical diversions of an American childhood. He swam at Audubon Park, played catch in dusty fields, and tossed a football with friends. Pictures of him around five years old suggest the possibility of a budding athlete. But Thelma maintained that her son never liked sports. "He was an artist," she declared. And she was happy for it because, while she "celebrated champions," she knew nothing about athletics. Besides, she had taken some measures to ensure her son would not fall into the brutish recreation of physical force. His baby book was bound in pink silk, and she had one of his baby pictures colored in hues of pink. And she had nurtured his love for Shakespeare and opera. He was intended to be a sensitive child. And while he showed some artistic talents in sketching, she identified he would be a great performer. Not only were his observations astute, but he proved to be a talented mimic as well. When he came home from school one day and impersonated the "stentorian voice" of the principal lecturing and reprimanding the student body, Thelma saw in her son a natural born actor.

It must have pleased her immensely when in 1948 he joined a youth theater troupe offered through the parks and recreation department. The Traveling Theatre Troupers was a rather large group of children and adolescents that performed plays on stages throughout the town. Thelma eagerly supported her son's interest in acting. When he was cast to play the minor role of a Chinaman cook in a performance of *A Leapyear in Arizona* around Mardi Gras season, Thelma had a Chinaman suit made for him to serve as both his costume for the play and his

Mardi Gras attire. Made of eye-catching lavender sheen, he proudly wore the costume in the production and paraded it through the streets of New Orleans during Carnival. He donned heavy makeup on his face to make his eyebrows look long and dark and his eyes appear almond in shape. When in character, he raised his cheeks, pursed his lips, and squinted his eyes, making all "the farcical expressions of the Asian face." The production took place at an outdoor theater in a park, and Thelma recalled how children playing in the distance looked at her son gesturing at the back of the stage. "Look at the Chinaman!" she heard them exclaim. For a moment, he had stolen the show. He took this character to Charity Hospital to entertain the elderly, a performance that was broadcast on the radio.

Racial stereotypes in performance art were despairingly common in Toole's day, especially in the Jim Crow South. In *Mystery at the Old Fort*, Toole played Dick Bishop, "a boy . . . full of adventure"; and of course there was Chief Charley Horse, "an old Indian," surely played by a white youth. And in a summer production of *Crinoline to Calico*, much of the entirely white cast, along with Toole, performed in blackface. Granted, blackface has an elaborate history in theater performance, especially in New Orleans where the krewe of Zulu, comprised of African American members, satirically parades in blackface every Mardi Gras. The musician Louis Armstrong even appeared as the King of Zulu in 1949. But in Uptown, the young actors were playing the traditional role of minstrelsy, one that would die away with the civil rights movement.

Whether her son gestured as a Chinaman, danced in blackface, or played more conventional roles, Thelma felt that the directors at the Traveling Theatre Troupers underappreciated her son's talents. So in the summer of 1949, when Toole was eleven, she started her own youth theater troupe, the Junior Variety Performers. She put together variety shows of music and dramatic interpretation, as opposed to full plays. Members of the group do not recall feeling Toole was given undue preference. However, in Thelma's own recollection, she intended to place him center stage from the first rehearsal to the last performance. When the troupe was to give a gala at the U.S. Marine Hospital to the theme of "romance in words and music," she searched the library for material, but ultimately decided to write it herself with her son cast as the star:

I composed various lovers for him, very quickly. When he came home . . . I said, "Son, you are going to do this for our gala performance." It was in two weeks. I said, "I am going to read it to you, and tonight you study and give it back to me tomorrow." He could memorize as I could. So he gave it back to me. It was a little better than my rendition. He was the star. It was a beautiful production.

Theater was serious business in the Toole home. Between the ages of eight and twelve, there were many photos of him taken that appear staged, almost professional, as if they might serve as headshots or promotional material to land much larger parts in theater or film. The newspaper featured his photo to promote performances. He appeared on television in a show called *TeleKids*. From September 1948 to May of 1949 he was a guest newscaster on a popular New Orleans radio station. And throughout his days as an actor, the coverage in the local media suggests that he now preferred being called by his full middle name, Kennedy.

As Toole strutted on stage at his mother's prompting, it is easy to cast Thelma as a typical stage mother, but many of her students cherish their memories of the productions they put on. One of her students, who later became an accomplished lawyer and returned to help Thelma with her estate at the end of her life, always attributed his clear speech to her tutelage. She made rehearsals and performances fun for the young actors. She expected much from them, and, in turn, they learned a great deal. In the end she made them feel like stars.

Surely her son enjoyed the theatrical endeavors, as well; he certainly gained many of his talents of expression from her example and direction. But it would only be natural for him to grow tired of memorizing lines, singing, and dancing on cue—especially if it never held the magic it did for Thelma. Jane Stickney Gwyn, the same classmate who recalled Toole's clear pronunciation of "arctic," witnessed this fatigue when she saw Toole every year at Cornelia Sansum's birthday party in her grand home on Constantinople Street. Sansum was an elderly woman with white hair, who always wore white dresses and white gloves. She loved to read the newspaper in her gleaming apparel, but she detested the black print that rubbed off onto her gloves. Gwyn would be dragged to the party to play a sonata on the piano, and Toole would have to recite some poems. Neither Gwyn nor Toole relished performing for the elderly woman, but she always had delicious cookies and punch. And the novelty of an elevator in her house provided a source of infinite amusement to two bored adolescents. After Gwyn and Toole satisfied Sansum and the other guests with their performances, they commiserated, loaded up with *petits fours*, and rode up and down the elevator, getting thrills from occasionally tripping the failsafe mechanism.

Such glimpses of Toole appearing like an average child, eating cookies, playing in an elevator, or being teased on the playground, are rare testimonies from this time period. Much of what is known of him in these early days comes directly from his mother. In her narrative, he appears as a person of perfection. In interviews she focused on stories about his early childhood. And many of her recollections, documented in her early eighties, verge on a hyperbole that can be difficult to believe. One of his grade school teachers supposedly confided in her that her son's "vocabulary is superior to Dickens." Any proud mother deserves the right to sing the praises of her child, but Thelma left a severely limited depiction of her son at a young age. From her memory, it seems as if her genius boy appeared on the earth to begin his brilliant undertakings, suffering the occasional fool who did not recognize his talents. Beneath this veneer was a powerful and complicated dynamic between mother and son. Undeniably, Thelma was his greatest advocate. From his first breath to her last, she believed his brilliance was limitless. But her drive could be relentless, and at times it must have risked overshadowing her son's own desires and interests.

While father and son bonded over automobiles, mother and son came together in performance art. But the years of his impressionable youth were coming to an end. And every parent-child relationship must navigate the inevitable current toward independence, especially during the turbulent teenage years. Near the end of eighth grade, Toole must have lost interest in acting. Thelma cast him in one more show that she directed for the Lakeside School of Speech and Dramatic Art, a school he did not attend. She recalled her son's "resonant, far-projecting voice, dramatic flair, and stage presence brought warm praise from the audience." His adieu came with honorable applause. But his final role as a young actor seems a more fitting end, pointing toward the scholar he would become. In the fall of 1950 he modeled for a public service announcement that urged the public to read and study in well-lit areas. With no costumes, props, or heavy makeup, he sits at a table doing homework under a lamp. Shortly after that appearance was published in the *New Orleans Item*, he quit the stage troupe, and Thelma shifted her classes to focus on elocution.

The glories of theater were the dreams of his mother. And she savored some notoriety from her labors as director. In November of 1948 a review of the Traveling Theatre Troupers, written with flattering enthusiasm, equates the two-hour variety show to "having a front row seat at a Broadway musical." It goes on to state, "The high quality of the entertainment was a tribute to Mrs. Toole's experienced and sustained coaching." There is no doubt her son enjoyed performing, donning characters, and doing impersonations. But the stage was not his forte. Besides, he would find his city so full of interesting people that one did not need the theater to experience rich characters and intriguing plots. His days on the stage would certainly help him in his future literary pursuits. He recognized that the most interesting stories occur through characters and dialogue, not lengthy narration. While he would carry such lessons with him, his entrance into high school was a time to explore his own life goals, to define who he wanted to be, as he narrowed his interests in observation, mimicry, and writing. And once he crossed over that threshold into high school, he asked his friends and family to call him Ken.

Chapter 3

Fortier

D uring the first eight years of Toole's schooling, the country had recovered from the Great Depression and emerged victorious from World War II. The ideology of sacrificing for the war effort subsided. And while the Cold War generated some unnerving fears and men still fought on battlefields in Korea in the early 1950s, the spectre of a world torn asunder by axis powers gave way to a growing desire for all things new. After all, one way to combat communism was to exercise the right to purchase. Families bought suburban homes, seeking some semblance of domestic utopia. These homes away from city centers necessitated new automobiles. As Toole had predicted, televisions became commonplace in the living rooms of the middle class. And New Orleans, now a foremost tourist city, was undergoing a renaissance. Canal Street bustled with shoppers; tourists crowded the streets of the French Quarter; and from the city that once served as the cradle of blues and jazz, the developing genre of rock and roll emanated from dance halls and music studios. An emboldened generation, tapping their feet, softened the social barriers of race as they danced to the supposedly corrupting, yet utterly intoxicating music. It was a great time to be young in New Orleans.

In the fall of 1950 Toole entered Alcée E. Fortier High School, named after the professor and scholar of Creole and Cajun literature. It resembled many of the brick and limestone schools built in the early twentieth century: a three-door entrance with hallways four stories high, forming a U shape—its arms extending to the rear to form a quad in the back. The tall ceilings and draft windows offered the only relief from the sweltering heat. Eventually, in 1969, Fortier would become a microcosm of the challenges facing the integration of whites with African Americans. But the civil rights movement of the 1950s, while gaining momentum in Louisiana, had yet to get its footing in the school systems of New Orleans, such were the rigid segregationist power structures of the city. Fortier was an all-white school, and for the first two years of Toole's attendance it was an all-boys school.

Only twelve years old, Toole looked much younger than his classmates, although he had slimmed down from days at McDonogh 14. And while he must have grown accustomed to the two-year age difference between him and his peers, he now walked the same halls with eighteen-year-old seniors who were nearing college life and adulthood. But whatever social bearing the age difference had on him, it did not impact his academic performance. He breezed through the four years of high school as one of those rare students who needs only to attend class and submit the assignments to achieve high marks. He rarely studied and spent much time reading books of his own interests. So impressed with his son, John Toole once declared, "There is not a classroom into which he would go that he wouldn't excel." Indeed, Toole maintained a high "A" average every quarter, passing all classes with flying colors. But yet, he never reached the top of his class or expressed a desire to prevail in that regard. Without feeling particularly challenged, he contentedly glided through courses with ease. Besides, his head was turning elsewhere. He proved to be a talented mathematician, and he loved books, but human behavior captured his interest above all. As his mother once observed, "The seeing eye and the hearing ear characterized him all his life."

Throughout his high school years, Toole set to observe and mimic the personalities he encountered in New Orleans. He had surely visited relatives living downtown, but he now had the independence and mobility to explore and observe other neighborhoods, often without his mother knowing of his adventures. Piercing through the façade of the city, exploring the intricacy of its culture, he began his ever-expanding catalog of characters. While tourists came to watch Carnival floats pass by at the Mardi Gras parades, Toole came to understand that the spirit of the city lay in a display of unmasked revelers dispersed throughout its many neighborhoods. He was beginning the long process of assembling his own parade. And there was no greater companion in this endeavor than his friend Cary Laird.

Much like Toole, Laird had skipped two grades. In their freshman year they shared a common bond in being the youngest students at Fortier. Both incredibly bright, their names always appeared every quarter in the honor roll column in the school newspaper, *Silver and Blue*. The two friends often competed with each other to get the highest scores on tests. They loved to read, and they both liked opera. But their sophistication was never beyond adolescent infatuations. They were both wild about Marilyn Monroe, although Toole developed a near obsession with her. In 1955 he wrote a letter of praise to the *New York Times* for an article by Bosley Crowther, who described the central tension in Monroe's new film *The Seven Year Itch* as "the primal urge in the male animal," meeting a "voluptuous young lady" for a "summer in the hot city." Any fan of Marilyn Monroe's would find his review titillating, but Toole felt compelled to compliment the author.

While Toole and Laird had much in common, they looked like opposites. Laird was blond, while Toole had dark hair. Laird was Southern Baptist, while Toole was Roman Catholic, although not devout. And while Toole was an only child with aging parents and a household that held itself up to a rigor of formality, Laird had a sister and a devoted mother and father who created a relaxed home life. Despite the differences between the two friends, Laird's sister, Lynda, remembers how their personalities complemented one another. Whenever Toole visited the Laird house, the family rollicked, as the two friends became a comic duo, mimicking everyone from their teachers to Hollywood stars. They would enter into impromptu skits, impersonating their teachers or people they had overheard on the street. And they left everyone in the Laird house in stitches.

One of their favorite duets was Bing Crosby and Louis Armstrong from the 1956 film *High Society*. Without warning, the two friends would break into song, recreating the quick jazzy exchange between the smooth, debonair Crosby and the wide-eyed, smiling Armstrong. In his later years Laird would sometimes do the routine on his own, bouncing back and forth from the velvety baritone of Crosby to the raspy improvisations of Armstrong. And when done, people stood astonished at how he could change his voice and mannerisms so quickly. Laird would often say, "If you think that was good, you should have seen Ken. He was even better."

Of course, living in New Orleans, Toole didn't have to look to the big screen to find great characters. Toole and Laird found a wealth of material in their immediate surroundings, which inspired them to embellish scenes they witnessed for the sake of humor. They talked about their busty Spanish teacher who always sat astutely at her desk. But whenever she opened her desk drawer, her breasts flopped in, making it impossible to close. Unaware of the obstruction, she would slam her breasts in the compartment, and yelp expletives in Spanish. And the Latin teacher seemed to blame all the misfortunes of the world on people who weren't studying Latin. Pretending to be newscasters, Toole and Laird would report a horrible tornado had ripped through Louisiana and killed hundreds of people, or a hurricane had carried away thousands of homes, or a horrific trolley car accident resulted in the deaths of dozens. Whatever the tragedy, the reason was the same: "Well it looks like somebody did not study their Latin."

Outside the bounds of their school, the two friends ventured around New Orleans, absorbing the flavors of the different neighborhoods and creating fictional characters based on their observations. Downtown, there was little Tammie Reynolds whose mother would tell her to play on the sidewalks, what New Orleanians call *banquettes*. "Awww—little Tammie," she would say, "go'on da banket by ya grammaw." From the Irish Channel there was Antoinette, the promiscuous girl who "always wore dangling earrings and smacked gum." She was just crazy about her beefy boyfriend named AJ, who was obviously an Italian because he used his initials as his nickname. And roaming throughout the city, looking for suspicious characters, was Captain Romigary, one of New Orleans finest policemen. He specialized in "hawtatheft."

Toole and Laird went to the French Quarter, downtown, and to the Irish Channel. They even crossed over the race line, at a time when segregation was prevalent. They attended a service at a black Baptist church, participating in the long, lively ceremony of music and dance. And one day they observed a jazz funeral, watching as the brass band, playing dirges, led the deceased to the cemetery while the second line—those following the slow parade—marched sadly behind. As the funeral ended, the brass band erupted in songs of jubilation and the second line of the returning parade danced in the streets, celebrating the life of the deceased.

From a Fortier Latin teacher to Mid-City burial ceremonies, Toole witnessed the wealth of inspiration in his city. And yet he found some of the most memorable personalities during his high school years right next door to the Laird home on General Taylor Street. On the other side of the Laird's rented duplex lived their landlady, a widow by the name of Irene Reilly. Her husband had died in World War II, and she now lived with her boyfriend, her son, and her mother. She worked at the corner market and talked to the neighborhood customers in that New Orleans Yat accent. "Where Ya't, honey?" she would ask a local shopper. "Aw fine. Just makin' some groceries." Her boyfriend held the steady job of a postman, but because Irene collected a government check for her husband's death, the two did not marry. The family was an amicable bunch until, as with many families, they started fighting. A disagreement quickly erupted into screams and bellows, and Irene's elderly mother had some of the foulest language in all of New Orleans. When she slung her colorful rants in her deep New Orleans accent, her words carried throughout the house, resonating through a shared vent and into the bathroom in the Laird household. If Toole happened to be visiting the Lairds, which he often did, and the Reillys got into a fight, he would sit in the bathroom with his ear to the vent, listening and chuckling, as the profanity poured from the old woman's mouth. Years later when he wrote *Confederacy*, Toole took the name Irene Reilly for Ignatius's mother, a woman of unending sympathy for her son. But Toole may have transferred some of the profane spirit of Irene's mother to the character Santa Battaglia, who shockingly exclaims, "Fuck Ignatius!"

Like a sponge, Toole absorbed all the different walks of life, all to be used in his repertoire of impersonations. The Laird family served as an aid and an audience to his impeccable portrayals. From the snobbery of wealth to the down-and-out man peddling wares on French Quarter streets, Toole recognized that his hometown was best understood through its unique people.

And yet as he sought out such colorful personalities throughout his city, he had a prime example of New Orleans eccentricity at home—although, in the case of his parents it seemed far less humorous. Laird

saw firsthand some of the odd ways of John and Thelma during his visits to the Toole house. Thelma made rigorous demands on her son
(Laird was always careful of his pronunciation around her), but her theatrical expressions made her interesting and enjoyable company. However, Toole's father, while always cordial, displayed sure signs of his
developing neuroses, signs that may have gone unnoticed when Toole
was a child but now could no longer be ignored. The same man who
once let his five-year-old son drive a car was now obsessed with safety
and security. He feared intruders could come in the home at any moment, so he installed deadbolt locks on all the internal doors of the
house. Once he felt safe inside, he made himself quite comfortable, preferring to walk about in his jockey shorts. Since Laird was a regular visitor, John made few changes in his attire for him, although it must have
cut a striking difference next to Thelma's formal reception of guests.
One day, as John walked through the house in his underwear, he spotted
a prop sword placed in the umbrella stand by the door—surely one of
Thelma's harmless items used in one of her productions. John identified
it as a deadly weapon that could be turned against the entire family. He
drew out the sword from the umbrella stand and turned toward
Thelma, scolding her for leaving it close to the entryway. "Someone is
going to break in here, find this weapon, and kill us all in our sleep!" he
yelled. Laird barely withheld his laughter as he watched the aged man in
his underwear wielding the sword above his head, chasing his well-
dressed wife about the room, reprimanding her on safety. Looking to
Ken, Laird could tell the scene mortified his friend. It was a moment of
humor and pain, a conflicted experience that must have permeated the
Toole home at times.

Whether or not they acknowledged it, his father was gradually sinking into a debilitating mental illness. For lack of an official diagnosis, his
nephew, Harold Toole, termed it senility. But the initial signs of his neuroses seemed to be exhibited in moments of slight paranoia throughout
the 1950s, although they were far less dramatic than the saber episode.
In addition to John's concerns over home security, he began displaying
extreme caution when selling a car. When Lynda, Laird's sister, went to
John to purchase her first vehicle, she had to meet some of his rigorous
criteria. Even though she had the money to buy the car outright, he
needed to ensure her finances demonstrated she could actually afford

the car. He then required her to drive down St. Charles Avenue, to prove she could handle the car. Once she passed his financial and driving tests, she said she wanted a convertible, and he replied he would sell her a white one only. That way people could easily see her coming down the street. It was the safest option, he explained. So Lynda left with her brand new white Oldsmobile convertible, and shortly thereafter John retired from automobile sales.

Such eccentric behavior eventually turned into more bizarre obsessions with safety and the apparent onset of paranoia. But this was a private matter. Thelma and her son kept John's illness largely a secret as it gradually worsened, perhaps to protect John or perhaps out of shame. And while Toole's father worked throughout the 1950s, Laird witnessed the early stages of the slow deterioration to come. Toole later confided to one of his adult friends that growing up he rarely invited friends over to his house for fear of embarrassment. Clearly, Laird was an exception.

While Toole may have felt bringing guests to the house was too risky, he still led an enjoyable social life in high school as he entered into a new and challenging world of dating. In 1952, when Toole was fourteen, Fortier opened its doors to female students. The mixture of boys and girls in classrooms and hallways changed the social dynamic in the school. The newspaper, *Silver and Blue*, received a telling facelift, adding the gossip sections "Cat Nips" and "Social Whirl," which covered student affairs. The first time "Cat Nips" appeared, the anonymous reporter wrote, "We are all one big happy family . . . and the gossip is about you." In that first column, Toole was snagged by the snooping gumshoe with the suggestive question, "Every morning JOSEPHINE T. meets KENNY before school to discuss lessons????" "Social Whirl" focused on who was seen about town on weekends. The sons and daughters of the social elite might still dance a waltz at formal balls, but a new sound was taking shape in New Orleans, which characterized the social scene of teenagers all over the country in the 1950s. It was a movement that arguably began in the alter ego of Uptown—the poor black neighborhood of the Ninth Ward—and it created just as much frenzy and fear as jazz did in the early 1900s.

While Toole was performing in blackface at an outdoor theatre in Uptown in the late 1940s, a young black musician from the Ninth Ward named Fats Domino was playing piano in honkytonk bars in New

Orleans. An undisputed innovator in music, Domino quickly cata-
pulted to a recording studio and began touring across the country. In
the mid-fifties, audiences went wild for "Ain't That a Shame" and "Blue-
berry Hill." Such success terrified old order white Southerners. Organizations such as the KKK attacked early rock and roll concerts, and they
urged parents to save their children from the evils of listening to "Negro
music" with its sexually suggestive language. But young people of every
color won out.

Despite its initial controversy, eventually white musicians, who were
inspired in part by Fats Domino and Professor Longhair, eased the music's transition to mainstream, predominantly white audiences. The nation tuned into the *Louisiana Hayride* broadcast in Shreveport,
Louisiana, to listen to Elvis Presley and Jerry Lee Lewis. And throughout
the fifties, American youth watched Dick Clark's *American Bandstand* to
learn the newest dances to the hottest songs. Like most teenagers in the
1950s, Toole listened to rock and roll. And any young man hoping to enter the dating scene in New Orleans would need to know how to dance
to it. Cary Laird asked his younger sister, Lynda, to give him some lessons, and Toole joined them to learn the latest moves. They cleared some
space in the basement where they had set up a record player. They practiced dances like the Jitterbug and the Cha-Cha. And to Toole's amusement, they covered the Dirty Bop, a provocative and taboo variation of
the Jitterbug that had been banned from many school dance floors,
which made it all the more interesting to teenagers.

By all accounts Toole was a wonderful dancer. Evenings out for the
students at Fortier usually included either going to a party, a school
dance, a dance hall, or, on special occasions, the Blue Room at the Roosevelt Hotel. Of course, taking those first few steps into the rituals of
dating can be awkward, especially as a teenager. But this meant the opportunity for new experiences and new humorous stories, which Toole
eagerly shared with Laird. In his senior year, Toole dated a girl everyone
called Buzzy, who, according to Lynda Laird, attended the prestigious
Holy Name of Jesus School, in Uptown. In January of 1954, "Cat Nips"
reported "Ken T. and Buzzy P" as "seen doing the town." But Toole may
have underestimated Buzzy's level of devotion to the Catholic Church.
One evening when Toole went to pick up Buzzy for a night out, she welcomed him into her house so he could offer the customary greeting to

her parents. Her mother, unaware of Toole's arrival, yelled down from the second floor, "Buzzy, you'd better get some romance before you become a nun!" Buzzy was humiliated. Toole was amused. But perhaps Buzzy's devotion to clergy life was not as firm as her mother believed. Toole told Laird that he broke up with her when she brought up the topic of marriage.

Whatever embarrassment Buzzy suffered paled in comparison to Toole's embarrassment over his own parents. In regard to dating, his father had an unobtrusive piece of advice: "Kenny boy," he would say, "you need to beware of loose women!" His mother, however, took a different approach. While she maintained that she stayed out of her son's business when it came to dating, Laird told a different story. According to his account, Thelma would sometimes follow her son on dates. This was not necessarily typical behavior but happened enough times for Laird to retell the story to his sister. Thelma undeniably coveted her relationship with her son. He was everything to her. And while she wanted him to be desired, she also harbored anxiety that he might one day abandon her. She often said that the ladies loved him, but "he only had eyes for her." And she was convinced that she was his only confidant. This intensity may have stifled Toole's growth toward independence. What was once heartwarming devotion between a young boy and his mother became somewhat distorted in high school—a crucial time when a young man explores relationships with others, as he envisions what form his life will take once out from under the roof of his parents.

Regardless of his mother's intrusions, Toole gained a reputation for being an enjoyable date—a good dancer, polite, always well dressed. It was a reputation he carried into college and beyond. But romantic interests always seemed secondary to his drive to achieve some form of greatness. What that form was still remained unclear. However, in high school, his energetic exploration of writing styles suggested a particular direction.

Toole's academic essays show his interest in both popular culture and history. In "Television, Tomorrow's Entertainment," he returned to the idea that he muttered to John Geiser on their way to school in kindergarten. Citing historical and statistical evidence, and noting the decline in attendance at cinemas, Toole argues for the growing trend and popularity of television. He declares at the end of the short essay, "Television is here to stay and soon it may be the world's chief entertainment." He was acutely perceptive. Around the time he wrote this paper, the Golden Age of television began, a time of innovation and experimentation in the medium.

Toole also understood well the language of patriotism, and for his teachers he embraced it in his writing, showing energy and vision. In a short essay on the Louisiana Purchase, he casts the American heartland in picturesque detail:

> On the Great Plains spring up the graceful, golden "gift of God"— wheat. Beneath the fertile surface lay the extensive pools of blue-black oil lying dormant until the greedy drill should pierce their slumber.
>
> These are the same plains that still bear the wagon tracks of the 1850s in the furious rush westward. Up from the virgin forests have sprung the great industrial and commercial centers. Above the banks of the Mississippi rise the smoke-blacked factory towers representing the nation's strength. . . .
>
> At the tip of this cornucopia lies New Orleans, the insuperable gateway to the Mississippi and America's region of prosperity.

After surveying the vast regions of the country, he casts New Orleans as the beginning and the end of it all.

He wrote his high school essays in idealized language about America and American history, which was quite common for the historical narrative offered at the time. In an essay titled "Democracy Is What We Make of It," the young Toole explores the citizen's responsibility to uphold the principles of "the greatest nation of the earth" and overcome "Communist tyranny." Without cynicism or humor he expresses a loyal affirmation of the creed of the country. The overtly patriotic voice he used in his class assignments does not indicate the skepticism he may have felt toward the ideal vision of the United States and the Cold War mentality.

In college he would directly undermine such idealistic precepts of the nation, a sentiment that eventually culminated in his character Ignatius Reilly whose New Orleans–centric vision of the world is laughable and who finds the country lacking in "geometry and theology." And Toole would also mock simplistic notions of government and economies, humorously voiced in *Confederacy* through the character Claude Robichaux, who is convinced anyone that opposes him is a "comuniss." While Toole maintained a patriotic line in his classwork, early traces of this cynical tendency appear outside of his schoolwork. In 1951 he joined the staff of the school newspaper, making his entry through a satire edition titled *Ess and Bee*, presumably an inversion of B.S. Taking on the character of a Russian ring-toss athlete Ivan Vishivsky O'Toole of the Russian institution Liquidate University, he offers testimony of losing to a Fortier student at the world ring toss championship held in "Upper Lower Slobbovia." O'Toole testifies in his Russian dialect:

Vhy, oh vhy, does effryting haff to hoppin to me?

Chust when I t'ought I had der voild's ring toss championship in der bag, Fortier's Villie Harrison (dorty capitalist) came from behind to win hands and feets.

Da, I vas sure dat I had von it, ven dot slob made a beautivul 10-foot toss mit der rink, and I vent down in dorty democratic defeat. Siberia, heer I come.

This is the first documented instance of his writing in a dialect, and his interest in commenting on current events through satire shines. In this case, he cast the competition between communism and democracy through the ridiculous metaphor of ring tossing. After writing this article, he stayed on with the newspaper until he graduated.

Toole employed the use of dialect in some of his creative writing in high school as well. In the John Kennedy Toole Papers at Tulane University (called the Toole Papers hereafter), there is an undated manuscript titled "Going Up" that is likely from this time period. His name appears on this manuscript as Kennedy Toole, which he started using again in print when he became the managing editor of *Silver and Blue* in his senior year. Told in the voice of an elevator operator who speaks in the downtown New Orleans accent, the narrator tells of a serendipitous event when he accidentally left a lady on the twelfth floor, although she asked for the thirteenth. He feared her reprisals, but because his mistake resulted in her securing employment, everything ended for the best. Despite the flaws of "Going Up," it demonstrates Toole's early interest in capturing the cadence of speech in the commoner of New Orleans.

These stabs at fiction and satire may have been a warm-up to his watershed moment as an aspiring author. By 1953 the Tooles had moved to 2226 Cambronne Street in a less desirable neighborhood on the edges of Uptown, away from the lush green archways and park spaces. Thelma later explained to reporter Dalt Wonk that they moved in order to be closer to Fortier, but Cambronne was farther away from Fortier than Webster Street was. Most likely, their move had more to do with a decrease in income. And leaving the heart of Uptown was a sacrifice Thelma would have met with bitterness. Perhaps the pressures of home primed Toole for some time away from New Orleans. In Toole's senior year the Lairds invited Toole on a family visit to an aunt and uncle that lived on a farm in Mississippi. Toole eagerly accepted. In 1954 he and the Lairds piled into their old Studebaker and headed due north to McComb, Mississippi. To the Lairds, there was little novelty in visiting the family farm, but to Toole everything teemed with the uniqueness of country life. The dairy farm and fields of crops offered new scenery. Toole rode on the back of a tractor and, as his best friend watched, eventually took his hand at driving one. It was no Oldsmobile. He struggled to shift the gears of the foreign contraption. Toole's enthusiasm made him a welcomed visitor. Laird's aunt Alice loved his company, which was in no small part due to his flattery of her. He commented that she had the look of the Italian actress Anna Magnani.

The weekend visit soon came to an end, but Toole didn't want to leave. He had seen another side of life, with different kinds of people. On the way back to New Orleans, he seemed invigorated by the whole experience. They passed road sign after road sign of religious platitudes, messages pleading for the moral sensibility of the passersby, signs that said "Drink and Drive and Burn Alive." The overt dogma emblazoned on highway signs spoke to the tension between salvation and damnation, between religion and commercialism. Toole looked at Mississippi and its staunch religious conservatism as ripe, literary material. It was not a reflection of his own beliefs. While raised Catholic in a city with deep ties to Catholicism, the Tooles were not avid churchgoers. The parade of wealth made of the religious ceremony in Uptown churches drove Thelma and her son away from attending mass, so she claimed. Although, she maintained that her son was always "a Christian in the true sense of the word." But what repulsed Thelma about the Catholic service intrigued Toole when he encountered it in another form in the Baptist church. The highway signs in Mississippi were religious messages blended with advertisements for products such as Burma-Shave shaving cream. And thus pleas to the faithful were simultaneous pleas to the consumer.

The young observer had seen a different worldview, not necessarily one to which he aspired, but one with significance nonetheless. One of his favorite writers, Flannery O'Connor, had grappled with conflicting messages of religion, but she had not placed it in the scope of a boy coming of age amid familial and social conflict. Somewhere between McComb and New Orleans, driving on a country road at night, Toole asked his friend to pull over. Laird, somewhat confused as to Toole's intent, did as requested. The New Orleanian who had spent most of his life seeing nights illuminated with street lamps that glowed in the river mist stepped out of the old Studebaker and looked up. He "gasped at the beauty of the millions of stars in the sky" and exclaimed, "'I didn't know there were this many stars in the heavens!'" It seemed a revelation had hit him. They all paused to appreciate the twinkling lights. Back in the car, heading south toward New Orleans, Toole told his friend, "I have to write a book." He started muttering to himself, making mental notes of what he intended to do. Laird encouraged his enthusiasm, although he did not realize the seriousness with which Toole would pursue his idea.

Back at home, Toole set to work on writing the book, distilling his impressions of Mississippi. The trip to the country sparked his interests in this world of God and land and the small Southern town. And for all the dozens of road signs blazing in his memory from the trip home, New Orleans provided him the central image to his novel, as well as the title. Along Airline Highway in Metairie, in the outskirts of New Orleans, a sign for Mid-City Baptist Church lit up at night. It was a radiant bible with red letters and yellow pages, opened to the passage of John 3:16: "For God so loved the world that he gave his one and only Son, that whoever believes in him shall not perish but have eternal life." The holy text beamed in commercial illumination like a commodity sold to customers. It embodied that tension between religion and commercialism. He had found the ironic symbol to place at the center of his book: *The Neon Bible*.

In this short novel, Toole drew upon tensions between religious virtue and the sins of the faithful in a small Mississippi town during World War II. Under the veneer of a simple country life, a boy named David is driven to the edge and, in the end, kills a preacher to protect the body of his dead mother. At the heart of the novel is a tent revival that compels the townspeople to "find Jesus."

While Toole never attended a revival meeting in Mississippi, at the invitation of his friend Cary Laird, Toole went with his mother to "hear Billy Graham at a revival meeting at the old first Baptist church on St. Charles near the old Touro Infirmary." He and his mother watched the impassioned evangelical preacher hold sway over the congregation. His mother recalled,

> We were fascinated—professing for Christ—young minister, very handsome, in a beige suit and a salmon tie showed how wicked social dancing was. I said to my son, "This is a fine religious meeting." And they laughed their heads off. I didn't think they were funny. My son gained a great deal from that.

Toole must have appreciated the theatrical quality of the tent revival. And while Billy Graham may disagree that his revivals were "shows," his organization used the same tactics that stage productions use to generate interest. Before coming to a city, a media blitz preceded him with posters and advertisements. Then for a series of nights, sometimes weeks on end, he preached the gospel. In Los Angeles in 1949, Graham spoke behind a huge stage prop bible opened toward the audience. And several years after his New Orleans "crusade" he would take Manhattan by storm, drawing in thousands upon thousands of audience members, filling Yankee stadium and Madison Square Garden. His preaching always culminated in the "altar call," which was when members of the congregation would step forward to declare their promise to Jesus. Toole stood on stage as a young boy, but he had never held such power over an audience. And while his Catholic church had the regal and austere theater of ceremony, it was nowhere near as lively as the jam-packed seats of believers calling to Christ and professing aloud their faith. But mixed with his appreciation, he showed some disdain for the simplicity of the believers to be swayed by such theatrics, and so, as Thelma says, "they laughed their heads off."

As Toole drafted *The Neon Bible*, he must have recalled Billy Graham. The evangelist in the book who comes to the small Mississippi town appears remarkably similar to how Graham looked in 1954. David, the narrator protagonist, explains his first impressions of the evangelist:

> The first thing I noticed about him, even before his clothes and how skinny he was, were his eyes. They were blue, but a kind of blue I never saw before. It was a clear kind of eye that always looked like it was staring into a bright light without having to squint. His cheeks weren't full like a boy's would be, but hung in toward his teeth. You could hardly see his upper lip, not because it was thin, but because he had a long, narrow nose that sort of hung down at the end. He was blond-headed, with his hair combed straight back and hanging on his neck.

And in the tent the spirits of the townspeople awaken. Even David nearly goes to the altar to profess his faith. The tent bonds the town together. But once it is taken down and the evangelist leaves town, everything begins to crumble. Having lost his father to the war, his Aunt Mae to the wind, and his mother, who died in his arms one night as he wiped the blood from her mouth, David, in the end, defends the family home when the preacher from the local church comes to take his mother to the mental hospital. Unaware of her death, the preacher's presence threatens to uncover their poor and secretive existence. So as the preacher ascends the stairs, David shoots him in the back and kills him, then flees town. Like Flannery O'Connor, Toole uses violence to twist the plot, moving it from the subdued, coming-of-age story of a Mississippi teenager to the tale of a boy pushed to the brink to defend his mother, resulting in his being ousted from the community he had known all his life.

While *The Neon Bible* has become known as a work of juvenilia, an accomplishment in respect to Toole's age at the time he wrote it, the novel remains a work that demonstrates his keen awareness of character and dialogue. Kerry Luft, senior editor at the *Chicago Tribune*, expresses this early talent: "Toole knew that the way to write about complex emotions is to express them simply." He likely gleaned this style of simplicity from one of his favorite novels at the time, *The Catcher in the Rye*. But his first novel also appears as a counter principle to Toole's introduction to verbal expression under the guidance of his mother. Thelma expressed herself in the most florid ways possible. She prided herself on the occasional, elaborate "literary sentence" that she would contribute to her son's school papers.

But Toole decided the voice of the narrator in his novel needed to sound like an average teenager of the time. When David explains the experience of being beat up by high school bullies, he does so using the straightforward vocabulary of a sixteen-year-old:

> The first sock came. It was on my head right above my eye, and I began to cry again, only this time harder. They were all on me at once, I thought. I felt myself falling backward, and I landed with them on top of me. My stomach made a sick grinding noise, and I started feeling the vomit climb up into my throat. I was tasting blood on my lips now, and an awful scaredness was creeping from my feet up my legs. I felt the tingling go up till it grabbed me where I really felt it. Then the vomit came, over everything. Me, Bruce, and the other two. They screamed and jumped off me. And I laid there and the sun was hot and there was dust all over me.

Toole clearly had the ability to describe this moment with more ornamentation, as is evident in his school papers, but he stays true to the diction of his character, describing the all-too-common experience of a boy terrorized by bullies.

For some reason, Toole never told his mother he was writing a novel. And she had no idea that he submitted it to a writing contest. She explained years later, "He didn't want me to worry, you see." She never explained what worries she would have had. The very fact that he had written a novel deserved some celebration, but he kept the whole thing a secret. It was his first serious attempt to write fiction, and from his return from Mississippi to completing the novel in New Orleans, he took measures to ensure his mother remained completely unaware of it. The novel is an expression all his own, a definitive departure from his performances as a speaker, actor, or singer, and drafted in an energetic burst of writing. He had successfully expressed himself as a perceptive observer and a writer. But perhaps he never told his mother about *The Neon Bible* for fear of what could happen and what did happen. When he received word he lost the contest, he tucked away the manuscript, hiding his failure, suffering the pangs of rejection alone.

Despite his perceived failure as a novelist, his senior year was a busy time, overall, as he garnered recognition and accomplishment. He was elected a state representative at Boys' State in August of 1953. He became managing editor of the school newspaper and assistant editor to the yearbook. In October of 1953 he appeared as a guest speaker at the Kiwanis Club. He was inducted into the honor society. He took fifth place in a Spanish language contest. And on December 16, the day before his sixteenth birthday, he appeared on local television with six other students to review the epic novel *Tree of Liberty*. A month later, *Silver and Blue* published a "Senior Spotlight" on him, naming him "one of Fortier's big wheels."

For all the awards and positions he held, his most seminal moment, one that would plant a seed for his future, came in May of 1954 when Toole left New Orleans with a school group to take a tour of historic sites along the eastern seaboard. He was one of thirty-one students from Fortier selected to receive a National Freedom Foundation award at Valley Forge, Pennsylvania. These students represented "how the ideals of the American way of life are taught in classes at Fortier." Boarding a train at 8 a.m., they made the long journey northward. They visited Washington, DC, taking in the sights of the Lincoln Monument, the White House, the Capitol, and ascending the Washington Monument. They watched the "solemn changing of the guard at the tomb of the Unknown Soldier." At Valley Forge they were honored in a ceremony, and they stopped in Philadelphia to pay tribute to Liberty Hall. And like true New Orleanians, they carried the spirit of their hometown with them. In the city of brotherly love, they enjoyed a "costume party at the Sylvania Hotel."

The most exciting part of the trip for Toole must have been the three days he spent in New York City. The group made the typical tourist stops, such as the Statue of Liberty, the Empire State Building, and the United Nations—all symbols of the American identity and its value of freedom, competition, and diplomacy. They took a ferry to Ellis Island, and they stepped into St. Patrick's Cathedral. But the highlight of his visit to New York was the glitz and glamour of Broadway shows. In an article Toole wrote for the school newspaper upon their return, he summarizes the trip, noting, "Entertainment was an outstanding feature of the tour. The gawking Fortierites viewed Cinerama, the new movie wonder, the world famous 'Rockettes' at the fabulous Radio City Music Hall, and one of the biggest musicals on Broadway, *Wonderful Town*."

While much of the trip was spent invigorating the patriotic spirit of the students, the rolling hills of Valley Forge and the then sleepy Southern town of Washington, DC, would be difficult to rival the heart-pounding verve of New York. In a promotional map of Manhattan that Toole saved in his scrapbook the tourist is informed, "Manhattan is the financial, cultural, manufacturing, and theatrical CAPITAL of the World!" It was a statement that Toole heard loud and clear, a statement that, for better or worse, returned to his ears throughout his life, both drawing him to and repelling him from New York City.

In primary school he had strutted upon the stage, but in high school he stepped into the world, observing his city, dating women, and making his first movements toward social critique through satire. Some of the key characters of *Confederacy* were beginning to germinate. Joel Zelden, a friend and neighbor, recalled how one afternoon they invented the name Ignatius Reilly, finding the mere sound of it funny. And perhaps even then he reflected on how he might use his impressions of Irene Reilly and her boisterous mother. He also gained a reputation for his wit and humor. Jane Pic Adams never forgot seeing Toole through the window and across the green in another class on the other side of the school. Locking eyes, Toole would make hilarious facial expressions. Adams struggled not to laugh, trying to keep her composure as she sang in chorus. And yet his antics never compromised his standing as a scholar. His classmates voted him most intelligent in his senior year, and he was awarded a full merit scholarship to attend Tulane University.

Most importantly, between writing a novel and managing the school newspaper, he pursued his interests in writing and had his first experience of New York City. And yet, despite his clear passion for literature and the arts, in his senior year of high school he decided to major in engineering in college. He must have understood his career path would likely have a direct impact on his family's future prosperity, one that had been compromised, resulting in the loss of their home. After all, there was no one else but Toole to take care of his parents when they would inevitably succumb to old age. His mother claimed that his father persuaded him to study engineering, but Thelma was not one to passively approach these kinds of crossroads, either. She dedicated her life to creative endeavors, and she also endured the instability of it. "He was an artist," but perhaps he could earn a respectable living creating works in a different discipline. Just like he tucked away his failed novel underneath his bed, he relegated his passion for writing to a hobby. Determined in his career choice, he announced his plans in the school newspaper.

But Toole would discover that Tulane, the university four blocks from Fortier, was undergoing major changes as it transitioned from a primarily New Orleans institution with a focus on applied technical skills to one of the leading liberal arts universities in the United States. As the university grew, students came in greater numbers from farther away, increasing diversity and bringing with them ideas of progress. The coeds enjoyed a city that unabashedly offered indulgences found nowhere else in the South. They also came to study at a university that was growing in notoriety as it added graduate programs and earned federal research grants, attracting high-caliber professors. The world of Tulane was about to open up before Toole, not just as a means to a job, but also as a place to refine and explore his ideas.

Chapter 4

Tulane

Before Toole started classes at Tulane in the fall of 1954, at the age of sixteen, he spearheaded the search for a new home for the family. Perhaps the scholarship along with the odd jobs Toole would pick up throughout his undergraduate career helped them stabilize their finances. He found a small and affordable second-floor apartment at 390 Audubon Street, and he helped furnish it. So the Tooles returned to the heart of Uptown, living on the opposite side of Audubon Park from their old Webster Street house and only seven blocks away from Tulane. On a nice day he could walk through the park, strolling under majestic live oaks and pass the well-appointed estates overlooking the green grass. At St. Charles Avenue the periodic streetcar would groan and sway down the tracks, lazily making its way to the French Quarter, as he approached Gibson Hall, the castle-like gray, stone building marking the entrance to campus and declaring the enduring tradition of the university.

Having grown up in Uptown, Toole was in familiar territory at Tulane. He had passed it countless times on the streetcar, traveled through its campus on his way to Fortier in his senior year, and played in front of Gibson Hall as a child. But now he was a Tulanian, one of the many freshmen looking for a place in the academic and social circles of college life. At sixteen years old, he stood in the midst of this co-ed university, his pudgy physique contrasting the seniors and graduate students who were well into their twenties. Toole usually met social situations with humor and wit; his four years at Tulane were no exception.

Unsurprisingly, the engineering program, which focused on mathematics and science, did little to stir his spirits. Unable to closet away his need to write, he sought an outlet, a place for his literary expression. In his first semester, he walked into a meeting of the Newman Club—an organization for Catholic students—and volunteered to help with its monthly publication. He submitted his first story to the president of the club, John Mmahat. Mmahat shared it with the other editors and they all agreed they "had never come across anything like that before." More than fifty years later, Mmahat is unable to recollect the subject of the story, but he vividly remembers his impression of Toole as a "gifted observer of the human condition." Mmahat looked at Toole, who was four years younger than he, and judged him to have a "superior writing talent."

Predictably, Toole quickly grew discontent with engineering. He could be an engineer no more than Thelma could be a secretary. Writing and reading were in his blood and bones. One day after school he came home upset and confided to his mother that he felt he was "losing his culture." The presumed financial security a degree in engineering offered could not outweigh his need to express and cultivate the talents he cherished most. The English department offered him an alternate path. No longer a mere support discipline at Tulane, the English department, with its fairly new PhD program, was training scholars and sending them into tenure track positions in colleges all over the country. And as universities grew throughout the United States, the likelihood of young scholars securing a coveted professorship increased. Toole needed only a guide to nudge him toward that career. Fortunately, he walked into the classroom of Alvin Foote, an English instructor who encouraged him to pursue a life in literature.

In a 1984 interview, when asked about her son's experience at Tulane, Thelma exclaimed, "Oh that Alvin Foote!" She went on to explain that her son suggested she visit with the inspiring instructor during Open House Night at the college. When they met, Thelma asked Foote what he thought of her son. She reported that he gushed with pride and exclaimed, "Mrs. Toole, the other students can't even spell!"

Thelma often embellished people's reactions to her son's abilities, but Foote did identify Toole as a prodigy. On the back of one of Toole's essays on Chaucer, Foote comments, "This is an extremely interesting and perceptive paper. It could, perhaps, be worked into something for publication in one of the scholarly journals." Toole was still a teenager, and yet a specialist in the field of literary studies had recognized him as a budding scholar, one who could have a future in writing. Certainly this placed balm on any remaining wounds from his experience with *The Neon Bible*.

Foote encouraged Toole to pursue a life in literature. Over the span of several semesters, both teacher and student left an indelible impression on each other. Toole offered Foote hope amid his growing fatigue with undergraduates. And Foote, seeing great potential in his young protégé, upheld Toole's talents as that of a professional, not just a novice. It must have been a sad day when Toole found out Foote was leaving Tulane. In the fall semester of 1956, Foote moved to California for a higher salary. Toole sent him a Christmas card, and on February 26, 1957, Foote replied. The nature of their relationship is reflected in this single letter:

Dear Ken:

Your xmas card came at a time when the muddy bottom of Morro Bay looked more inviting than the nearest bar to A. Foote—and bars have always had an attraction to him. In other words, the kind things you wrote helped lift me out of a depression that threatened my insanity. Believe me, I am grateful.

Foote makes light of his mood, but he conveys his sincere appreciation. Whatever Toole wrote helped him weather his unhappiness. In California Foote found himself longing to be back at Tulane, longing for students like Toole. He describes his current students in a manner that Toole must have found most entertaining:

We turn out technicians here—the men who are educated enough to be able to turn the little wheel when the gauge shows red: "Giver a lil more naptha, Charlie, the mixtures gittin bad." Unfortunately these men receive the M.S. degree—equivalent to the B.A. I suppose—and go out into the world armed with the conviction they are "engineers."

Toole developed a similar style of banter as written by Foote—a blend of imitation and disdain. Years later, Toole would write similar lines about his own students in Puerto Rico. And the sarcasm pointed at engineers may echo their discussions about Toole's career path. God forbid Toole could have been the one turning that little wheel when the gauge turned red.

Foote goes on to reaffirm his dedication to teaching, despite its challenges. He also reiterates his vested interest in Toole's future, clearly regretting his decision to leave Tulane:

> I would enjoy a letter from you. I'd like to know how
> Tulane goes, and how your plans are shaping up for the
> teaching profession. I'd still recommend that profession,
> but I'd add a little counsel and guidance: don't be fooled
> into thinking that higher salaries mean more interesting
> students. . . .
>
> My best to your mother, and please write.

This letter, the only one from Foote in the Toole Papers, offers a suggestive glimpse into the relationship between teacher and student. Their bond, however brief it might have been, likely had a resounding influence on Toole. Foote was one of his few male mentors. He pointed to a track, rather than a paycheck, that suited Toole's talents. He encouraged Toole to turn away from engineering and pursue a degree in English.

By the end of his freshman year, and with his mother's blessing, Toole changed his major. Just as Ignatius in *Confederacy* drafted his invective against the modern age in his Big Chief Tablet and scribbled on the front, "MOTHER DO NOT READ," Toole claimed a place in his studies where his parents would not tread: his father had an interest in mathematics and engineering, and while his mother tried to follow his studies in literature, she later mused, "In grade school, I was my son's tutor. In college, he became my tutor." Her son would bring home his reading lists from classes, and she tried to keep up with them. It soon became clear he was blazing a trail of his own choosing. After all, if he already felt duty-bound to eventually care for his parents, he would at least do it working in a field that he enjoyed.

Having declared his own path in his education, perhaps feeling a bit more liberated, Toole planned to take a trip to New York City with his friend Stephen Andry. It was to be a short trip at the end of the summer, but one that was free from parents, teachers, tour buses, and itineraries. Even if only for a few days, Toole would see New York his way. He plodded through the New Orleans summer, looking forward to his trip north, and by September 5 he was in Manhattan, enjoying the fair and mild weather. Almost every night he took in a show: *Damn Yankees*, *Cat on a Hot Tin Roof*, *Silk Stockings*, a taping of *Coke Time with Eddie Fisher*, and *The Vaughn Monroe Show*. He saved playbills, ticket stubs, and subway maps, placing them all as mementos in the back of his scrapbook from his 1954 high school trip, like an addendum, filling in the gaps from his previous visit. As planned, Andry and Toole left New York on September 9, along with another friend who had a car, taking a couple days to cover the thirteen-hundred-mile journey south. Despite the long trip, the car ride home in a convertible Chevrolet Bel Air was a thrill. As a devoted fan of automobiles, Toole captured the moment. In a snapshot taken somewhere between New Orleans and New York, Toole poses at the wheel of the sporty convertible with the top down and the sun shining bright. Carrying on down the road, the wind in their hair, Toole bid adieu to the summer, his last hurrah before classes resumed and he set to work on his bachelor's degree in English.

In the fall of 1955, the beginning of his sophomore year, he took the expected courses for an undergraduate: English, Spanish, history, and biology. He also took a philosophy course with E. Goodwin Ballard, a phenomenologist interested in aesthetics, among other topics. While Ballard covered the obligatory philosophers such as Plato and Aristotle, he also posed questions about American society and economy, providing a fertile ground for Toole's contemplation over the tension between his scholastic success and the lack of money that perplexed him for much of his life. Granted, his scholarships secured his way through school, but the pressure of money relentlessly hounded his family. Their income fluctuated, depending on how many cars his father sold and how many students his mother taught. He saw, year after year, the rotating wheel of Fortuna in the family finances. This experience seems to have colored his interpretations of philosophy and American society. He held an early interest in medieval philosophy, and he expressed growing resentment toward modern America. It seemed to him that the learned pauper was a uniquely American invention. Certainly the medieval era, with its clear social structure, would not allow such an injustice. But in America, a fool could become a millionaire, while the genius lay destitute, all under the guise of economic freedom. He expressed this frustration in Ballard's philosophy course. In response to an exam question on freedom and equality, Toole writes,

> Our government tells us we are equal, even though we enjoy economic freedom. There are, of course, many citizens who believe wholeheartedly that this is true. It is taught to all school children as the catechism of our government, as dogma.
> But when these children are faced with the stark reality that school is over, that they are no longer "actives" in their fraternity, that they have their degree in Business Administration and that the regular checks from home are no longer forthcoming, the dogma which they so firmly believed explodes in their faces.

Such notions would have shocked the patriotic core at Fortier. Nowhere in his surviving high school writings did Toole indict with such hostility, but at Tulane he was far freer to express his ideas. Clearly, he resented the more privileged students who were spared the woes of "a working boy." With no regular paycheck from home, Toole endured the indignity of a variety of jobs, one of which was selling hot dogs at Tulane football games. While he didn't push a hot dog cart through the French Quarter, like Ignatius Reilly, Toole was a scholar, steeped in medievalism, selling wienies to his peers. Even Bobby Byrne, the person who would serve as the model for Ignatius Reilly, recognized Toole's feelings of disgrace. However, Toole's critique of the privileged was not only fueled by animosity; it seems he envied them.

A few months after writing the bitter words above, Toole decided to pledge Delta Tau Delta, a small but growing fraternity. In many ways, the fraternities and sororities were the entry points to social life at Tulane. Fraternity brothers would stand at the back of the auditorium during student assemblies and hand out cards, actively recruiting new pledges. Anyone could be swept up in rushing. Delta Tau Delta selected Toole as a potential member, and he decided to explore his options in the Greek system. In the fall of 1955, Toole posed for a yearbook picture with his fellow pledges, sitting on the steps of the brick portico outside the cafeteria. Resting his right hand on his knee, he holds a cigarette between his fingers, while his left hand casually displays his class ring from Fortier. With a slight smile, he looks into the distance. In the caption, they misspelled his name, Ken Tolle. In another photo taken that same day, which did not make the yearbook, the pledges and the brothers pose together. While many of the other men lean toward each other, signaling their alliances, Toole awkwardly sits in the middle of the group, separate as if floating alone amid the ties of brotherhood. And for the privilege of pledging, he received his monthly bill, expenses totaling $18.20, comprised of a house fee and board fee—all this for a fraternity with a house one block away from his home on Audubon Street. He started the process of pledging, but he never officially joined the fraternity. Financially, it made little sense. Besides, as an observer with artistic inclinations, he needed to find his circle off center, somewhere on the margins, giving him the vantage point to watch and critique the society in which he lived.

As with most undergraduates in the liberal arts, Toole spent the first two years of college establishing a foundation in a variety of disciplines. In his first year he redirected his career path, and in his sophomore year he wielded a sharp critique at American society. Perhaps through the temperance of gained wisdom, he restrained and focused his frustration in his junior year when he bloomed intellectually and artistically. While it would be well over six years before he would write *A Confederacy of Dunces*, his undergraduate work from this period indicates his exploration of the philosophical and aesthetic underpinnings of his novel.

Toole dove into his junior year grappling with clashing philosophies that would shape his approach to literature. In the fall of 1956 he honed in on the conflict between medieval philosophy, a system of understanding the world based on hierarchies, and pragmatism, a system of understanding the world that, as Toole defines, "focus[es] on the *results* of things, the *utilitarian aspect* of actions." For Toole, medieval philosophy presented order and harmony, while pragmatism became the intellectual validation of a Darwinian approach to society. The discourse between these two worldviews would echo throughout his academic and creative work.

He largely based his understanding of medieval thought on the sixth century Roman philosopher Boethius, who wrote *The Consolation of Philosophy* from prison as he awaited execution. This work is central to the worldview of Ignatius Reilly in *Confederacy*. Boethius scholar and Toole's friend Bobby Byrne, whom he would meet a few years later after graduating from Tulane, claimed Toole had a superficial knowledge of the medieval philosopher through his reading of Geoffrey Chaucer. But Byrne does not give Toole enough credit. Both Byrne and Toole studied under one of the leading medieval scholars in the South at the time, Robert Lumiansky, who also served as the dean of graduate studies and would go on to teach at New York University (NYU). On the final exam of Lumiansky's class in 1957, Toole demonstrates a clear understanding of the metaphysical order that explained the human condition, according to *The Consolation of Philosophy*: "Fortune and nature are, together, on the bottom rung of what might be called the Boethian hierarchy. . . . Destiny directs God's will directly through them to man." He also employed Boethius in a Shakespeare class when he wrote, "The wheel of Fortune is the old medieval device of explaining the rise and fall of illustrious men . . . *De Casibus Virorum Illustrium*. It is the Boethian philosophy of a blind goddess, Fortuna, spinning a wheel on which man's fortune rises and falls." The same Latin line appears in *Confederacy* in the journal of Ignatius when he recounts his attempts to rally the factory workers in the Crusade for Moorish Dignity. But by the time Toole wrote *Confederacy*, he no longer had to display his knowledge of Boethius to professors or fellow academics. He understood the philosophy well enough to push the metaphor of a "great man falling" into the literal and grotesque:

> *De Casibus Virorum Illustrium!* Of the Fall of Great Men! My downfall occurred. Literally. My considerable system, weakened by the gyrations (especially in the region of the knees), at last rebelled, and I plummeted to the floor in a senseless attempt at one of the more egregiously perverse steps which I had witnessed on the television so many times.

As a counterpoint to Boethius, pragmatism gained an unavoidable presence in Toole's education, although much like Ignatius in *Confederacy*, Toole grew suspicious of it. He owned a collection of academic essays titled *Pragmatism and American Culture: Problems in American Civiliza-tion*, which documents a discourse between supporters and opponents of pragmatism. In the collection, some philosophers uphold pragmatism, validating its focus on ends and results. Others, like Mortimer Adler, who focus on a medieval sensibility of philosophy, deem pragmatism antithetical to morality, a sign of the "anarchic individualism" that has led to the "cultural disorder . . . of modern times." This book of rivaling arguments must have weighed in Toole's judgment of the philosophy. In another assignment he argues pragmatism was an influential precursor to the Great Depression. As pragmatism emerged at the turn of the century, "America had found a national philosophy. It looked towards *ends*, rather than *means*, and that was all that the larger capitalists and their guardian, the pre–Great Depression Republican Party, could ask of a nation's philosophers." Toole continued to apply this philosophy in other classes; he grappled with its meaning and the way it both reflected and influenced American society. During his years as an undergraduate, he clearly developed an appreciation for the medieval interpretation of life. And yet, he was immersed in a country whose pragmatic worldview was antithetical to the medieval notions of Fate and Fortune.

These contradicting philosophies play out in *Confederacy*. The underlying tension in the novel, which plagues the mind of Ignatius, is a conflict between Boethian philosophy and pragmatism. Caught between his mediaeval worldview of Fate and Fortune and the pragmatic worldview of economic mobility, jobs, and social reform, Ignatius believes he is the fallen man awaiting Fortune to send him on a trajectory upward. But he is pushed to act, endeavoring in plots of social reconstruction at whatever cost, which would be a medieval absurdity, but of central value to the pragmatist. The medievalist morally lives with his fate and seeks order, whereas the pragmatist molds his fate for a happy end, even if that means creating disorder. Ignatius expresses this conflict when he writes in his journal,

> A debate between morality and pragmatism rages in my brain. Is the glorious end, Peace, worth the awesome means, Degeneracy? Like two figures in the medieval Morality play Pragmatism and Morality spar in the boxing ring of my brain. I cannot await the outcome of their furious debate: I am too obsessed with Peace.

Morality and pragmatism. Ignatius Reilly and Myrna Minkoff. New Orleans and New York. In *Confederacy*, Toole layers two opposing philosophies in characters, dialogue, and the two most intriguing cities he had ever experienced. But unlike his undergraduate days, in the novel, Toole would not support or declaim either philosophy. In fact, through the ridiculousness of Ignatius, Toole mocks an investment in a single thought system as a means to construct a view of the world. Thereby he seems to ridicule the often-overreaching methods of an academic who applies a formula or method to order the intrinsic chaos of the universe. Of course, he had years of experience to gain before arriving at that conclusion.

As Toole refined his philosophical stance, he also examined the relationship between literature and society, an important approach for him as he narrowed his focus on a career as an English professor, but did not necessarily dismiss a future as a writer. This exploration culminated in an essay wherein he surveys movements in literary history that correspond to shifts in Western society. Unsurprisingly, he finds that each time period responds to the trends and values of the previous age. But these responses do not create a true progression. He observes, "Man behaves in cycles. The great sociological phenomenon of action and reaction is quite unassailable." While this reading of history is by no means profound, Toole distills his interpretation to arrive at the role of the writer in society. Since he positions literature as an indicator of social change, he asserts, "A writer is a mirror to the temper of his times."

Such an observation clearly speaks to his mode of writing *Confederacy*. One of the lasting criticisms of the novel is that the characters remain unchanged; in essence, they do not progress. But as a mirror to his society, Toole seems to have determined that he could not reflect the idea of lasting change or redemption when such graces rarely occurred in the world as he knew it. And like any good satire, this notion of unattainable reform flies in the face of the prevailing sentiments of his time, which was an era of intense social activism. As an undergraduate, Toole came to the realization that, regardless of how a society projects itself, the writer must reflect what he observes.

Of course, Toole always preferred to color his reflective lens with humor, which made some of his cynical sentiments more palatable. He has moments of wry wit in his academic essays, but literary criticism is typically an unsuitable medium for comedy. So in the fall of 1956, Toole found an artistic venue for his caustic humor. As he contemplated Hawthorne, Shakespeare, Chaucer, and the condition of America in his academic classes, he contributed satirical cartoons to the student newspaper *Hullabaloo* and the student literary magazine *Carnival*. While he would become the most well-known literary satirist that New Orleans ever produced, he ventured into satire through comics, which certainly impacted his way of writing.

As a boy, Toole had shown talents in visual art. In high school and college, he drew some thoughtfully designed sketches on the margins and backsides of his class notes. And he sustained an interest in comics well into his college years. He owned a copy of the 1955 illustrated edition of *Archy and Mehitabel*, a poetic satire that begins much like Kafka's *Metamorphosis*. A poet awakes to find himself reincarnated as a cockroach, but at night he continues to write verse on the typewriter of a journalist. Interestingly, George Herriman, a New Orleans–born Creole, contributed the single-frame illustrations to the edition that Toole owned. Herriman was the creator of the famous and highly influential comic *Krazy Kat and Ignatz*. Of course, Ignatz is the German form of Ignatius. As in Herriman's syndicated cartoon, *Krazy Kat* remains devoted to Ignatz, despite his verbal and physical abuses, much like Irene and Myrna Minkoff remain devoted to Ignatius. The characters also speak in an accent remnant of the New Orleans Yat dialect.

Like Herriman's illustrations in *Archy and Mehitabel*, as a cartoonist for *The Hullabaloo*, Toole drew single-frame scenes that captured humorous moments accompanied by a line or two of dialog. But unlike Marquis and Herriman, Toole did not use the vehicle of animal characters. He drew sharply critical images of Tulane students and professors, most of them with glasses and sharply pointed noses.

Through these comics, he uses the people of Tulane, often the female students of Newcomb College—the all-female affiliate of Tulane—as a means to critique the university and popular culture. No topic seemed forbidden to him. Addressing Cold War politics in the university setting, he depicts a sizeable Russian sorority sister picketing in front of a professor with a sign that reads, "Workers Unite!" The oblivious professor reviews the student's transcript and dryly observes that she has not taken

American Government. Toole presented the meeting point of religion and modern society when he drew a determined Moses at a movie theater entrance, cradling the sacred tablets in his arms and pointing his staff that parted the Red Sea toward the box office window. The biblical prophet demands free admission to view *The Ten Commandments*. He is directed to speak to a manager.

Above all, women were his favorite subjects in his comics. Toole depicted the uptight, sweater-wearing women of Newcomb College: the loose lily stumbling into the scene, as if she just returned from a night on Bourbon Street, and the rare beauty, the ephemeral delight, ostracized for her otherness. In one comic, a young, beautiful woman, whose face Toole practiced drawing to perfection, walks ahead of two Newcomb students with short, cropped hair and unshaven legs. The two ladies comment that the new girl will "never fit in." In another series of comics, Toole references the 1957 film *Bus Stop* with his beloved Marilyn Monroe. In a three-part installment, he depicts a voluptuous Monroe leaning in ecstasy against a bus stop post. In the background, two Newcomb students observe her and whisper, "I don't know who she is, but she's been there for two days." The next week the same frame was published with the caption, "What! She still here?" Two weeks later, the same image appears with the caption, "NOoooo!" The homely ladies appear threatened by the beauty that simply will not leave.

His jabs at Newcomb students, Tulane professors, and others were typical of his acerbic humor. As Mmahat recalls, Toole "delighted in picking out the eccentricities in people and poking fun at everything he encountered." But he was not beyond making fun of himself, as he did in an illustration published in the student literary magazine *Carnival*. In the fall of 1956, Toole served as nonfiction editor, reviewing newly published books. He also provided small illustrations as accents to stories and poems. In the ninth edition of *Carnival*, Toole contributed "Portraits," a visual parody of the *Carnival* staff. On the first floor of a decrepit building, the artistic editor, a busty woman sitting on a stove, cuts out images from a page of "easy cut-outs." The business office has a vending machine with selections of martinis, beer, gum, candy, and *Carnival Magazine*. Outside a curtained doorway, a motley group of contributors waits for the editors' decisions. But below, in the basement den, the editors crowd around a television. They watch *Superman*, which seems to take their minds off their own rejection letters pasted haphazardly on the wall. Toole appears in the background with dark hair and sunglasses. His tongue hangs out the side of his mouth as he holds up a beer bottle. He lampoons the entire group, including himself, humorously casting the way would-be writers cope with rejection: they call themselves editors, watch television, and drink beer.

Toole's comics are the first creative materials that demonstrate his versatile and scathing satirical wit. And the sensibility developed as a cartoonist for *The Hullabaloo* and *Carnival* is present in *Confederacy*. In his comics, he caricatures the world of Tulane. In *Confederacy*, he does the same to New Orleans. The characters, the plot, the dialogue, almost everything is exaggerated in *Confederacy*, except for the setting, which Toole depicts realistically. As he wrote in 1957, "Social satire, to be effective, must be based upon realistic aspects of the society being satirized." He applied this maxim with precision in blending the beauty of New Orleans with the cartoon-like absurdity of the characters. For example, Patrolman Mancuso ridiculously dressed in a T-shirt, Bermuda shorts, and a fake red beard rides on his motorcycle that could, at the sound of its siren, "make suspicious characters within a half-mile radius defecate in panic and rush for cover." And yet, he passes under the "ancient oaks of St. Charles Avenue arched over the avenue like a canopy shielding him from the mild winter sun," and he thinks to himself it "must be the loveliest place in the world." In the end, it is not the place but rather the people who live, laugh, and die in that city that create the tragicomic play of New Orleans life. The real-life characters so often seem as outlandish as Ignatius Reilly, standing in front of D. H. Holmes, "with a green hunting cap squeezing the top of the fleshy balloon of a head." It is no coincidence that the covers of *Confederacy* have been adorned with cartooned versions of Ignatius. The 2002 Grove Press paperback depicts a cartoon Ignatius walking down a French Quarter street, with the wrought iron galleries in the background taken from a real photograph. It is that meeting point between the unreal and the real, in other words the absurd, where Toole rooted his humor—an approach that first sprouts in his comics.

*   *   *

Clearly, 1957 proved a seminal year for Toole. While he explored
his city in high school with Cary Laird, creating a variety of characters
from their observations, at Tulane his eye focused on the people at the
university, and his creative ideas took more substantive shape. Furthermore, he refined his ideas in philosophy, literature, and humor that he
clearly drew upon when writing *Confederacy*. In the yearbook of 1957,
Toole no longer appears in the fraternity pages. He poses among a group
of writers and editors from various university publications. Wearing a
pea coat with a popped collar and his shirt slightly unbuttoned, he looks
the part of a young and bright artist. It seems he had found his place.

After such a successful school year, Toole certainly deserved a break.
Unsurprisingly, he got an itch for New York City. He still kept in touch
with his high school friend Cary Laird, although Laird was pursuing a
degree in geophysics at Tulane, a far cry from English coursework.
Laird's father had just bought a new Chevrolet and they asked Mr. Laird
if they could take his car to New York. While they were only nineteen
years old, Mr. Laird trusted them, and, much to the consternation of
Mrs. Laird, he simply replied, "Okay, go ahead." So Toole was off to
New York again, and from what Laird's sister recalls, they both enjoyed
it immensely.

In his senior year, Toole dedicated his time to his course work, writing an undergraduate honors essay and securing funding for graduate
school. In fact, he pursued his studies like a professional, enrolling in a
graduate-level English course and deciding to leave *The Hullabaloo* and
Carnival. In one of his classes he met Nick Polites, who recognized that
Toole "must have had special permission to take a graduate seminar
course while an undergraduate." Indeed he did. Professor Richard
Fogle later wrote that Toole "was the only undergraduate I can recall we
let take a 700 level course." Despite his youth, he kept pace with the
graduate students. He socialized with a group of them, often eating
lunch in the cafeteria, discussing matters of literature, history, and culture. The professor complimented his work years later when he recalled
that he "wrote a surprisingly good essay on Coleridge for me." And like
most professional academics he felt the drive to contribute something
original to literary studies. In his essay on Nathaniel Hawthorne he

writes, "I have attempted some original work in the field. . . . It is an attempt to find Hawthorne's representation of the reality he might not have found apparent in his society, a reality from which Americans might be hiding even today." Toole felt compelled to reflect on modern society, even as he discussed a nineteenth-century author. And his desire to contribute something new to his discipline likely led him to the subject of his undergraduate honor's essay: the obscure British playwright John Lyly.

In the essay Toole argues that Lyly, a playwright of the late sixteenth century, remarkably depicted women as empowered, educated, relatively independent, and often the equal to male characters. Lyly also brought the convention of euphuism—an ornate, witty style of writing—into English literature through his two novels, which Toole argues influenced both the high society for whom he wrote and other playwrights at the time, including Shakespeare. Toole may have taken interest in Lyly as a personality as well. "He seems always to have been determined to maintain his reputation as a clever figure . . . who would impress courtly circles with his understanding and extremely timely interpretations of the contemporary scene." The same description could be aptly applied to Toole.

The essay on Lyly as a culmination of Toole's work at Tulane also accents his interest in the role of women in society. In his cartoons, he depicts mostly women, either frumpy or sultry. In the margins of his class notes, he sketched faces and figures of women, studies of the female form. And in his honor's essay, he focuses on women during the Elizabethan era as seen through the eyes of a male writer. These contemplations may have been a reflection of his own ponderings of women in his life. At home, his mother was the dominant personality, and while she contended that she never pried in her son's business, others remember that she was quite overbearing. While attending Tulane, Toole brought a young woman home on one occasion. His mother deemed that she had a "hoity toity" way of talking. Would another woman ever be welcomed into the Toole home? Or must they remain as unreal as Marilyn Monroe? Toole offers no personal musings on this subject. But his query into the nature of woman throughout his work at Tulane, from his cartoons to his honor's essay, surely signifies something more than an intellectual interest. These female characters mark the beginning of an inquiry in which, years later near the end of his life, he would contemplate the role and the meaning of a mother.

That is not to say that his exploration of the female sex was confined to pen and paper. He connected with several women at Tulane. While working at *Carnival* and *Hullabaloo*, Toole was reacquainted with Emilie "Russ" Dietrich, a childhood friend who had lived next door to the Tooles when they lived on Webster Street. She was an aspiring writer whose "Bacchanalia" was featured in *Carnival*. On Mardi Gras day in 1957, Toole asked Dietrich to dance while she waited for her date to pick her up. She mused years later, "It would be easy to fall in love with a man that could dance like John Kennedy Toole." Their brief dance was not the end of their relationship. They would reconnect several years later in New York City.

On another occasion, he escorted Marcia Suthon to one of the final church services at St. Paul's Episcopal Church, before it was destroyed to make way for a ramp onto the Crescent City Connection, the bridge that spans the Mississippi River, connecting downtown to Algiers Point. It was a historic moment, one of the unfortunate compromises that New Orleans made as it attempted to step toward modernity. On the winter evening of the last service in 1958, Toole and Suthon saw Jane Gwynn, another Fortier alumna and the same girl who used to ride with Toole up and down the elevator eating *petits fours* in Cornelia Sansum's house. After the service, they went to the Napoleon House in the French Quarter for some drinks. They shared an evening of laughter, reminiscing over their high school days.

And according to a biographical article on Toole by Dalt Wonk, the most enduring relationship he had with a woman began at Tulane when he started dating Ruth Lafranz who also worked on *Carnival* and *Hullabaloo*. They had first met on a blind date. Mmahat recalls the couple coming to meetings of the Newman Club. Eventually they started going out regularly, to the movies or to dances at the Roosevelt Hotel. They enjoyed sipping "tall drinks at the Napoleon House, where they laughed about the unrelenting 1812 Overture on the record player." She majored in journalism, and Toole took four journalism classes in his junior year. As the chapter president of Theta Mu, Lafranz sent him an invitation to join the honorary journalism fraternity. While it would be far more fitting than his Greek venture into Delta

Tau Delta, Toole still did not join, but their relationship would continue long after graduation.

While Toole was no socialite, by all accounts he was great fun to be with. He danced well, from the waltz to the Jitterbug. And he made people laugh with his impersonations of professors, fellow students, and anyone who struck his fancy. But as a gentleman, he took care not to impersonate people in his company. His friends during this time recognized that he saw the world in a most unique way. He delivered his observations as hilarious one-man skits, teasing out the absurdities in everyday life, bringing his friends to tears with laughter.

Above all, Toole proved to be an exceptional student at Tulane, from his first day to his last. And his reputation as a scholar supposedly extended past the bounds of the university. His friend Cary Laird reported that, one day, as the two friends contemplated life after graduation, Toole told him the agent of Yul Brynner had asked him to serve as a personal tutor to the Brynner's children as the family traveled about the country. Of course, in 1956 Brynner famously played Ramses in *The Ten Commandments*. And in 1958 he starred as Jean Lafitte in *The Buccaneer*, a remake of the Cecile B. DeMille film that premiered in New Orleans a few months after Toole was born. The Brynner film also made its world premiere in New Orleans, and considering Toole's interest in the movies and his ancestral connection to the pirate Lafitte, he likely attended. Upon hearing of the remarkable offer made to Toole, Laird believed that his friend was telling the truth. But had this offer actually been made, Thelma Toole would have surely gloated, as it would be another validation of her son's talents. Thelma never publicly mentioned such an opportunity offered to her son, or perhaps he had kept it from her. Toole was likely trying to impress Laird. It would be one of many incidents to come in which Toole exaggerated in order to impress a friend, even through his friends rarely doubted his talent. Perhaps Toole needed to reassure himself that he was on some grand path toward greatness.

In his final semester, Toole lived up to his reputation as an exceptional scholar. On one of his papers, his professor, Dr. Fogle, commented, "You have done an excellent job, I think; if you were a graduate student I would still give you perhaps an A- on this paper." He was inducted into the Phi Beta Kappa honor society, and a faculty member nominated him for a Woodrow Wilson National Fellowship. He had secured the key to his future in graduate school.

He probably could have stayed at Tulane to get his master's degree, but Toole felt it was time to move on. At the time, job prospects after graduating from an Ivy League school were much brighter than what Tulane would be able to offer. The fellowship would help him attend a school that he could not otherwise afford. According to Thelma, he wanted to attend Harvard, but he was not accepted. So once again, the electric lights and the energy of New York City beckoned. In late March he opened a letter welcoming him to Columbia University. Luckily, he would not be alone in the city as Ruth Lafranz was also heading to Columbia for her master's in journalism.

After graduation from Tulane, he secured a summer job. The fellowship was generous, but he knew the expense of New York would be challenging. He was hired at the Haspel Brothers, the company that made seersuckers famous. He worked at the factory, located on the east side of the city. Toole was accustomed to the low wages of temporary jobs, and working at the factory was certainly better than selling hot dogs at football games. Such jobs were the pragmatic means to an end—a little more money in his pocket so he could reach his goal of one day becoming a writer, or a professor, or both. Best of all, the factory and its array of characters made for ripe storytelling material. While his friend Laird never envied the conditions in which Toole labored, he loved it when Toole would tell him about the people and the absurd conflicts unfolding at the factory. Toole had found his model for Levy Pants, the first place of employment for Ignatius in *Confederacy*. Although, unlike Ignatius who negotiated a sixty-dollar-per-week salary, Toole's payroll stub suggests he made $34.10 after taxes. It was a rate closer to that of the character Miss Trixie, the aged office worker with rheumy eyes.

Fortunately, his summer before leaving for New York was not all work. Toole visited the Gulf Coast, piling into a convertible with friends, heading east out of the swampy environs of New Orleans to enjoy a day at the beach. The Mississippi coast has long served as a retreat for summer-worn New Orleanians, who long to wade in the water, feel the cool breeze, and watch as those ancient-looking pelicans gracefully fly in low formation across the horizon. But in 1958, viewing the common scenes of the gulf, Toole must have reeled with the excitement of his future prospects. He would trade beignets for bagels, the streetcar for the subway, and the slow, easy pace of his sultry town on the Mississippi River for the bustling thoroughfares of New York City. In several pictures taken at the beach during this summer, Toole shows off his "brawny physique," as his mother had described. His body had filled out from his freshman year. He stands triumphant, ready to take on the world.

Chapter 5

Columbia University

The Manhattan skyline emerges out of the Hudson and East rivers, an American symbol of human ambition. Businessmen, restaurateurs, artists, all manner of disciplines come to New York, hoping to carve a legacy out of this labyrinth; and the city, unforgiving, demands their best. Toole's successes in New Orleans served as stepping-stones to this moment. Far removed from the quaint temper of Tulane, he entered another kind of world at Columbia—a mammoth institution that drew people from every walk of life, students from more than sixty-three nations, and a star-studded faculty from the forefront of knowledge. To a young scholar from the South, Columbia must have seemed a place of limitless possibilities. Here, Toole pursued his dream vision of New York, the place where he would cast a mold for himself far from the comforts and burdens of home. His previous visits to the Big Apple had offered him an introduction to the city, but he understood graduate school in New York would be quite different from a weekend taking in Broadway musicals.

Distanced from the tourist centers of Manhattan, Columbia is situated in Morningside Heights between the Upper West Side and Harlem. Originally named King's College, the school was established in 1754 by a charter from King George II and located in lower Manhattan.

It was renamed Columbia out of patriotic fervor that followed the Revolutionary War, but one can still sense its regal distinction while walking through its current campus. The columned, neoclassical buildings surround green lawns, where students stroll from class to class, from genius lecture to genius lecture. And during Toole's time at Columbia, when the graduate student searched for "overtly social occasions," the *Graduate Student's Guide* suggested visiting "the Graduate Student Lounge . . . about tea-time" where one would find the knowledgeable Mrs. Edgar Grim Miller "presiding over the students and staff members gathered there." With the crown emblem and lion mascot, the faculty and students sat upon their thrones as urbane kings of an urban jungle. In this royal sanctuary, a world apart from the frenzy of Times Square or the bohemian quarters of Greenwich Village, Toole could quietly study in the libraries or ponder literature while sitting along the Hudson in Riverside Park. And yet, the endless diversions of the metropolis were at most a subway ride away. For a young man at the age of twenty, it offered the best of both worlds, serene and exhilarating.

But for all its opportunities, Columbia offered no escape from the sobering, financial reality of living and studying in Manhattan. Even with the good fortune of a fellowship, the imposition of money determined Toole's course from day one. The Woodrow Wilson National Fellowship covered tuition and awarded him fourteen hundred dollars for the entire year, from which he had to pay for room and board, books, and supplies. But it lasted only for the fall and spring semesters. In two semesters it was possible to complete the degree, which required ten courses, writing a thesis, and passing two comprehensive exams. But according to the student guide such an achievement was "unusual." Most master of arts candidates completed the degree requirements over three semesters, usually finishing in the summer. If Toole followed the typical track, he would need money to pay for a summer session. Put into perspective, the student guide presented financial figures for a student with a university loan, savings from a summer job, and income from a part-time job on campus, which still left the student seven hundred dollars short. These funds would "have to be filled from 'outside' sources: [such as] help from family or sponsors, savings, other loans." Toole had no outside sources, certainly no substantial help from his family; they simply could not afford it. It was clear, he had to accomplish the unusual.

He had to graduate in two semesters, after which, if approved, he could continue on to the PhD program at Columbia.

With his deadline established, he began his life as a graduate student. He moved into Furnald Hall, room 1008. It was sparsely furnished with two beds, a sink, and an alcove at the far end, offering enough space for a desk or a chair, positioned under the bay windows. The top floor room offered a view over Broadway. Out of the windows he could see the bell towers of the Union Theological Seminary and Broadway Presbyterian Church, the soaring gothic tower of Riverside Church, and the new high-rise dorms under construction at Barnard College. Ten floors down, the wood-paneled lounge of Furnald Hall with its grand marble fireplace and huge chandelier offered students a spacious escape from the confines of their small rooms. Crown emblems embossed on the coffered ceiling subtly reminded students of their privileged place.

Unpacked and settled in his room, Toole set his sights on the work ahead. He had lectures to attend, much reading to do, and a thesis to write. In the brisk autumn air, he headed to class. His short walk across the South Lawn to Philosophy Hall soon became commonplace. But each day he passed the buildings and statues that ever so clearly evidenced his elevation from Tulane. Upon exiting Furnald, he passed the Graduate School of Journalism, founded by Joseph Pulitzer and where the famed Pulitzer Prize annually originates. To the right, on the south end of the lawn, Toole could see the Butler Library, the giant columns upholding the names of poets and philosophers Homer, Plato, and Socrates. On the north end of the lawn, he passed the iconic Alma Mater statue, sitting upon her throne on the steps of the Low Library with an open book in her lap, her arms outstretched, welcoming all her chosen ones. Finally, approaching Philosophy Hall, he passed an original cast of Rodin's *The Thinker*, the timeless statue prompting contemplation. Renowned academics, poets, and writers had made a similar trek to arrive at those same oak doors. He walked in the footsteps of Allen Ginsberg, Jack Kerouac, Joseph Heller, J. D. Salinger, and Upton Sinclair. Here it was that great thinkers came to study and teach, as they had for decades. Inside, professors sat in their offices, the doors slightly ajar, as they worked on their latest projects. The faint clacking of typewriters echoed into the wood-paneled corridors. Lecture rooms filled with students quietly chatting, awaiting professors. Taking his seat, Toole set his course for something greater than what New Orleans could offer him.

Over the next nine months, he spent much of his time in Philosophy Hall, taking five graduate courses each semester, almost all of which reflected his declared focus on British Literature. His professors for these courses were among the luminaries of Columbia. In their own way they contributed to his development as a scholar, teacher, and writer.

He enrolled in an eighteenth-century British Literature class that was taught by the department chair, Marjorie Nicolson, a "short tank of a woman" often seen "drawing on a cigarette with her thin lips." She declared her independence through her fierce dedication to academic rigor. But never a tyrant, she tailored her questions so as to challenge students, not demoralize them. Students affectionately called her Miss Nicki behind her back.

He also took two courses with the lively William Nelson, another ranking official listed as the department representative in the *Graduate Student's Guide*. Robert Parker, who studied extensively under Nelson, remembers him as an underrated scholar and gentleman. In the seminar on British poet Edmund Spencer, Nelson would often read passages of poetry. He maintained that when read aloud, Spencer's *The Faerie Queen* becomes one of the great joys in literature, despite its intentional archaic language and reputation for difficulty. Nelson's lectures became a kind of literary theater, which may have demonstrated to Toole a way to blend both performance and teaching to create memorable classroom moments. And any young scholar harboring aspirations of a writer in the mid-twentieth century would benefit from William Tindall's Contemporary British Literature course. Under Tindall's guidance, Toole leapt into the world of James Joyce, reading *Finnegan's Wake* and *Ulysses*. Tindall encouraged students to discard the confines of historical context and read a work of literature in its present-day significance, an approach that differed from Toole's undergraduate instruction. But such a challenge may have provided him an opportunity to appreciate Joyce in a new light. As an author steeped in the place of his birth, Joyce used his city, Dublin, to parallel the roots of Western literature in *Ulysses*. And yet, Tindall argued, one need not understand those roots to appreciate the work. Similarly, in *Confederacy*, Toole would compose a reflection of

New Orleans, while connecting the work to the long line of his literary predecessors, from Chaucer to Dickens, and yet he would achieve an accessibility open to anyone with a sense of humor.

By far the most important professor he met at Columbia was John Wieler who taught a course on sixteenth-century literature, the area of Toole's particular interest. Wieler was a graduate of the PhD program at Columbia and must have been teaching there as a part-time faculty member. By 1959 he was already acting chairman at Hunter College, an all-girls school located on the east side of Manhattan. Wieler would prove integral in Toole's professional life, essentially opening the door to his transition from student to professor. The two would spend an academic year getting to know each other, a year in which Wieler became very impressed by Toole.

It is quite possible Toole also attended other lectures outside the courses for which he registered. At that time, graduate students did not earn grades for each class. There was no attendance taken and most lecture courses required no term papers. The English department held the philosophy that "Students devote themselves to preparation for final examinations and to Essays or Dissertations. Courses . . . are designed as aids to their progress, rather than as ends in themselves." One need not appear on a specific class roster to partake in the learning; they just needed to show up early enough to find a seat. Many graduate students registered for courses, as they needed to pay for thirty credits of coursework, but they attended other classes out of interest. William Cullen Bryant II could be giving a lecture on Romanticism, or Mark Van Doren might be discussing his recent book *Don Quixote's Profession*. Toole could take full advantage of the intellectually rich environment.

Clearly the opportunities for learning at Columbia were abundant. But as a student sitting in a class among eighty peers, and as a young scholar trying to navigate the ways of a new institution, Columbia could also be a lonely place. It offered little warmth in its welcome to graduate students. Toole had received the *Graduate Student Guide* in June, giving him sufficient time to read what the dean of the graduate faculties referred to as "the law." Therein students were forthrightly told,

There is no disgrace in acknowledging that you are not cut out for a scholarly career; and the sooner this discovery is made, the better. . . .

Far better to be in doubt and withdraw than to "grind out" a degree by brute persistence.

According to this handbook, the successful student would read incessantly, type to perfection, not burden his professors with inane questions of policy, and, most importantly, become an independent scholar. It preemptively forgives the professors burdened with thought if they overlook the questions of students. "If it should happen that in the welter of . . . multifarious and yearly increasing demands, an officer of instruction should accidentally overlook a student's legitimate need of consultation time, it would not be surprising." Another graduate student in the English department in 1958, Robert Bozanich, took away from the handbook the lesson that "one should not greet a professor in a casual encounter on campus and . . . one should not feel rebuffed if ignored." Like many students at the time, Toole must have found this abrasiveness off-putting. He wanted the rigor and prestige of Columbia, but he would tire of this institutional condescension.

Furthermore, the English department ran a massive operation where MA candidates often felt insignificant. Thelma Toole referred to it as a machine, churning out graduates. The clear sense of hierarchy between the PhD and the MA students could make the graduate experience "very impersonal." And the "huge lecture classes" offered "few opportunities for student-to-student or student-to-professor" interaction. At Columbia, Toole learned much from his professors, and he fortunately found a mentor in Wieler, but such a bond was not the usual for everyone, especially at the MA level.

Despite the institutional shortcomings of Columbia, Toole had at his doorstep one of the invaluable benefits of coming to New York, the artistic and cultural capital of the country. When not in class, he reveled in his explorations of the city, especially in the autumn when New York appears most alive. Trees arch over walkways; yellow, red, and orange leaves burst with color, a vibrant spectacle against the backdrop of black pavement and gray concrete. Ruth Lafranz, his romantic interest from Tulane, accompanied him on some of these excursions. As Dalt Wonk reports, "The two Southerners did up Gotham. They went to Coney Island, rode the Staten Island Ferry. They frequented Roseland, a dance palace. They took in plays and operas and the Bronx zoo."

And naturally Toole enjoyed wandering through Greenwich Village, the artistic hub of New York in 1958. While New York had the Quarter, New York had the Village, and both places attracted colorful characters. Within the first few weeks after Toole arrived in New York, he strolled through the Village and reported some of his observations in a letter to Dave Prescott, an acquaintance and graduate student from Tulane. Prescott responded, "Your first reactions to life at Columbia and to the Village proved most interesting reading." In a four-page reply letter, Prescott offered Toole a detailed update of Tulane, reviewing new graduate students, additions to their "lunchroom coterie," and other New Orleans news. He also tells of an occurrence in the French Quarter, a story of violence and dark humor Toole likely found amusing. Prescott sets the scenario with the well-publicized murder of a Mexican tour guide by three Tulane students. Amid the subsequent tensions between whites and Hispanics, a friend of Prescott's was victimized. A new graduate student to Tulane named Shmuel Barovsky was walking in the Quarter when three Latinos "bludgeoned . . . his skull three times with a lead pipe and robbed" him. Prescott writes that Shmuel "began screaming at the top of his lungs causing a resident to open her window and in turn cry out." The attackers grabbed what looked like his wallet but was really his address book and ran away. A patrolman soon came, and the two "were off to Charity" hospital. But on the way to Charity, they saw the three assailants, chased them down, and caught them as other police converged on the scene. The officers began to push the "disturbers-of-the-peace" into a police van. And as Shmuel stood "dazedly beside the patrol car with blood pouring down over his shoulders" a policeman started pushing him toward the van. Another officer noticed the commotion and yelled out, "That's the victim!" Shmuel was let go, spent a few days in the hospital, and returned to school, "wearing his beret everywhere to cover his stitches."

Dimwitted burglars, a victim mistaken for the criminal, a comedy of errors in the Quarter—even in Toole's absence New Orleans remained the same. And with such an unusual name as Shmuel, the original Hebrew version of Samuel, it seems beyond coincidence that Myrna Minkoff mentions a Shmuel in a letter to Ignatius in *Confederacy*. In Toole's novel Shmuel is the writer of a "bold and shattering movie" about an "interracial marriage." The screenplay, as Myrna reports, is "chock-full of disturbing truths and had the most fascinating tonalities and ironies." Prescott tells Toole of Shmuel suffering from racial tensions in New Orleans, and Toole puts him in New York commenting on interracial marriage.

The letter exchange between Toole and Prescott also illustrates a primary connection between New Orleans and New York that attracted Toole to both cities. They are places where all the complicated characteristics of the human condition are on display all the time; one merely needs to walk through the streets to find the tragically funny scenes of everyday life.

But even for a seasoned urban dweller such as Toole, someone who was much more comfortable riding a streetcar than walking through the woods, both cities could overwhelm him. At times, he needed to get away from the bright lights and clamor. In New Orleans he would retreat to the Gulf. While in the northeast, he took a November sojourn to Massachusetts. Snapshots from this trip capture views of boulders and tree-lined beaches on Marblehead Neck, the bayside estates across the water, and the Marblehead lighthouse that he ascended to capture a shot of the crashing waves of the Atlantic Ocean. The huge rocks along the coast, just outside Salem, made for a scene quite different from the creeping waters of Louisiana. This was the same seaside town that inspired H. P. Lovecraft's fictional town Kingsport. He was the same writer from whom the phrase of Ignatius Reilly—"theology and geometry"—stems. Toole also visited Cambridge, taking a snapshot of the recently built Kresge Auditorium at the Massachusetts Institute of Technology, a building praised as a prime example of modern architecture. Interestingly, no pictures from this trip capture an image of Toole or, if present, traveling companions. Perhaps, after months in Manhattan, he cherished these moments because they were solitary.

If his cool November day on the rocky coast of Massachusetts offered him respite from New York, it also signaled the coming of winter. The winds had stripped the weakened leaves from the trees. With no exams or final papers at Columbia, the semester ended quietly, and he began the long holiday break. He now had more time to venture about the city. But the frigid northeast winter brought out an aspect of New York he had never witnessed. People covered from head to toe, their eyes pointed downward, averting the cold air; they quickly ducked into buildings and into taxis, escaping the winter winds. The homeless curled into corners, sitting on greasy cardboard, their shaking hands sticking out from mismatched layers of coats and blankets. His dream vision of Manhattan faded as he tried to make sense of this disturbing collage. And Toole turned to poetry to express what he saw. In his poem "New York: Three Aspects," he surveys the city and its people, focusing on the tensions between the cold winter and the glistening sunlight that hit the windows of skyscrapers, between "An East Side Heiress" and the "Hopeless of Third Avenue." At the end of the poem he brings together this incongruous diversity: "New York / is today's Noah's Ark." And while Noah's Ark stands as a symbol of rebirth and hope amid devastation, Toole originally ended the poem with the line that cynically defines New York, as "The American way in a biblical bank." In the typed version he struck that line, ending the poem with more ambiguity.

As time passed, Toole no longer found humorous observations of life in the city as he did in his first weeks at Columbia. The winter set the contrasts between the rich and the poor, the light and the dark, the high and the low in harsh relief. In "New York: Three Aspects," his perspective takes on shades of what the French call a *flâneur*, like Charles Baudelaire wandering about Paris, an observer of humanity, finding a bitter existentialism in all that he sees. The rosy-colored glasses through which Toole once viewed New York darkened. And if his poems were expressions of his perspective, then his view of academics darkened as well.

During the winter break, he drafted a poem titled "The Arbiter," wherein he expresses misgivings over the role of the literary critic. The speaker of the poem cynically summarizes the argument of a literary scholar and author who echoes Nietzsche's Zarathustra in proclaiming poetry dead. The critic asserts that "writers sought to mirror their existence," which was not worthy of poetry but "mere ritual / Falsely spiritual." In the retelling of the argument, Toole mocks the conventions of literary scholarship with parenthetical references to other works. And ironically the scholar seems wholly unaware that his position undermines his own legitimacy. A poetry critic has no purpose if poetry is really dead. But it becomes evident in the poem that the critic has no intention of enriching people's understanding of literature; he wants to

sell copies of his book, even at the expense of poetry. The poem ends
with these lines:

> *The book sold well, we understand,*
> *Although the cover itself would command*
> *A buyer's attention: a large, abstract bee*
> *Crushing a butterfly with a typewriter key.*

Through the act of writing, the critic violently kills the beautiful
and transformative spirit of the poet. Toole may have seen himself as
the butterfly. After *The Neon Bible* failed to win the contest, he determined the work lifeless and put it to rest. In this poem, he attempts to
revitalize his creative pursuits. And just as he did with his novella, he
intended to submit the poem to a contest. On February 1 he wrote to
his mother:

"The American Scholar" is sponsoring a poetry contest.
With the long holidays here and a degree of free time on
my hands I figured, why not try?

Enclosed is the first poem I wrote (in 2 hours). I know
that some of it may seem esoteric to you, but please
read it and let me know what you think. I first wrote
"thing" as that last word. Must be the Lawrence Welk
influence.

Love—and read it, please. Ken.

He never let his mother see *The Neon Bible*, but now he sought her
opinion on this poem. He repeats his request of her to read it, as if
something in it was meant for her, perhaps a veiled confession of his wavering confidence in his academic pursuits. The poem looks with suspicion at the scholar who "consistently attacked / the writers of reaction."
As such, "The Arbiter" springs from a query into the relationship between artist and critic. Was Toole being groomed by scholars who dismissed contemporary literature, attempting to wield power over it? And
if a division exists between writer and critic, what side would he choose?
This poem seems to signal his growing discontent with literary criti-

cism. These questions would resurface throughout his life, as he repeatedly stepped into and fell out of the pursuit of a PhD. And this inquiry ultimately led to larger questions. "New York: Three Aspects" and "The Arbiter" are two of several unpublished poems and stories likely written in New York during this time. On these manuscripts, as well as on his college essays, he uses varied forms of his name—Kennedy Toole, Kenny Toole, John Toole, and J. K. Toole. Considering his first name comes from his father and his middle name from his mother's grandmother, these choices may well indicate self-reflective questions of identity. He appears to be asking himself: Who am I? Who do I want to be? How will I be remembered?

Writers of a new literary movement that was taking shape in the New York neighborhood in which he lived proposed similar questions. While Toole attended classes and wandered about New York City, Jack Kerouac, Allen Ginsberg, and others were enjoying their newfound literary fame, which had roots in their days at Columbia. In fact "The Arbiter," with its description of the poet as a "poetical Bramin and self-conscious intellectual," may have been inspired by the conservative reaction from critics who deplored the Beats. While there are few parallels to draw between the writings of the Beat Generation and the writings of Toole, in 1959 he evidently took an interest in Beat writers, particularly Kerouac.

While in New York, Toole purchased Kerouac's newly published novella *The Subterraneans*. Since it was by no means recommended reading for his graduate courses, he must have selected it out of his own interests. His copy, inscribed with his Furnald address, resides in the Toole Papers at Tulane. It is the only book from his library that was not sold or given away after his death. *The Subterraneans* deals with the contradicting forces of an artist's need to create and his desire to maintain a steady relationship with a woman. The opening lines illustrate the battle between ego and insecurity in a "self-conscious intellectual." Toole fought a similar battle until the end of his life:

> Once I was young and had so much more orientation and could talk with nervous intelligence about everything and with clarity and without as much literary preambling as this; in other words this is the story of an unself-confident man, at the same time an ego-maniac.

The narrator recognizes there is meaning in love, and yet he has to "rush off and construct construct for nothing." In the end, he makes his decision that fills him with regret: "I go home having lost her love. And write this book." It was a message that may have spoken directly to Toole. As he explored the city with Lafranz, he still found himself compelled to achieve some greatness he had not yet fully designed, perhaps at the compromise of a relationship he held dear.

Toole also had the opportunity to see Kerouac in New York. On November 6, 1958, Kerouac sat on a panel at Hunter College (where his mentor John Wieler chaired the English department) to discuss the question "Is there such thing as a Beat Generation?" *On the Road* was published in 1957, and *The Subterraneans* had just been released by Grove Press, catapulting Kerouac from an obscure drifter to a leader of a literary movement that was gaining momentum. British novelist Kingsley Amis, a writer that Toole also admired, sat on the panel that night, along with anthropologist Ashley Montagu and journalist James Wechsler. By all accounts, it was an odd mix. Amis earnestly questioned the meaning of the Beat movement, while Kerouac, under the initial impression he was going to lecture and read from his works, drunkenly responded to questions and identified some comical roots of the Beat generation. He named influences such as Harpo Marx and Krazy Kat, from George Herriman's *Krazy Kat and Ignatz*.

As the literary wild child of the day, Kerouac was an iconoclast, discarding the restraints of tradition in both his works and his life. In reading Kerouac, and perhaps witnessing his antics at Hunter, Toole encountered an alternative track toward a literary life. Rejecting the narrow walls of academia, Kerouac searched for America, taking a physical and spiritual journey, the basis for *On the Road*. His travels westward inspired a generation to follow his lead—perhaps influencing Toole to take his own trip across America ten years later. In the late 1960s, Toole would incorporate the Beats into his class lectures, particularly praising the work of Kerouac. And both writers share some compelling biographical similarities. They both attended Columbia; they both struggled to make the world see their unique genius, often heeding an editor's requests to make their work "publishable"; they both retreated from a society that no longer made sense to them; and they both took their final journey to the grave in 1969.

If Toole missed seeing Kerouac at Hunter College, he had another opportunity to witness the Beat poets on February 5, 1959, a short walk from his dormitory at Columbia. Five days after Toole sent his poem "The Arbiter" to his mother, Allen Ginsberg returned to his alma mater for a controversial reading. It is not certain that Toole was in the audience that night. He was not one of the self-identified Beats, unshaven and dressed in black, but he surely knew about the event taking place less than a block away. The obscenity trial over Ginsberg's poem *Howl* made national news, and Ginsberg's return to Columbia created chatter on campus among faculty and students. The English department officially disassociated from the whole event. However, Diana Trilling, the wife of Ginsberg's former English professor Lionel Trilling, sneaked away to the reading, while her husband held a meeting in their home with far less controversial literary figures such as W. H. Auden. As Diana reports, the time drew near for the reading, and "word spread of vast barbarian hordes converging on poor dull McMillin Theater from all the dark recesses of the city, howling for their leader." When she arrived at the theater, she expected to see a congregation of degenerates. Instead she found a group of nearly fourteen hundred people, mostly inoffensive youth who, to her surprise, "smelt clean."

That night Ginsberg read "Kaddish," a poem about the consuming insanity of his mother, her commitment to a mental hospital, and her eventual death. It is a wrenching narrative that would speak to any young man, particularly an only child caught between a sense of filial duty and a longing to fulfill his own life dreams. At the end of the reading, Ginsberg, in tears, embraced his father who sat in attendance. Trilling expresses the overwhelming pity of the audience, which was a surprising emotional response from supposed foul-smelling rebels. Granted, Toole may have been inclined to mock such displays of emotion in the company of friends. But he was not heartless. In some ways, Toole would be able to relate to Ginsberg. Toole's father was developing neuroses, which would fester into a full-blown mental illness that relegated him to the backroom. In Toole's most private moments, he proclaimed his love and expressed his exhaustion with his parents, much like Ginsberg had done with his mother on that Thursday night in 1959.

Ginsberg also offered a vociferous reproach of academics at Columbia. During the question-and-answer period, Ginsberg proclaimed, as

Trilling paraphrases, "No one at Columbia knew anything about prosody; the English department was stuck in the nineteenth century, sensible of no meter other than the old iambic pentameter." This diatribe was soft compared to his rant against Columbia in September of 1958. In a letter to his friend John Hollander, Ginsberg writes, "What a Columbia instructor can recognize in Pound he can't see in Olson's method, what he can see in Lorca or Apollinaire he can't see in *Howl*— it's fantastic. You call this education? I call it absolute brainwashed bullshit." Ginsberg wanted to reclaim poetry from the hands of the arbiters at Columbia.

Even if Toole missed Ginsberg's reading, the event evoked the spirit of the times in New York City. Fred Kaplan, author of *1959: The Year Everything Changed*, identifies Ginsberg's reading as one of the keystone moments that preceded the social upheaval of the 1960s. Indeed the changing tides moved about Toole in New York City in 1959, although what that change would mean was yet unclear. Miles Davis recorded *Kind of Blue* at Columbia 30th Street Studio; Harry Truman gave a three-day lecture series at Columbia; Fidel Castro toured the Bronx Zoo, and the owner of Grove Press published the uncensored version of *Lady Chatterly's Lover*. Toole was no anarchist or experimentalist, but in New York, on the home turf of the Beats, he must have heard his generation growing discontent by the old order of its elders. It was the generational difference, as Trilling puts it, between the aged scholar, sitting in his comfortable living room, dressed in a suit, dryly critiquing literature, while his protégé passionately reads poetry on the school stage, bringing audience members to tears. If Toole was there that night, he witnessed the butterfly emerge from the typewriter in his full brilliance, refusing to be crushed by the arbiter.

Ultimately Toole found his style in refined wit and slapstick humor. In fact, Toole playfully mocks the beatniks in *Confederacy*. Myrna Minkoff, an angry revolutionary looking to usurp the establishment without any clear sense of why she rebels, is a classic beatnik. And in the last pages of the novel, as Ignatius and Myrna run for the car to make their escape to New York City, the next-door neighbor calls out from behind the shutters, "Hey, where are you two beatniks going?" While he pokes fun at followers of the Beats, he does not take aim at their works. And to whatever degree he sympathized with the discontent of the youth generation, at the very least he considered the complex layers of New York, just as he saw the complexity of New Orleans. It would be all too easy for him to entrench in the libraries and halls of Columbia for his short time in the city. But Toole was too interested in humankind to be so obtuse. He cultivated a vision of New York that stretched from the ivory tower in Morningside Heights to the subterranean realm of the "angel-headed hipsters" of the Beats.

By spring Toole had to narrow his expansive vision of the metropolis. He put to rest his winter of poetry to focus on fulfilling the requirements of his degree. By then he had the attention of John Wieler, who named Toole "the number one student in the sixteenth century seminar in which there were nine students, three of which were Woodrow Wilson Fellows." And he was also well prepared for his master's thesis. Already approved in October of 1958, it was to be another essay on the women characters of John Lyly's plays. Scholars and biographers have noted that his thesis was a "rewrite" of his undergraduate honor's essay, but it is, virtually, the same paper. He changed the title, and he added a three-page introduction. He changed some words, and he shifted around some phrases and a few paragraphs. Essentially, he edited it. Even his conclusion reads nearly verbatim from his undergraduate essay, except a sentence he added at the end where he claims Lyly's works as a predecessor to Shakespeare's. Submitting an essay originally written for another purpose was uncharacteristic of Toole. Of course, it may have been a choice driven by finances. A thesis in need of only a few touchups would help him complete the program in two semesters. And the choice may have been affirmed by his winter suspicions of the role of the critic. He had dissected Lyly before. He would not have to heft another work of art onto his examination table. And the fact that the essay he essentially wrote at Tulane satisfied the degree requirements for his MA from Columbia testifies to his academic virtuosity in his undergraduate days. Surely he could have crafted another essay, but as usual, time and money worked against him. In March of 1959, his thesis was approved. Professor Wieler commented that his work "reflected wide reading, critical acumen and literary sensitivity."

During his last few months at Columbia, he prepared for the final examinations. On May 18 he took the six-hour essay test that covered literary theory and literary history. His nine months of reading and attending lectures had boiled down to these essays. Like most challenges in his life thus far, he excelled. He passed the exam and was approved to graduate. But not all graduates were equal at Columbia. The English department had a ranking system, tied to continuance into the PhD program. As the *Graduate Student's Guide* explains, "The Third Class is considered a Pass; the Second, Honors; the First, rarely awarded, High Honors." Toole graduated with High Honors.

With this distinction he could have continued on to the PhD program, but this would mean he would need funding. Many PhD students in the English department taught at other colleges to make ends meet. Wieler tried to secure Toole a teaching position at Hunter College. But Hunter maintained a rigid rule of hiring only professors with experience. Despite his attempts to convince Hunter to make an exception in the case of Toole, the college was unyielding. Without experience, his prospects of landing a teaching job in New York were grim. But a break from graduate studies may have been a welcomed reprieve as well. The winter season had provoked serious questions over the role of the literary critic. And he did, after all, harbor aspirations of becoming a fiction writer. In the Woodrow Wilson fellowship directory, his listing appears as "John Kennedy Toole . . . MA 1959; Columbia University; Graduate studies interrupted—plans uncertain." Despite the completion of his degree, Toole still found himself in limbo, somewhere between scholar, writer, and teacher.

With his future unclear, Toole graduated on a cool spring day in Manhattan. On June 2, more than six thousand students gathered to participate in commencement at Columbia. Usually the ceremony would take place on the South Lawn under the watchful eye of the goddess Alma Mater, but with light rain drizzling throughout the day, graduation was moved to St. John the Divine, the nearby Episcopal cathedral. Like most graduations, the president praised students for their accomplishments and sent them forth to work for a better tomorrow. He reminded them that they were an elite group, graduating from an institution undistracted by the lunacy of sports or socializing, fully invested in intellectual growth. The graduation ceremony in the cathedral, jam-packed with nearly ten thousand people culminated an intense year for Toole. It had tested his intellect and his fortitude for living in New York, a city he found both exhilarating and exhausting.

Regardless of where he would end up, New York left its imprint on Toole. He adopted a rapid cadence in his speech, discarding his Southern drawl. He picked up the Ivy League style—a form-fitting coat and a slim tie. He also heeded the advice of the *Graduate Student's Guide*, which suggested upon graduation the student should "leave the institution he has learned to consider his intellectual nest and fly under his own power in a new academic environment, no longer a student but an officer of instruction."

However, he took an opposite direction from the subsequent advice in the handbook, which snobbishly states, "Better to teach first-rate minds in a good preparatory school than to waste one's spirit on the tenth-rate in an inferior college." As a graduate of one of the premier institutions of higher education in the country, he applied for his first job teaching English at Southwestern Louisiana Institute, a small college with open enrollment admissions in the backwaters of southern Louisiana. Toole tapped his professor at Tulane to write a letter of recommendation. Therein, Richard Fogle comments on Toole, "He is certainly a good bet. . . . He is attractive in a slightly dour fashion (heavy eyebrows) and talks well. . . . He seems an extremely solid fellow who has developed a great deal in the past couple of years. . . . All in all . . . you'll be lucky to get Toole as far as prospects go."

Wieler also wrote a glowing letter, recounting Toole's stellar year at Columbia and offering his "unqualified recommendation." But that letter suggests Toole may have understood this to be a temporary move. Wieler indicates that Toole would have a place in New York once he gained some teaching experience. "If Mr. Toole ever returns to Columbia to complete his Ph.D.," Wieler writes, "I shall make every effort to give him some work while he completes his degree." As Toole prepared to leave New York City, he was likely aware that the doorway back to Columbia was clear and open to him.

The job offer from Southwestern Louisiana Institute came quickly. They would pay him four thousand dollars for the academic year, teaching five freshman-level writing courses per semester. Toole accepted, and the department was thrilled to have him on board. Professor Paul Nolan wrote to Toole in the summer of 1959, suggesting that he would enjoy Lafayette. He warned Toole the town was small, but "in matters of personal and academic liberty it compares favorably to both" New York and New Orleans. However, Nolan draws one major distinction between New Orleans and Lafayette. In Cajun country "the crawfish is better."

So Toole packed his belongings and left his tenth floor room with the view of the high rises and bell towers. He returned to the second-floor apartment on Audubon Street, the family home under the canopied green of Uptown New Orleans. Back in his hometown, he spent the rest of his summer counting the days before moving to the bayou, a journey that would change his life forever.

Chapter 6

Cajun Country

D riving west out of New Orleans in the late summer of 1959, Toole crossed over the undulating land of southern Louisiana, watching as it sank into murky brown waters then rose to the flat fields where plantations once grew sugar cane and rice. He crossed the Atchafalaya swamp, open and expansive, where water and land mingle, where alligators lurk beneath the surface, and where the warm breeze gently moves through the cypress trees. In his epic poem *Evangeline*, Henry Wadsworth Longfellow imagined this same ancient place "resplendent in beauty" with "numberless sylvan islands" and air "faint . . . with the odorous breath of magnolia blossoms."

For centuries, the bayous of southern Louisiana have been home to the Cajuns, descendants of the French settlers who were banished from their homes in the eighteenth century, following the British invasion of Acadiana, the land now called Nova Scotia. Seeking refuge under a French government, the Acadians arrived in New Orleans to find the ruling Spanish pointing them toward the wild western territory, a land left to the native tribes and freed blacks willing to attempt a life in its treacherous beauty.

For much of Louisiana history, Cajuns have been viewed as the rural poor, cast in popular culture as bumbling and toothless hicks. To outsiders they appeared ignorant and uncivilized. But in truth they hailed from a rich cultural history. Perhaps through the isolation of the bayou or from their shared story of exile, they kept their French legacy alive, while incorporating the African and Native American traditions of their neighbors. They blend the flavors of those varied cultures in pots of gumbo, crawfish *étouffée*, and jambalaya. They dance and sing to the earthy sounds of Zydeco, to another day alive. They seem to celebrate their understanding that all human endeavors slowly slip back into the water.

At the western edge of the vast swamp, the land ascends to an elevated plateau, and there sits Lafayette, the capital of Cajun country. When Toole arrived, French was still spoken in the shops and restaurants, but the Cajun way of life was quickly changing. Since the early 1950s, Texas oil companies that had moved into the region had been propelling the city toward modernization. Sons and daughters left their family farms, their flat-bottom boats, and their kitchens to attend Southwestern Louisiana Institute (now the University of Louisiana at Lafayette), hoping to secure a future with more money and less hardship. The school that once focused on agricultural studies and was still completely bordered by farms now bustled with mostly Cajun students taking all manner of courses, seeking a different kind of life.

In early September the annual frenzy of course registration took over the campus. Meanwhile, Toole settled into his new home. He had found a two-room ground floor apartment in a converted carriage house outside the home of Elisabeth Montgomery on Covent Street. His landlady, "a hyperactive widow in her sixties," came from a wealthy family, but she kept her guesthouse in modest condition. Toole once described it to his friend Joel Fletcher as "a cramped heart of darkness with cockroaches and a linoleum floor." The dark dips and crevices of the pecky cypress wall paneling made perfect homes for spiders and other little bugs. But for all its discomforts, it was a place of his own, absent the clamor of dorm life or the presence of his parents. On the second floor apartment lived the artist Elmore Morgan Jr., with whom Toole could discuss literature and art in the lazy moments of an evening or a Sunday afternoon.

It would take some time for Toole to adjust to life in Lafayette. He had to slow his New York pace. And on the first day of class, he reckoned with his new place of employment. From the front of the campus, SLI looked like many colleges— distinguished red brick buildings with white-columned porticos connected to arched walkways, offering the architectural accents that dignify an institution of higher learning. But Toole would have no corner office overlooking the green lawn where undergraduates mingle between classes. His post was with the rest of the English teachers at the back of the campus in an orderly collection of decomposing army surplus buildings. Originally constructed as a temporary training facility during World War II, SLI had purchased the buildings to accommodate the increase in students. It seemed so far away from the main campus that students named it Little Abbeville after the town twenty miles south of Lafayette. It was the home of the English department.

Isolated from the rest of campus, the push for modernity in Lafayette did not reach the decrepit little "town" on the edges. Few of the classrooms in Little Abbeville had the luxury of a fan; most depended on open windows in the summer and a potbelly stove to keep warm in the winter. Paint peeled from the thin walls, water dripped from the ceilings, and wood desks were crammed into every space available. Humidity and termites had fed on the buildings so badly that if female students wore high heels the wood floor would crumble under their steps. Occasionally, in the midst of a lecture, a professor would go to write on the blackboard and under the pressure of his hand a small section of the wall would give way.

And yet, despite the condition of the buildings, SLI was in many ways a perfect place for Toole to gain experience teaching. While much of the South remained racially segregated, holding on to the delusion of "separate but equal," SLI had opened its doors to black students a few months after the 1954 *Brown vs. Board of Education* decision, which made it unconstitutional for black students to be segregated into separate schools. It was the first college in Louisiana to do so. So Toole walked into racially integrated classrooms. And because the students largely came from segregated school districts, teaching required patience and tolerance in order to address the disparities in their varied skill levels.

Regardless of race, the rural roots of the students were obvious. Many of them primarily spoke Cajun French, even though speaking French had been banned in the school systems. Many of them came from families adept at life in southern Louisiana—able to hunt alligator, trap crawfish, tend to crops, and make a perfect *roux*—all-important skills in the bayou. Writing an academic essay, however, posed a formidable challenge. It was clear his labors in Lafayette would differ drastically from honor's classes and graduate seminars. Just a few months prior, Toole had strolled between the towering skyscrapers of New York and conversed with the sophisticates of Columbia; it all must have seemed like another life once lived in a vague past. And yet, even as he carried the air of an Ivy League graduate into his remedial English courses, he treated his students with unequivocal respect. "He was always gracious to them," his friend and colleague Patricia Rickels remembers, "and they loved him."

But for Toole, courtesies rarely overshadowed the humor of humanity. He found daily comical moments as his students, many of them well into their adulthood, periodically stumbled in attempts to sound scholarly. They would try to impress him with elaborate vocabulary that they clearly misunderstood and often misused. He once shared with friends a quote from one of his female students. In a slow, deliberate Southern drawl, he repeated, "*Intrinsically*, I knowed it to be true." The conviction with which she expressed her nonsensical statement amused him. Of course, he would have never mocked her to her face. Such humor was shared and kept between colleagues.

As a new teacher, Toole also benefitted from a department that took its mission of teaching seriously—more than it pressured the faculty to publish or conduct research. The faculty's dedication created a robust camaraderie between its members. In fact, many of them recognized they could learn a great deal from each other. Rickels remembers how faculty members used to sit outside of classroom doors, listening to their colleagues lecture. Closing her eyes, imagining back to 1960, she recalled, "Dick Wagner, Ken Toole, Bobby Byrne . . . you would always learn something." Far from the seats of authority, in Little Abbeville, professors made their classrooms self-contained worlds that they could shape with their students, even if that world was physically crumbling around them. With the support of colleagues passionate about teaching and without worries of overbearing administrators, Toole had the freedom to refine his skills as a teacher.

But just as the isolation of the Cajuns created some of the colorful culture in southern Louisiana, so too the English faculty, largely left to their own means in Little Abbeville, seemed to attract and cultivate eccentrics. Toole would later playfully call them a "faculty composed of fiends and madmen." Shortly after his arrival in Lafayette, he must have marveled at the madcap personalities, like most new faculty members did. George Deaux, an aspiring novelist who came to work at the college a few weeks after Toole left, never forgot the "peculiar behavior" in the department. Reviewing some of the most memorable moments, Deaux recalls,

One guy had a fixation that he could only grade papers after he had found a four-leaf clover. As hundreds of freshmen essays piled up on his desk, he searched even at night with a flashlight for a four-leaf clover. Another colleague became convinced that the voice of Dorothy Wordsworth was speaking to her from the radiator in her room.

Joel Fletcher and several others at the college recall the hallucinating instructor was actually a "skinny young male" who believed Emily Dickinson, not Dorothy Wordsworth, spoke through the radiator. Regardless of the instructor's gender or what nineteenth-century author communicated from beyond the grave, one day George Deaux and a small group of faculty "gathered around the radiator to debunk this nonsense only to hear the voice speaking from it." They "finally concluded that the radiator was picking up a radio signal."

This eccentricity even extended to some of the students. "Deaux recalls one student named Ted, who for unknown reasons emptied his .38 revolver into his TV set while his seventy-year-old mother in her rocking chair egged him on: 'Shoot it agin, Ted. Shoot it agin!'"

Of course, not all the strange behavior was so humorous. English professor Thomas Sims suffered a mental breakdown the year after Toole taught at SLI. Bereaved by his wife's early death from cancer, Sims "stopped talking altogether, would meet his classes, sit silently at his desk for an hour, and then leave the room." The college transferred him to an administrative position.

While some faculty showed the fragility of the mind, most exhibited foibles of outrageous hilarity. By far the most memorable and monumental specimen of eccentricity who left an indelible impression on Toole was Bobby Byrne, a mustached medievalist, tall and burly with dark hair. He lived in a little cabin behind the house of a fellow professor, where he played his harp, his *violà de gamba*, and a harpsichord he had custom made in England. As an avid devotee to Boethius, he assigned *The Consolation of Philosophy* to every class he taught, even freshman composition. As Professor Rickels remembers, "He believed the climax of civilization occurred sometime during the fourteenth century; it had been on a steady decline ever since." Byrne often said of people their "geometry and theology are all wrong," echoing a favorite line of his from an H. P. Lovecraft short story. And while he had completed his doctoral course work at Tulane, he never wrote his dissertation. At one time, one of Byrne's professors is reported to have said to him, "Bobby, just give me a piece of paper with something written on it, and I will give you your PhD." But he deemed the exercise of a dissertation unnecessary. "I wasn't going to learn anything from it, and besides I already had tenure," he admitted in an interview in 1995 with University of Louisiana graduate student Carmine Palumbo. "Ya see," he explained further, "I have a birth defect. I am amazingly unambitious." And yet this supposedly unambitious man taught himself to read Welsh and ancient Japanese, simply because he had heard they were the two most difficult languages to learn.

Behind his supercilious posturing, Byrne was also known for his ill-timed flatulence, and he harbored a deep devotion to hot dogs. He once told Rickels a story from his childhood that explained and justified his passion for the common street food. When he was growing up, his mother had become convinced that "wieners were not good for children." But taking pity on her son, she would occasionally yield to his pleas. Preparing the rare and savory treat, she carefully buttered both sides of a split bun as the young Bobby watched with anticipation. Then she nestled the sanctioned sausage into its soft throne. But as she handed it to little Bobby, she would squeeze the bun so the hot dog would slip back into her hand, leaving the child only the buttered bun to eat. "I felt cheated all my life," he would say, thinking back to all the hot dogs that had eluded him in his youth. In adulthood, he reclaimed those lost wieners.

Whether by chance or choice, Byrne and Toole shared an office at SLI. They actually had much in common. Byrne was hired the year before Toole, so he was relatively new to the faculty. They were both raised in Uptown, had an interest in medieval thought, and graduated from Tulane, although Byrne had finished his undergraduate studies nearly a decade prior to Toole. They also felt a fierce sense of devotion to their hometown. And like any two New Orleanians, their histories connected long before a formal introduction. Byrne's aunt was Toole's second-grade teacher, who remembered the bright child and his hovering mother.

Their similarities of background aside, one could not conceive of a more opposite pair sitting together in an office. Toole's average height and trendy fashion sense contrasted with Byrne's burly physique and his incomprehensibly bizarre manner of dressing. Byrne cared little about coordinating his attire. And his blatant disregard for appearances occasionally shocked Toole, who always had his clothes "fit, tapered, neat as a pin . . . carefully fitted pants with a good crease in them." One day Byrne came to their office "wearing three different kinds of plaid and an absurd hat." Toole later told his friend Joel Fletcher of the shocking vision that had materialized in front of him. He could not help but comment, "My God, Bobby! . . . You look like the April Fool cover of *Esquire!*"

Byrne usually dismissed such comments, especially from a young man who clearly put stock in appearances. But as a faculty member with higher rank, Byrne need not suffer reprisals from his junior colleague. When Toole once reproached him for the loose fit of his clothes, Byrne responded with a pointed and detailed lecture on the sartorial philosophy of the Arabs, who, he argued, wear flowing fabrics in order to retain moderately warm body air and keep out the desert heat.

Indeed, with his encyclopedic knowledge and bellowing voice, it seemed Byrne could dissertate on any topic. Those who kept company with him learned to endure his preaching. But Toole not only enjoyed Byrne, on occasion he provoked him, as if to test his reaction. In an article published in *Acadian Profile*, Trent Angers interviewed several of Toole's friends who recalled one cool spring morning Bobby Byrne, J. C. Broussard, and Toole sat at "an outdoor table next to the concession stand . . . engrossed in a bull session." Angers describes the scene:

> Bobby Byrne, was giving a verbal dissertation on the lack of taste and social redeeming value in music and literature created since the Medieval period. . . . John Kennedy Toole, was sitting across the table with his head cocked to the side with eyebrows raised and with a smirk on his face as if he were trying to break in with something like,

"I can't believe that's coming out of your mouth!" Byrne continued pontificating, and Toole began trying to harass the orator with facial contortions that reflected increasing incredulity at what he was hearing.

Accustomed to Byrne's tirades, Broussard sat at the table silently drinking his coffee. Then Broussard noticed that Toole "seemed to be studying and subtly mimicking the speaker's gestures." In his year at Lafayette, Toole found in Byrne a New Orleans character almost too much to take, the ironies and absurdities layered into his larger-than-life existence. The contradictions of his bizarre clothes and his demeanor of sophistication made him ripe for the plucking. Toole closely watched Byrne, taking note of his sayings and inflections. And Byrne remained unaware of the impressions he made on Toole for decades. In recalling their many conversations, Byrne admits, "I didn't know I was under observation."

Almost twenty years later, when Rickels read an excerpt of *Confederacy* published in the *New Orleans Review*, she immediately recognized the basis for the slovenly character Ignatius Reilly. "Oh my God!" she exclaimed to her husband, "This is about Bobby Byrne!" She worried Byrne would read it, and find out what Toole had done. But Byrne made it a point not to read popular fiction, especially not best-sellers. He finally gave in after someone leant him a copy, telling him he must read it because obviously Toole based the main character on him. Byrne recognized some likenesses between himself and Ignatius. The devotion to Boethius, his passion for hot dogs, the motto of "theology and geometry," and his dress all seemed to be derived from him. Toole even seemed to have recalled Byrne's lecture on Arab dress when describing the fashion philosophy of Ignatius Reilly whose "voluminous tweed trousers" had "pleats and nooks" that "contained pockets of warm, stale air that soothed" him.

But Byrne also recognized clear differences between himself and Ignatius. As a tenured professor, he enjoyed professional success. He was a true academic. His colleagues recognized him as a walking encyclopedia. These were not the accomplishments of a lazy man loafing off his mother. And while Ignatius claims devotion to Boethius, Byrne actually held *The Consolation of Philosophy* as his creed; to a degree, he lived the principles of Boethius who accepted the meaninglessness of the body and focused on the mind and soul. For Byrne, pretentions in appearance exhibited mere vanity.

Upon these differences, Byrne denied he was the inspiration for Ignatius. Rather, he identified Ignatius as the alter ego of Toole, imbued with all the characteristics that Toole feared he might become: messy, alienated, fat, and such a tremendous failure that everyone laughs at his blunders. In fact, Byrne believed that Toole envied him in some ways, citing a conversation he had with Rickels where she admitted that Toole once marveled at Byrne's ability to dismiss the materialism of the world and still be content. "He has it all figured out," Toole commented. Alas, tenure at a small rural college, a cabin in which to live, and spending free time playing fourteenth-century music, would never satisfy Toole. Byrne noticed a burning drive in his young colleague to become "rich and famous," to achieve greatness. This drive deprived him of a lasting sense of contentment.

Interestingly, in the same interview that Byrne offers this psychoanalytic reading of Ignatius Reilly, he rails against the absurdity of using Freudian psychology to interpret literature. Byrne might have a point in Ignatius being the alter ego of Toole, but he seems to miss the more likely possibility of why Toole grinned and reveled in his observations of his over-the-top colleague. To any medievalist, Byrne could be seen as a textbook rendition of a medieval clown: a character both of the mind and of the body, humorous in that he speaks with knowledge and eloquence but still succumbs to the whims of the belly, much like Shakespeare's Falstaff.

With Byrne at the forefront of absurdity, Toole watched this great play of humanity at SLI. He could not stop himself from mimicking such a rich palate of colorful personas. His colleagues were astounded at his ability to mirror the mannerisms and inflections in a person. People he spoke with, conversations he overheard, everyone was potential material to Toole. At dinner parties or interludes between classes, he would tell entertaining stories about people at SLI or sometimes people from New Orleans, impersonating them with precision. Eventually his colleagues started to wonder if anyone was safe from his observations. One night at dinner with Rickels and her husband, Milton, two of his dearest friends in Lafayette, Milton asked him directly, "Ken, you make fun

of so many people. Do you make fun of us when we aren't around?"
"Certainly" he replied.

Toole had no misgivings over mimicking someone, even friends for
whom he cared deeply. His friend Nick Polites, who was in Dr. Fogle's
graduate class with Toole at Tulane and who also joined the SLI English
department in the fall of 1960, saw Toole's full repertoire of SLI professor impersonations. Because Polites never mingled much with the rest of
the English faculty, Toole was free to tell his stories of the faculty, and he
did so with enthusiasm. As Polites recalls,

> Ken used to regale me with his tales of his evenings with members of
> the English faculty, where he was always the star, and he would
> mimic the personalities of each person. . . . He told a story of one
> of the senior members of the English faculty, a very proper sort of
> woman. . . . One evening at a party when he was carrying on, she
> waited for a pause, then pursed her lips and said to him, almost coyly,
> "Oh, Ken, you're so droll." He mimicked her tone and gestures with
> dead accuracy.

In the course of an evening, Toole might repeat his impersonations
several times, as if refining them to perfection. Like many of his friends,
Polites made a good audience, laughing and marveling. Of course, Toole
maintained a steadfast rule to never turn his mirror of imitation on
someone in his presence. Had Polites ever asked a question similar to
that of Milton Rickels, Toole would have likely confirmed; of course he
mimicked Polites when he was not around.

* * *

So with the pressures of success somewhat alleviated, he enjoyed
working and socializing with department members. In doing so he
reaped much material for his future novel—he had his main character
Ignatius Reilly in the works. And while Toole probably thought of
Lafayette as a pit stop on his journey elsewhere, either toward a writing
career or back to graduate school, it became much more to him than a
way station. Observing the absurdity and hilarity in Lafayette, he
quickly became quite the entertainer at parties, but this is only one side

of his experience there. The other side is a story of the heart. In Lafayette, he made endearing and long-lasting friendships. Many of his colleagues cared deeply for him, but no one loved him more than Patricia Rickels.

Toole appeared to Rickels as the impressive new hire, fresh in from New York City. She knew he originally came from New Orleans, but everything about him emanated a Manhattan vogue. He dressed in the Ivy League style, and while most faculty and students strolled along the walkways, Toole would throw his tie over his shoulder and dash across campus "as if he was off to some place important, or running for office." When Patricia met Toole she quickly recognized his brilliance. "He was young. He was handsome. He was flashy . . . smart as a whip and funny as hell." She often invited Toole over to eat dinner with her husband and child. And while he received many dinner invitations, usually from his married colleagues who were sympathetic to the loneliness of bachelorhood, he favored the company of the Rickels family.

It's not surprising Toole was so fond of them. By all accounts they were an extraordinary family. Patricia, having endured a regretful marriage to a Mississippi man, had divorced, finished graduate school, and moved to Lafayette where she fell in love with and married Milton Rickels, a successful professor whose mind was sharp, but whose legs had been crippled by polio. Together they doted on Patricia's son from her previous marriage, Gordon, who was thrilled to have "a real father" in Milton. And Milton, who was unable to have children, now felt the joy of fatherhood. In some ways they mirrored the Toole family: a strong mother, a father who struggled with illness, and a beloved son. However, the Rickels home was filled with an evident unconditional love between husband and wife and between parents and child. Patricia never chided Milton for not being the man she wanted him to be. While he depended on crutches to walk and physically struggled with common tasks like standing up from a chair, his disability never stopped him from living a full life of publishing, researching in archives all over the country, teaching, and of course being a dedicated husband and stepfather. Gordon, like Toole, was an extraordinarily bright child. And Toole felt a particular connection with him, perhaps seeing something of himself in the only child. On occasion, with Patricia's permission, he would pick up Gordon in his small two-door car, and they would "play bachelors for the day." Gordon liked to ride fast in Toole's sporty Chevy, and Toole enjoyed having company while grocery shopping, a chore he loathed. Before leaving Lafayette, Toole gave Gordon all of his childhood books—*Alice in Wonderland, The Yearling, Heidi*, and others—some of the stories that his mother used to read to him before bed, those same works that had sparked his own imagination at a young age.

The Rickelses must have provided Toole a welcomed escape from the pressures of his own family. Toole rarely spoke to anyone in Lafayette about his home life, but on occasion he opened up to Patricia. He told her of his days acting on the stage when he was a boy. And he told her of his father's odd behavior, sharing with her that, for a period, his father became obsessed with the virtue of apples, handing out the shiny red fruit to visitors, all the while "preaching at the difference it would make in them and how regular their bowels would be." Such a story was funny for a moment, until it was clear the humor in the absurd behavior of his father was never far from the pain that it caused him.

But Patricia didn't need anecdotes from Toole's childhood to see that even as he cared deeply for his parents, they could distress him. One weekend his parents came to visit, seeing their son for the first time in the environment of his own home. Toole introduced them to the artist-tenant upstairs, Elmore Morgan, who remembered them in good spirits as they laughed and made jokes. But during their stay, Toole's father noticed that his son's apartment lacked sufficient protection from intruders. Over the weekend John installed deadbolt locks on the external and internal doors. In the event of a break-in, he explained, one would have a plan of retreat. This strategy may have made sense in their apartment in New Orleans with its rooms branching off a long hallway. But the extreme measures made little sense in a two-room apartment in a small rural community, where few people locked their doors at night. Patricia witnessed the new locks on the doors and the embarrassment behind her dear friend's half-smile when explaining his father's behavior.

An evening with the Rickelses meant some moments with a stable family that was genuinely content with spending time together. On the weekends, Toole often joined them on their days in the country, clearing the plot of land they had recently purchased to build their dream home. Because of his weak legs, Milton could not do strenuous labor, so Patricia, Gordon, and Toole hacked away at the thick overgrowth. After hours of work, they would have a picnic, eating together as they watched the Spanish moss sway in the trees and the slow steady stream of the Bayou Vermillion make its way toward the Gulf of Mexico. After lunch they returned to clearing the land. Occasionally, Toole showed his true colors as a city boy. One day as they cut through thick vines and tall weeds, Pat heard Toole shriek, "Snake!" She looked up to see him running away from the area he had been working. Expecting a venomous serpent to greet her, Patricia carefully approached the cleared section to find a common garden snake. She killed it, and they all had a good laugh at Toole. After all, they bordered the swamps of Louisiana that had been home to reptiles long before humans arrived. With Toole's help, they cleared the land to build the house where, years later, he would come to visit, taking retreat from his life in New Orleans.

Toole survived days in the countryside with the Rickelses, but clearly he felt far more comfortable in the social setting of the dining room. Over modest meals of pasta and wine, the Rickelses relished his witty conversation, lively impersonations, and his stories. Sometimes he would tell them of his shameless pranks he played on the department chair Mary Dichmann. A tall and proud woman, Dichmann had been an officer in the Navy in World War II. As Patricia remembers, "You didn't want to mess with her." But Toole did. On occasion he would sneak into Dichmann's classroom as soon as the doors in Little Abbeville were opened in the morning and write a message on the board, inoffensive, but sure to embarrass the proud professor. His favorite line was, "Mary Dichmann eats Fritos." Minutes later, as the students entered and took their seats, they tried to make sense of the cryptic message on the board. When Dichmann arrived and read the message as the students laughed under their breath, she was outraged and embarrassed, but she had no way of knowing who did it. And with her blind devotion to any graduate of Tulane, she would never suspect Toole. Knowing this, he could carry on his pranks and confess to other faculty members, hopefully over dinner, that he was the culprit.

To his friends' enjoyment, Toole also made up stories of two androgynous, globetrotting friends, Flip and Sandy, who were always visiting exotic locales like Buenos Aires or Rio de Janeiro. He would begin each tale with the line, "I got a letter from Flip and Sandy today." Then he explained the colorful adventures they described in the letter and what he had written back to them. Intrigued by his most interesting friends, Patricia would sometimes ask if they would ever have a chance to meet Flip and Sandy. "I'm afraid not," Toole always replied. They finally figured out that Toole was making it all up, but they didn't care. The stories and characters were so interesting they enjoyed losing themselves in the fiction.

From harmless pranks to imaginative storytelling, Toole seemed like an unending wealth of entertaining conversation. But his charm had its limits in the eyes of his colleagues. In addition to his frequent visits to the Rickelses, he visited the homes of other couples in the department. Nearly everyone played host to the young bachelor, and after a meal the wives would often sew buttons on his pants and coats for him. Everyone appreciated his company and conversation, but their sympathies started to wear thin, especially when they recognized his miserliness. "He was a cheapskate!" Patricia Rickels remembers, "He would sponge off of everybody, and everyone would invite him to dinner." Toole offered good company, but he seemed content to dine at the expense of his friends. Of course, with all these invitations to dinner, and with the convivial sort in what he once called "the fattest English department in the lower Deep South," Toole experienced a common side effect of moving to Cajun country. Having gone through school as a portly adolescent, he was horrified to discover he was gaining weight. The slim-fitting jacket with which he arrived in Lafayette began to bulge, and his white shirt started to show through the slit in the back. Perhaps that is why the buttons on his shirts and pants kept popping off.

As his body showed signs of his indulgences, the faculty had had enough of his willingness to consume and not contribute. They demanded Toole throw them a party. At first he resisted, saying, "I don't know if I can." Regardless of his hesitation, they informed him, "You have to!" With an apartment far too small to entertain the English department, he asked his landlord, Mrs. Montgomery, if he could have a party in her garden. After some persuasion, she agreed, and Toole welcomed his colleagues to a small affair with few refreshments. He seemed out of his element as a host. When one of the professors accidentally broke one of Mrs. Montgomery's lawn chairs, Toole became nervous, exclaiming, "She's gonna kill me!"

The party ended without another incident, except for Toole's own flirtatious behavior. Emboldened by cocktails, he focused his attention on Patricia Rickels, as Milton ushered her into the car. Patricia vividly remembers the scene that ensued. Toole positioned himself in the car window, preventing their departure. "He didn't want me to go," Patricia recalls. "He was leaning over me inside the car and wouldn't leave." Milton liked Toole very much, but like many of the other husbands in the department, he found his company irritating at times. He had a way of stepping too close to the bond between husband and wife. Milton had enough of Toole's flirtations. "Get out of the window, Ken. We want to leave!" he said. Toole replied, "Well, I'm not through saying goodbye." "Yes you are!" Milton shot back as he rammed the window up, choking Toole at the neck. "I'm gonna strangle you to death if you don't get out of the window," he yelled. Toole nodded, removed his head from the window, and returned to his apartment. It was, by far, the boldest move he ever made on Patricia and fairly out of character for him. But on another occasion, when he forgot himself in the company of another bachelor, he expressed in crude terms his attraction and desire for Patricia.

Patricia took Toole's affection as flattery, not temptation. She was devoted to her husband. But she also cared deeply for her friend. Looking back on her many years at SLI, she said, "There have been people I have known here for thirty, forty years, but they didn't leave the impression that Ken left on me. It's hard to believe he was here only for one year." Her eyes glimmered as she remembered her friend who walked into her life in 1959. She even saw some part of herself in his novel. She was convinced Toole recalled her Civil Rights activities on campus when he wrote about the Crusade for Moorish Dignity in *Confederacy*. She, too, wanted some lasting connection between her and her friend.

In Patricia, Toole found a smart, warm, loving, and at times maternal woman. She never sought to manipulate or gain anything from him. She simply wanted his company. And Milton eventually overlooked the episode in the car window. After some time apart and a little distance, they, too, became close friends again. The Rickelses offered Toole an enthralled audience and an example of what a family life could be, the kind for which he may have yearned.

His relationship with the Rickelses, his honorary Lafayette family, did not alleviate him from the devotion he felt to his own parents. Throughout his year in Lafayette, he often returned to New Orleans on weekends. Usually one of the other professors wanted to go, too, so a few people would split the cost of gas and share company during the drive. Nick Polites often traveled with Toole. Initially they would go their separate ways, spend time with their families, and return to Lafayette together for Monday classes. But as they grew closer as friends, Polites invited Toole to meet his mother. In turn, Toole invited Polites to meet his family. On that day Polites entered their small apartment on Audubon Street, "furnished in the inexpensive, period-style furniture at the time." He saw in passing Toole's father, who "just glided through and went into one of the back rooms." Mrs. Toole came to the living room and, at her son's request, sat down at "the tiniest baby grand piano" Polites had ever seen. For months Toole had bragged about his mother's musical talents. "My mother could have been a concert pianist," Toole once said to Polites. But what Polites heard bewildered him:

She played the first movement of a Haydn sonata. The instrument was out of tune, she had the score on the piano's music rack, and her playing didn't make musical sense at all. She'd stop when she had to turn a page, and slow down when she couldn't play the eighth or sixteenth notes at tempo.

Perhaps she was losing her touch with the ivory keys, although, her students would not speak so critically. But her playing is not what surprised Polites most of all; it was his friend's ability to overlook it. "When Ken could be dismissive about so many things, it was interesting to see the mother/son relationship expressed so totally uncritically and unrealistically." Perhaps this unwavering devotion to each other's talents was how Thelma and her son expressed their unconditional love.

Over the course of a few months, spending time in Lafayette and traveling back and forth to New Orleans, Toole and Polites eventually breached a conversation on sexuality. Toole was aware of Polites's "gay side," so it came as no surprise when he invited Toole to a gay party in the French Quarter. And Toole expressed interest in going. "There were a lot of silly people there," Polites admits. But there were also "a few thoughtful people that he might have had a really good conversation with." However, upon entering the apartment Toole became visibly uncomfortable. The personality that blossomed at social events in Lafayette now shriveled into a corner. Even after Polites introduced him to a few acquaintances, Toole sat without saying a word. He "talked to no one, and no one talked to him." Soon after they arrived, Toole mentioned to Polites his intentions to leave. Recognizing his discomfort, Polites agreed to leave the party as well. Later that evening, Toole "expressed his negative feelings about the gay world, or gay life." Polites detected that his friend saw it all in stereotypes; he determined Toole "was intimidated" by what he saw at the party. But Polites is also quick to mention that, while they spent a lot of time together, they were not close confidants. Much of what Polites concluded from that conversation, he warns, is conjecture.

It is interesting that as a teenager Toole boundlessly explored his city, and he now found a place that discomfited him. It is tempting to deduce some conclusion about Toole's intent in going to the party, but that presumes more than even Polites would surmise from that night. "Toole kept his own counsel," as Bobby Byrne once observed. Whether disgusted, intimidated, enticed, or shocked by what he saw, no one knows for sure, and it matters little. He likely used his impressions of the party to create the scene of the gay soirée in *Confederacy*, where Ignatius tries to organize the Army of Sodomites. Whatever Toole's reasons for going to the party, his curiosity, from wherever it stemmed, spurred him to see all sides of New Orleans life, even if that led to some discomfort.

Joel Fletcher, another friend from SLI, also witnessed this innate curiosity in Toole. Near the end of the academic year, Fletcher, who was working in the basement office of the news bureau at the college and was also the son of the president of SLI, met the young scholar from New Orleans. Polites had suggested that the two meet, but they didn't get around to it until the beginning of the summer, months after Polites left for the army in January. As predicted, Fletcher and Toole sparked an immediate friendship. They were both Tulane graduates, cultured intellectuals, and held much higher ambitions than Lafayette, Louisiana. Throughout the remaining weeks of the school year, they drove to bars and talked about literature, music, and art. And every so often they traveled to New Orleans.

In July of 1960 they took a trip to the Crescent City where Fletcher saw Toole observe a unique New Orleans scene. The day after they arrived, they met up at the Napoleon House to eat lunch. They spent the rest of the afternoon meandering through the Quarter. They browsed bookstores and had a memorable encounter with the sizeable posterior of New Orleans writer Frances Parkinson Keyes. And they walked to Elysian Fields, the childhood neighborhood of Toole's parents, where his aunt and uncle still lived. They strolled through the once respectable section of town, which had since become depressed. They walked by people standing in doorways and "dirty-looking mothers screaming at their much dirtier children." As it started pouring rain, Toole became "transfixed by the scene" of a mother who violently struck her child in an attempt to protect him from the downpour. Fletcher recounts in his memoir,

> "GET IN OUTTA DAT RAIN, CHA'LIE" one of the mothers yelled at her child, and (WHAP!) struck the child with a convenient board. "GET IN OUTTA DAT RAIN! YOU'LL GET SICK!" (WHAP!). She struck again.

Later that day as they drank coffee, Toole "mimicked the Elysian Fields mother braining her child while voicing such concern over his welfare, chuckling to himself, delighted by the comic irony." Fletcher had witnessed Toole's process of observation. Heeding a moment unfolding before him, Toole watched and then shortly thereafter rehearsed the narrative and the voices, working his way to the spirit of the moment, not to merely report or accurately represent it, but to boil it down to its most humorous essence. And then he likely cataloged it somewhere in his mind, ready to recall on another occasion, at a party, talking with friends, or when he finally sat down to write his novel.

Such a mentality requires a degree of detachment. Instead of expressing sympathy for the child or judgment of the mother, Toole recognized it as one of the many tragi-comic vignettes that abound in New Orleans on any given day. Elmore Morgan, the artist who lived in the apartment above Toole, concisely described this character trait in Toole when he said in an interview: "He had a sort of detached view, in a sense; he was an observer. Rather than get terribly upset by some situation, he would be more likely to deal with it in a sort of humorous way, to see the absurdity and irony and humor in it. . . . Humor was a way of dealing with things that he couldn't do anything about."

Toole's reactions suggest his recognition of forces in this world he could not change, and laughter was the way to overcome them. In comparing the two moments of New Orleans life, Toole was far more comfortable watching a scene in the street than sitting in that party with Polites, but in both cases, this was his city to absorb and reflect, in all its unsettling humor. And regardless of the situation, from watching a scene of domestic violence unfold on Elysian Fields to awkward moments at a party in the French Quarter, during this period Toole is said to have had a constant "half-smile on his face, as though he were up to something, as though he were amused by the people in the world around him."

Toole and Fletcher returned to Lafayette to finish out the remaining days of the semester. At SLI Toole found companions with whom he could discuss art and literature. He relished the eccentricities of his colleagues. And he had the joy of partaking in life with the Rickels family. As Patricia recalls, Toole was "in his season of glory" in Lafayette. He was coming closer to his own spark of innovation, collecting the voices that would echo through his own work. Joking with Patricia, he once commented that "he couldn't stay at SLI more than a year because he didn't want to get any fatter." But truthfully, he must have felt that nagging compulsion toward achieving something great, whether in writing or in teaching. And it was not going to happen in Cajun country, or at any college at this point. As Toole well understood, a master of arts, even from Columbia, walks in limbo. He could teach classes, but rarely would an MA gain promotion or achieve tenure. So he set his sights on returning to graduate school to get his PhD.

In May of 1960 the SLI English department newsletter announced that Toole was "resigning his position . . . at the end of the summer semester to return to Graduate Studies." He would attend the University of Washington on a three-year university fellowship and "do his specialized study in the field of Renaissance English Literature." Washington was an odd choice for him, but for a penny-pinching scholar such an offer would be difficult to refuse. According to Patricia Rickels, "He wanted to be in New York more than anything." He also wanted the prestige of Columbia. The logistics of finances created a substantial barrier between him and New York. Fortunately, in June, word came from his mentor, John Wieler, who was able to make good on the promise stated in his recommendation letter to SLI a year earlier. The English department newsletter announced that Toole would "return to graduate school at Columbia University this September . . . [after receiving] an appointment to the faculty of Hunter College, and he will teach at Hunter while attending Columbia." Even with a job in New York, between tuition, living expenses, and a schedule stretched between teaching and taking courses, the stage was set for a life of intense financial pressure. But after a year in the bayou, New York may have once again appeared a luminous city in the distance, a metropolis of aspirations ascending into the sky.

He taught for the summer session at SLI in order to save some money, and he enjoyed the leisurely pace. He went out to Cajun bars with Fletcher and Broussard, and over cold beers they would talk about literature. He had recently become obsessed with British novelist Evelyn Waugh. Fletcher appreciated Waugh's dark humor as well. Although Nick Polites remembers with some irritation how Toole was so infatuated with the "brilliance and economy of his writing" that he "talked incessantly about Waugh." On occasion he met with his high school friend Cary Laird, who was finishing up his graduate degree at Tulane. One weekend in New Orleans, Toole heard of a party taking place in Lafayette. Eager to show Laird the popularity he had gained in the small town, Toole convinced his friend to borrow his sister's white Chevrolet convertible, the one Toole's father had sold her, and the two cruised westward, crossing the Atchafalaya Basin with the wind in their hair. He must have enjoyed his corner of Cajun country all the more now that he was about to leave.

As the sweltering heat of the summer hit its August peak, Toole packed his belongings and bid adieu to his friends. Heading east, the mud of the Louisiana swamp dried from his shoes as he prepared his return to the fast-paced frenzy of Manhattan.

Chapter 7

Hunter and Columbia

Returning to the realm of brick and limestone, Toole found little had changed in Manhattan since he'd left. The skyscrapers still towered over the people who still hurried along sidewalks. The bohemians of Greenwich Village still gathered in Washington Square Park. The Beats still preached their anti-establishment message in cafés and dive bars. And Columbia still held its regal poise in Morningside Heights. But Toole had changed. As an experienced instructor, he could now manage a classroom, not just ace a course. And the terms of his survival in Manhattan had changed, too. No longer under the wing of the Woodrow Wilson fellowship, Toole intended to work while attending Columbia part-time until he earned his PhD, which would take at least three years—three years of bouncing between the west and east sides of Manhattan. With the pressures of earning enough money to survive and his rigorous daily routine, it would be a year vastly different from his first foray to New York City. And yet there remains a mirrored dynamic between those two years. They both began with his initial excitement but led to his eventual dismay with a place that he found hard to love at times, despite his best efforts. And at some point in the midst of his mind-spinning schedule, he would begin sketching his ideas for what would become *A Confederacy of Dunces*. It was to be Toole's busiest year. For the first time he took on the roles of student, teacher, and writer all at once. And after donning all three hats that year, he would leave New York with a clearer sense of what he wanted to do, what he *had* to do with his life.

He began his semester with intense focus on his studies. He rented a "large and bright" room on Riverside Drive, which offered him "a limited view of the Hudson and New Jersey across the river." He registered for four graduate courses, a daring endeavor in combination with his new teaching post. And while his courses were all on aspects of British literature, he selected ones that reflected his expansive interest in various time periods of history. He registered for a course with William Nelson, the same professor from his MA studies who read *The Faerie Queen* aloud. Under the guidance of the energetic Jerome Buckley, he studied Charles Dickens in Victorian Prose and Poetry. And he took a seminar on the Augustan satirists with James Clifford, a course aligned with his creative interests as a humorist more than it was with his academic pursuits. In this class he likely encountered the epigram by the master of satire Jonathan Swift:

> *When a true genius appears in the world,*
> *You may know him by this sign, that the dunces*
> *Are all in confederacy against him.*

These lines would inspire the title of Toole's novel.

* * *

Again taking his seat in the lecture rooms of Philosophy Hall, listening to erudite professors postulate on form, genre, and aesthetics, he had resumed his place in the city he so desperately craved. "He loved New York, and he loved Columbia," Patricia Rickels remembers. "He wanted nothing more than to return." Yet, unexpectedly, Morningside Heights proved quite sedate compared to his post at Hunter College on the Upper East Side. In the fall of 1960 the affluent neighborhood became a stage for the Cold War capers of the premier of the Soviet Union, Nikita Khrushchev. On September 19, the first day of classes at Hunter, Toole approached the campus on Park Avenue to find police had barricaded the road and posted guards in front of the Soviet embassy across the street. The security detail remained for several weeks, keeping watch over Khrushchev, who was in New York to attend the United Nations General Assembly. The *New York Times* reported that classes at Hunter remained undisturbed by the presence of the Soviet leader, but the calm did not last. As Toole reported home, "Refugees from communist controlled countries in Europe demonstrated here every day, screaming, singing, chanting. . . . " The refugees acted on the fundamental American freedom to protest, an act that may have resulted in execution in their homelands. But the civilized residents of the Upper East Side, accustomed to the serenity of their corner of Manhattan, found the protests bothersome. Toole observed how they "retaliated (in the cause of quiet and order) by pouring water from their apartment windows onto the demonstrators below." From September to October, as Toole watched the comings and goings in and out of the Soviet embassy, he saw the key players that would throw the United States into the most intense years of the Cold War—"Krushchev [sic], Malenkov, Kadar, Castro, and the others in their clique." Abandoning the decorum of diplomacy, Khrushchev made headlines with his zany antics. Upon hearing "The Star-Spangled Banner" blaring out of an apartment window, which was obviously timed for his passing by, he stopped on the sidewalk and moved his hands in rhythm like the conductor of an orchestra. And he made a desperate attempt to derail a United Nations session when he removed his shoe, "brandished [it] at the Philippine delegate on the other side of the hall" and then "banged the shoe on his desk." Initially humored by the insane behavior of Khrushchev, Toole expressed an underlying sense that the "carnival atmosphere . . . could have, of course, erupted into something more serious." Most New Yorkers, particularly those living near Hunter, were eager to see Khrushchev go and their lives returned to normal.

One morning in mid-October, Toole found the police barricades removed. The departure of Khrushchev had "restored peace" to the Upper East Side. And feeling optimistic about his place at Hunter, he sat down in his twelfth-floor office, with its nice view of Midtown Manhattan, and wrote a letter to his Aunt "Nandy" and Uncle Arthur, detailing his current situation in New York. He compared the appearance of Hunter to Charity Hospital in New Orleans in its "institutionalized aspect" remnant of "the late 1930s." He conveyed the intrigue of Khrushchev and the demonstrations that took place in the streets. And he described his first impressions of his students, who had far more potential than what he encountered in Lafayette. He reports,

The students here are—for the most part—very sharp,
very eager and interested, very worthwhile. The all-girl
student body is principally Jewish and Irish, balanced in
about a 50-50 split, and all drawn from the New York
metropolitan area. I'm teaching a Dominican nun, Sister
Martha.

As he wrote the letter, looking outside the window, he observed, "I
have a fine view of Midtown Manhattan, which at the moment is hidden
somewhat by usually present blue-gray haze that hangs over the city."
The initial optimism that usually began his ventures to New York City
still shines, but something ominous brews in the air above Midtown.

To a new arrival, Manhattan can create an odd sense of alienation as
one finds his way through the throngs of people constantly moving toward some unclear end. Toole confesses, "I find that I must readjust to
this maelstrom after my leisurely stay on the Bayou Teche." Longing for
some Southern warmth, he contacted a few fellow Louisianans living in
New York at the time. When Toole told Mario Mamalakis—Nick Polites's aunt and a librarian at SLI—of his return to New York, she suggested that once he got settled he call Clayelle Dalferes, a native of
Lafayette. So, Toole called Dalferes one afternoon, waking her from a
nap. She picked up the phone, and before Toole could say a word, she
sleepily asked, "Is this business or pleasure?" Toole thought her greeting
"was hilarious," Dalferes remembers. "He never let me forget it. He repeated the phrase to me throughout our friendship." Together they went
to movies, browsed bookstores, and dined. On one occasion she ate
lunch with him at Columbia, and she was struck by how he "treated
women in the cafeteria the same way that he treated professors. The
women loved it." Even amid the masses of New York, he remained "very
much a Southern gentleman."

Toole also contacted Emilie Russ Dietrich, who had shared that impromptu dance with him during Mardi Gras in their Tulane days, a moment impressive enough for her to remember how talented a dancer he
was. She was living and working in New York City, so Dietrich joined
Toole at movies or at the Roseland Dance Hall, where people danced
"cheek to cheek" to the tunes of big band jazz. And one night they went
to Harlem—an adventurous outing for two white Southerners in the

early 1960s—to see "Moms" Mabley perform at the Apollo Theater. That night they were welcomed to that shrine of African American performance art. And they laughed at comedy derived from the African American experience. And, of course, they had engaging conversations. Dietrich (now Emilie Griffin) fondly remembers, "Toole's way of smoking his cigarette hidden behind his hand and his way of talking without looking straight at you, but smiling a little superior smile." There must have been a certain comfort Toole took in exploring New York with his friend—they were in an exciting place that could quickly become lonely and cold without fellow companions with similar sensibilities. In a letter to her mother in late November, Griffin confessed that she "just had one of the funniest phone calls ever with Ken Toole." As she remembered, he spoke with speed, and his humor was just as quick. She explains what it was like to be in his company:

> With great skill and without warning, Ken would move from being a "colored cat" to being what New Orleans people now call a "yat" (as in "Hey, dawlin' where yat?"), jumping from one impersonation to another with little explanation. I was expected to follow him. I was supposed to know. Moments later, leaving me in stitches, Ken would return to his own character, asking me if I wanted a Coca-Cola or if I wanted to dance.

His pursuits at Columbia and Hunter provided few opportunities for his energetic, comical skits, but his friends from New Orleans understood his humor. Evenings at a movie or a dancehall likely offered him much needed relief from studying and teaching. For a short time he had a personal audience, something he periodically desired, not out of vanity, but rather out of a need to express his observations and release the apparent comical energy that was central to his conversations.

In November, when he spoke to Dietrich with such spirited hilarity, Toole had reason for excitement. A few days after presidential candidate Richard Nixon paraded down Broadway while celebrants threw paper streamers into the air, his opponent, John F. Kennedy, was announced the next president of the United States. Toole wrote to his friend Joel Fletcher months later, feeling encouraged about the new president with whom he shared a similar name and religious identity,

"It looks as if Kennedy may justify my faith in him, although I'm only very grateful that we were spared Dick and Pat." For the first time in American history, a Catholic with Irish roots would hold the highest office in the nation.

Socializing with a small circle of friends and appearing hopeful over the future of the country, Toole enjoyed the "cool, clear autumn" of New York. In fact, it was that same season in New York that the iconic film *Breakfast at Tiffany's* was shot. In mid-October of 1960 Audrey Hepburn was spotted throughout the city shooting the adaptation of the novel by New Orleans–born writer Truman Capote. On one occasion a crowd gathered as Hepburn walked to a window in Tiffany's on Fifth Avenue, wearing "a stark Givenchy evening gown." The crowd appeared disappointed that it was not a jewelry heist or Khrushchev in one of his curious episodes. But once released, *Breakfast at Tiffany's* crystallized the glitz and glamor of New York for millions of Americans. It presented a bedazzling city, where writers and elegant socialites walked the streets in the latest fashions, all set to the backdrop of the city in the fall of 1960. It was a vision of the city Toole would have loved to live. But after eight days the cameras stopped rolling, Hepburn returned to sunny California, and, as it always did, the lovely autumn made way for the cold winter nip that moved eastward from the Catskill Mountains.

New York grasped at the last moments of vibrancy with bells jingling and the Rockettes jollily kicking in unison at Radio City Music Hall. But holiday fanfare did little to ease Toole's daily commute. Every day he passed the same stores, the same delis, traveled through the same dark tunnels of the subway—a commute that was more than an hour long with two subway transfers. He coursed back and forth through the subterranean bowels of Manhattan, professor in the morning and student in the afternoon, only to discover that after tuition, rent, and food he barely had any money left over. The ominous blue haze he saw from his twelfth-floor office in mid-October descended, and he saw the city as "its usual busy, preoccupied, hustling self."

By the end of the fall semester it was clear he needed more income to survive. He decided to teach four classes at Hunter in the spring and take only one class at Columbia. This would substantially delay his degree for years. The Columbia *Graduate Student's Guide* fairly warned,

"A program of less than three courses puts study so far out in the margin of one's consciousness that it seldom leads to tangible results." But as was often the case, financial practicality took precedence.

With the weight of his spring semester shifted to teaching, it made sense for him to move closer to Hunter. He found a fourth-floor apartment and roomed with fellow Tulane alumnus Kent Taliaferro at 128 East 70th Street—a slender, red brick house on a quiet side street, shaded by an overarching canopy of trees. Ironically, while Toole struggled for financial viability, he now lived in the Upper East Side, one of the most affluent sections of Manhattan. Granted, the block of 70th Street he lived on was originally built in the 1870s for stables and stable hands. The relatively modest homes, for Upper East Side standards, created a quaint feel to the block. At the corner of Lexington and East 70th Street, the neon sign of Neil's Coffee Shop glowed, even in the blurry white of the winter snow, welcoming students and professors, a place where Toole could get a hot cup of coffee before walking a block to Hunter.

Toole spent Christmas and New Year's Eve that year in New Orleans and Lafayette, enjoying the calm pace and mild weather of Louisiana. Fortified with home-cooked meals, he returned to blustery Manhattan. At first the novelty of snow brought him some enjoyment. He went sledding with friends in Central Park, where they climbed the hill of the pilgrim statue near the entrance at 72nd Street, and they could see the three towers atop the Beresford—an upscale apartment building on the Upper West Side, which hovers like a dreamy castle keeping watch over the urban forest. During this playful winter day, Toole plopped into a mound of snow. A companion snapped a photo: the New Orleanian sits in his frigid New York throne.

But his proud smile withered as he returned to his routine during days that seemed successively colder and snowier. He walked to class against the frigid winds that whipped between the buildings—that burning winter air that creeps into one's bones. The *New York Times* declared the snowfalls in January and February of 1961 created "the worst winter in 80 years." Toole observed that New Yorkers developed a "snowbound mentality." Bundled under layers of clothing, he saw the millions of faces walking the streets and casting their gaze downward to avoid the chilly blast. For a man accustomed to the subtropical climate of Louisiana, the winter of 1961 proved nearly insufferable. He wrote to Joel Fletcher, "In my present snowbound condition, I find that letter writing alleviates some of the drabness and discomfort of the below-zero temperature." During this period of reflection, his track in New York started to mirror his previous experience. In the autumn he had absorbed and observed the character of the city, but winter bred bitterness, reflection, and questions of meaning and purpose. His New York endeavor grew tiresome. He confides to Fletcher, "As time passes, the tedium of graduate school magnifies; the Ph.D. looks like a nebulous and questionable reward for financial scrimping, stultifying research, and meaningless seminars." When he had finished his teaching contract at SLI in the humid haze of the Louisiana summer, it seemed he had understood the purpose of his return to Columbia; but now, once again entrenched in the reality of life in Manhattan, it all lacked a clear point. Of course, his financial struggles colored his perception. Egos volleying across a graduate seminar table, displaying one's own brilliance and seeking to gain the approval or even slight recognition from a professor, can seem pointless when compared to the weight of surviving in the city.

While Toole had come to New York for Columbia, now Hunter College took much more of his time and energy. By the spring semester he rarely spoke of Columbia in letters home. In March he writes, "I can only write about work, work, and work." Being so close to his place of employment meant he could teach in the mornings and be available to substitute for night classes at Hunter. Of course, more classes meant more students. And after completing one full semester, he gained a far more complex picture of Hunter than his initial assessment in October. Like many teachers, he expressed mixed feelings about his students. He varied from excitement over their potential to a view no more flattering than his cartoons of the Newcomb College women at Tulane. But his vacillating reactions indicate his students held his interests more so than did his professors at Columbia. And, in turn, his students found him an engaging and refreshing teacher.

Ellen R. Friedman took only one class with him, but he she never forgot him. On the first day of class he walked into the room of all female students and issued a writing assignment. "Answer this question:

What profession would you like to pursue and why?" He knew many of them wanted to be schoolteachers, the basis upon which the college was founded. Predicting cliché responses he stipulated, "And don't tell me you want to be a teacher because you like children. That is not a sufficient reason." Little did his students know, he was struggling with his own career path. Reflecting the same question he asked of himself, he pushed the students to think deliberately about their answers and their futures. "He turned on an intellectual light," Friedman remembers. "He began a chain of thinking for me. . . . He was one of the first professors that actually made me think." Years later, after reading *Confederacy*, it became clear to Friedman that there was another side of Toole she had not seen in class. She does not recall humor as central to his teaching. He was more caustic in his responses. "He had a way of letting you know that what you said was not that good or that you missed something." Considering he was only a few years older than his students Toole had to walk a fine line; he had to maintain his professional stance and focus, never to be misinterpreted as a friend. Friedman recalls how young he looked, and yet he carried himself in the classroom with the ease of a confident professor. He dressed in a tweed jacket with a collared shirt and tie. Sitting on the edge of his desk, one foot propped up and the other dangling to the ground, he lectured with clarity. Inevitably, some of the students developed a crush on him.

One woman, apparently a student from this time period, expressed deep feelings for Toole in a handwritten letter sent to him shortly after his return to New Orleans. The letter suggests a romantic relationship or at the very least an intense friendship. It remains one of the most puzzling letters in the Toole Papers.

Dear Ken,

I took my last exam today, followed it with a voice lesson "chaser," and then found your letter waiting for me, as effective as a soma holiday.

I spent Tuesday reading, sunning myself, and playing a terrible game of tennis at Sebago Beach. I'm not sure whether its sunburn, windburn, or frostbite, but I did lose my "nightclub pallor."

It has been suspiciously quiet around here. Today is Henry's birthday and I'm sure that 42 relatives are going to pop out of closets when I'm not looking.

If you happen to receive a loaf of rye bread in the mail, don't mistake it for a displaced "care" package—it would more likely be from my mother. She misses serving dinner to you, but not possibly as much as I miss being with you. I love you, I love you, I love you.

    Ellen

p.s.: the package hasn't arrived yet—I can hardly wait. My love to you darling—Ellen.

The author of this letter remains a mystery. It was not from his student Ellen Friedman at Hunter, nor would he normally invite one of his students to call him Ken. In fact, he usually reserved Ken for his friends in Louisiana. But this woman appears to live in New York, considering her visit to Sebago Beach. And Toole apparently charmed her mother and became familiar with her family. But who was Ellen? A fellow graduate student? A person he met at a bar? Perhaps an undergraduate at Columbia or Hunter? Whoever she was, she energetically bounces from school to vacation to her family and repeatedly declares her love for him. It seems he developed some affection for her, as well, after seeing her "night club pallor," likely during an evening of dancing.

It has been said that Myrna Minkoff is a composite character of the Jewish students at Hunter. As Fletcher suggests, Toole looked to his Hunter students and "Myrna Minkoff, the unlikely heroine of *Confederacy* was under observation." Thelma Toole understood that Myrna Minkoff was an actual student of his at Hunter. In fact, she worried a lawsuit would come out of publishing the novel with the actual name of the student. And Anthony Moore, who served with Toole later in the army and was in his company during the period that he wrote *Confederacy*, remembered that Myrna was "based off a girl that was infatuated with him in New York." Moore felt it mean of Toole to mock a woman who loved him, as Ellen clearly did. Of course, there is no spirit of revolution in Ellen's letter. It has no plots for social upheaval or unsolicited advice like the letters of Myrna Minkoff's to Ignatius Reilly. But it does suggest that Toole had a relationship with a young lady in New York City. And if he used her for Myrna Minkoff, it would certainly illustrate his boundless satire.

As a professor, Toole clearly earned the respect of both the students and the administration. His supervisor, John Wieler, filed a "highly favorable" report on his teaching. And in the spring semester they awarded him a literature course, a rare honor for a part-time faculty member without a PhD. As he admitted to Fletcher, "The Hunter hierarchy has been more than kind toward me." At least for one course he could delve into what he loved. In a letter to his parents he refers to this course as the Stein class, likely referencing Gertrude Stein, either in the character of the students or the content of the course. "Classes are all proceeding perfectly, The Stein Class, after a little slapping about the head and shoulders has developed into one of the most interested, alert of the four classes." In general, students enjoyed his classes, or so he tells his parents when he reports evidence of his virtuosity as a teacher:

> The professor whose classes I assumed in night school last week phoned me this afternoon to ask, "what did you do to those classes? They said they were the most exciting classes they'd ever had, covering psychology, philosophy, history and literature. All the classes want you back. They spent all the time telling me how thorough and fascinating you were." (One of the classes applauded when I finished one night!) So there's some recompense—aside from the financial—for all this fatigue.

As Patricia Rickels often said of Toole, "Always on stage. . . . He was always on stage." Wieler praised him, and his students adored him. But like any teacher he had moments of frustration. Ellen Friedman sensed that Toole was "a little baffled by New York girls. We were a bit more independent, not Southern belles." Dalferes remembers some moments where he felt he could not get through to them:

> He used to get very annoyed with the stupidity of Hunter. He felt the students were only interested in anti-Semitism. He wanted to bring the glory of literature to people. If people couldn't recognize that he would get depressed.

It is no surprise a young, bright professor, one who had a remarkable writing talent in his first year of college at the age of sixteen, would lament a crop of freshman or sophomore papers. But Toole had not forgotten where he had taught the previous year, which offered him some perspective on the skill level of the Hunter students. Nick Polites notes that Toole "acknowledged they were a lot more sophisticated and brighter than the students in Lafayette." And if he was unimpressed by their writing or preoccupation with politics he at least found some pleasure in observing them. At first he found in the students an amusing strain of reckless rebellion. He admits to Fletcher, "I like Hunter—principally because the aggressive, pseudo-intellectual, 'liberal' girl students are continuously amusing." Like many college students, their rebellion was often enacted under vague and half-formed notions of the world. While students picketed for everything from academic freedom to the cost of tuition, they also fought against oppressive traditions like the onerous yearbook dedication page. In the 1961 *Wistarion* the staff dedicated the yearbook to "friendship," declaring, "This is the year we are free from such shackles" of dedicating the book to a person. It was this kind of absurd rebellion that Toole found amusing and silly.

The influence of Judaism at Hunter and New York also intrigued and at times unsettled him. In the drafts of his poem "New York: Three Aspects," he sketched three Stars of David and compared the entire city to a mixed metaphor of both a biblical ark and a bank. And many students were declaratory about their Jewish heritage. They had a robust Jewish identity the likes of which Toole had not faced in Louisiana. Their intense sensitivities toward anti-Semitism blended with their aggressive political statements tried his patience at times.

Polites remembers, "[When] Ken spoke of his students at Hunter . . .
I recall a somewhat derogatory note in his voice. Maybe it was that he
thought them 'pushy.'" Toole, in his own way, pushed back. Emilie
Griffin remembers visiting one of his courses in May of 1961 when he
wrote on the board, "Anti-Catholicism is the anti-Semitism of the liberal." It was a line she would quote back to him years later in a letter,
having never forgotten the provocativeness of the statement. Griffin
identified Toole as a liberal, but she is quick to point out that the liberal way of thinking in New York City troubled Toole. He felt that
New York liberals quickly cast a Southerner as a racist and a Catholic
as a papist. As he saw it, while they railed against bigotry, they failed
to understand their own prejudice.

In Louisiana Toole avoided declaring a particular political persuasion, preferring to observe and satirize people. But the North seemed to
thrust him into political commentary. When it came to the South and
the escalating social upheaval in the Southern states, combined with the
brash comments he encountered in Manhattan, he could barely hold his
tongue. Dalferes tells of one occasion when they went to see *Birth of a
Nation* at the New Yorker Theatre. During intermission they overheard
a conversation between a man and a woman. The woman remarked,
"The movies take a grain of truth and blow it out of proportion." The
man replied sarcastically, "What truth is there in the South?" Unable to
restrain himself, Toole interrupted the conversation and began a passionate tirade in the likes of Bobby Byrne. "During Reconstruction," he
bellowed as he began his sermon, recounting the injustices dealt to
Southerners at the hands of the Yankee carpetbaggers and the policies of
the federal government aimed at punishing the Southern states. Dalferes
was as surprised with his eruption as the man and woman were. But she
recognized, "It took guts to do that in New York at the time." She eventually determined, "In New Orleans he was a liberal—but not in the
North. He was Southern to the core."

For as much as New York grated his social and political sensibilities,
it also provided him opportunities to see artists he would not otherwise
witness. It was one of the reasons he originally fell in love with New
York. He had access to forms of entertainment available nowhere else in
the United States at the time. And aside from the obvious Broadway

productions, Toole loved a good concert. In New York he saw one of his favorite singers, Frances Faye. As Polites recalls,

> He was a great admirer [of Frances Faye], and his admiration was infective. . . . He had seen her in performance at a nightclub during his New York days. He had all kinds of stories about her, how she fell off a stage during one performance and broke a leg, which he thought hilarious.

Polites probably references Faye's broken hip, not from a fall off stage, but rather from slipping on the bathroom floor in her hotel room. It caused her anguish, but she continued playing, at times using medication for the pain. The accident itself was no joke, but much like Toole, when performing, Faye turned everything into a laughing matter. In June of 1959 the *New York Journal American* reported that Faye opened at the Crescendo, a famed nightclub in Los Angeles, while "still on crutches, but that does not affect her repartee."

Her banter drew audiences, especially Toole, to her shows as much as her singing did. She was quick witted, an absolute parody of gender roles, and confident beyond measure. While no scarlet beauty or nightingale, she was a masterful satirist. At a time when sexuality and gender remained a cloaked and closeted conversation, she held a mirror up to society and made them all laugh at the reflection of the sexual complexities around them. In one of her most famous songs, "Frances and Her Friends," she strings rhyming names together, twisting gender roles, and turning relationships into a string of lovers: "I know a guy named Joey / Joey goes with Moey / Moey goes with Jamie / And Jamie goes with Sadie. . . . " This could go on in limitless variations, each verse ending with, "What a drag, what a drag / I'm not mad / I'm too hip to get mad." In the gay community, Faye has been celebrated as a pioneer for her openness. But her audacity and fearlessness on stage attracted both gay and straight listeners. As the *Washington Post* reported of her concert on February 18, 1961, "Frances Faye hit the New York scene with the impact of a 10-ton truck smashing through a concrete wall." Her shows were nonstop adrenaline-infused jazz sessions. She cranked out riffs on the piano, bellowed her lyrics, playfully changing lines here and there, adding jokes as she went along. It was precisely the kind of humor Toole loved—fast, witty, and unpredictable. And yet critics observed she achieved a balance of intensity and intimacy. *Variety* reports of her March concert in 1961, "She makes the big 750-seater an intimate room, turning the stint into one big house party." Having started performing on stage when she was fifteen, she knew how to hold masterful control over her audience.

Much like Faye, Toole fostered his talents of quick wit, interpretation, and satire at an early age. He was attracted to this artist that projected her style: bold, raw, and unrefined. Polites observes, "It wasn't necessarily the voice [he] admired, it was the style." In other words, it wasn't the aesthetic of what she created, as much as how she created it. So impressed with her, Toole once wondered aloud to Fletcher, "Is Frances Faye God?" As Toole lifted Faye on high as a deity of artistic creation, he reflected on his dream of becoming an artist who, like Faye, would burst onto the New York scene.

He began drafting "sketches" of a character he named Humphrey Wildblood, who would eventually become Ignatius Reilly. He left no detail of these sketches, although from what friends remember of his stories, they were likely short narratives, quick comical vignettes, a method of creation similar to his comics at Tulane. Since the earliest reference Toole makes to working on the book is described as "sketches," it is no surprise that *Confederacy* is a picaresque, a series of episodes, akin to the method of storytelling he preferred. Here were the beginnings of Ignatius, drafted in New York City, the place to which he would send Ignatius at the end of the novel, exiling him from New Orleans.

Unfortunately, all that remains of these "sketches" is the name Humphrey Wildblood, mentioned in a letter. Were the sketches set in New Orleans? Were they set in New York? What did Humphrey Wildblood look like? Nobody seems to know. Perhaps they were sketches only in his mind, narratives crafted from observations and drafted in his imagination to pass the time on the subway between Columbia and Hunter. Whatever the case, his movement away from academics and toward a creative endeavor in the early months of 1961 mirrors the winter season of 1959 when he wrote "The Arbiter," critiquing the role of the scholar-critic through poetry. In the winter of his discontent he makes his turn toward becoming a novelist. And New York, the epicenter of publishing, was an appropriate place to do it.

While he had yet to compose something he considered worthy of publication, he now entertained the life of a writer more seriously than the life of a scholar. And perhaps an attraction to the "literary life" in New York offered him some incentive. Along these lines, Polites recalls Toole telling him that he had become friends with the novelist James Purdy in New York. Purdy's novel, *Malcolm*, had been published in 1959 to international acclaim. And Polites remembers Toole being "impressed knowing a published writer." But Toole also "talked about how strange, almost weird, Purdy seemed to be."

In 1960 Purdy moved to New York, so their encounter was possible. And Purdy could certainly speak to Toole about the struggle to find one's own voice as a writer and the challenges of getting published. He had worked for years as an aspiring novelist until he sent his privately printed short story collection to poet Dame Edith Sitwell who jump-started his literary career. Undoubtedly, Toole could have learned a great deal from Purdy. But if they had been acquaintances, there is no record of it in the Toole Papers. And he never mentioned Purdy to Fletcher or Rickels. Like his supposed offer from Yul Brynner that he once bragged about to his friend Cary Laird, Toole may have been trying to impress Polites, which he often tried to do. Whatever the case, the story suggests that Toole wanted to see himself in the literary circles of New York. How he saw himself fitting into that scene, if at all, is unclear. He was far too straight-laced for the Beats. Purdy may have been a bit too off-beat for him. One thing became clear, though; he did not see himself traveling the long road to the PhD.

Perhaps that was just as well. As Toole questioned the point of his academic pursuits, the army called his number. With growing tensions in Berlin and Vietnam, Toole could no longer defer the draft. In June he packed his belongings in his apartment. The neighborhood that gave way to the raucous Cold War scenes nine months earlier, offered little excitement as he prepared his departure. Dalferes came to his apartment to see him off. To save money, he told Dalferes, he had sent his belongings on a bus and then would take a flight to New Orleans. He despised long rides on buses. Dalferes and Toole parted ways in Manhattan, and he quietly left the bustling metropolis behind.

* * *

Some people say that New York has a way of breaking people. The friends closest to Toole sensed that he saw the city as much of a convoluted cultural mélange as his own hometown. But Dalferes noticed he seemed restrained in Manhattan. She knew that he, "Loved to party. But he couldn't do that in New York. He was more formal." Ultimately, she resolved, "He didn't feel comfortable there," largely in part due to the cultural abrasiveness he found in the north. While Pat Rickels claims he wanted nothing more than to return to Columbia, Dalferes claims, "He preferred New Orleans. He just wanted the prestige of Columbia." Perhaps Polites got it right when he concluded, "While New York obviously meant a lot to Ken, I suspect he may have had something of an ambivalent relationship with the city." In that regard, it paralleled his relationship with New Orleans. From far away, the city glows in myth and memory. Distance reinvigorates the spirit of the place. But once returned, the reality of the city rarely achieves those expectations.

So with the sketches of Humphrey Wildblood either in hand or mind, and perhaps some inspiration for Myrna Minkoff, he returned to New Orleans. He had until August before reporting for basic training at Fort Gordon, Georgia. Early in the summer, Fletcher had invited Toole to come visit him in San Francisco. Toole declined, explaining, "I'm finally getting around to doing the writing I've postponed for so long. Whatever comes of the creative endeavor, I will now at least be able to say I've tried."

Since his undergraduate days, Toole had pondered the role of the writer in society. But critiquing a story or a poem is quite different from actually writing one. Therein lay the rub. As a master of mimicry with exceptional control over written and spoken language, he still struggled with the development of a narrative sustained over the course of hundreds of pages. When Emilie Dietrich returned to New Orleans for a visit, they spoke about writing. They exchanged some ideas as they tried to crack the code of composition, sharing in their ultimate dream of becoming fiction writers. After her return to New York, she wrote Toole excitedly, confessing that she had begun a promising writing project. In her letter she offers Toole advice, perhaps alluding to their previous conversations about the writing process. "I think it must be just that you have to be saying something that you really mean . . . not just dredging characters and situations up because they are charming." She strikes at the heart of his struggles as an aspiring fiction writer. He had a knack to quickly identify the absurd and to mimic it. But how does one bring it all together to form a cohesive story with true meaning? This question would hound Toole for years.

His summer was not nearly as productive as he had hoped. Before long, he was packing his belongings for basic training. After weeks of marching, firing weapons, and learning survival skills, Toole lined up to get his orders. Most of the recruits received the typical assignments—Fort Sill, Oklahoma; Fort Eustis, Virginia; and, least desirable, Berlin, Germany, in the midst of a Cold War crisis. Toole opened his papers: Fort Buchanan, Puerto Rico, English Instructor, Company A.

Chapter 8

The Army and Puerto Rico

What a mad universe I am in at the moment.
However, the politics and intrigue are
fascinating in their way—and I have intelligent
and very witty friends with whom the evening
can often be spent savoring all of this. . . .

—Letter to parents, 1962

Once again Toole assumed the role of teacher, although he traded in his professorial tweed jacket and slim tie for an army uniform. Considering the other possible assignments he could have received, his orders to teach English in Puerto Rico were fortunate. And his position, which inherently held rank over the students, necessitated an immediate promotion once he arrived at Fort Buchanan. This came with the benefit of access to the officer's club, a privileged gathering spot on base. Furthermore, he had access to beautiful beaches and other tropical islands in the region. While he regretted the draft intruding on his career, he could certainly endure the Caribbean for two years.

And according to David Kubach, his close friend at Fort Buchanan, Toole actually lived a charmed life in the army. He was liked by his students, and he enjoyed remarkable success, earning the rank of sergeant in less than two years. Most importantly, Toole faced challenges and moments of loneliness in Puerto Rico, but he also achieved his long-standing ambition to write the quintessential New Orleans novel. While stationed at Fort Buchanan, he wrote *A Confederacy of Dunces*. Quite

119

unexpectedly, his experience in the army proved crucial to both his personal and artistic development. As Joel Fletcher explains, "It was the best time of Ken's life, though he didn't know it."

He arrived in Puerto Rico in late November of 1961, the beginning of the dry season, before the torrential downpours of the summer months. On the grounds of Fort Buchanan, palm trees with white-washed trunks swayed over well-manicured lawns. Boxwood hedges lined the roads and pathways. And at the far end of the base, Monte de Santa Ana marked the beginning of the mountainous island interior. The barracks were a series of white, single-level, A-frame structures with louvered windows, akin to the shotgun houses of New Orleans, only longer. Inside the building marked Company A, dark green cots with footlockers lined the walls, creating a long, narrow aisle down the length of the room. Small desks and steel wall lockers stood between each cot. And a track of bare lightbulbs ran the length of the ceiling.

As he settled into his new residence, unpacking his books, his uniform, and his favorite gray suit, Toole met his fellow instructors. There was the charismatic socialite Bob Young. There was Joseph Clein, a Harvard graduate from Alabama. Tony Moore hailed from New Jersey and, fondly embracing Puerto Rico, met his wife on the island. Bob Schnobel, with his plastic-rimmed glasses and baby face, seemed unusually young, especially in contrast to older instructors like the blond-haired, slightly balding Jerry Alpaugh. And Bob Morter was a good-humored man who seemed awkward and troubled at times, especially in the culture of the army. He devotedly inserted a picture of a male instructor he admired into a small copy of the *Mona Lisa* on the inside of his locker door. They were a collection of unlikely suspects for the army: recently graduated English majors, intellectuals grounded in the liberal arts, hopeful writers, and aspiring college professors. They all shared an appreciation for literature, music, and film. They discussed books and movies with witty repartee. And each personality added dimension to their social dynamic: dandies and dilettantes, urbane conversationalists and daredevils. Toole described them as "a hilarious group. All college graduates (some with advanced degrees), they exist here in an alien society."

Introducing himself as John (reserving Ken for his Louisiana friends), Toole took his place among the personalities of the group. As typical, he kept a certain distance from the social center. He participated in the impromptu soirees of Company A, but he rarely craved an audience like some of the other more loquacious instructors. Candid pictures from the time depict him socializing at parties and dinners but never as the center of attention. In one picture he stands and smiles contemplatively, tapping his cigarette over an ashtray, as the other instructors, drinking at small, circular tables, cheer the arrival of a new guest. In another picture taken at the Officer's Club Christmas dinner a few weeks after his arrival, Toole holds back laughter as he looks at Bob Young, who appears to have just made an amusing comment. A momentary enthusiasm shines in Toole's eyes. He appears on the verge of offering some hilarity to complement Young's joke. He likely interjected with his trademark wit, the guests probably laughed, and Young would once again take center stage of the dinner conversation.

The poise that Toole maintained offered him that slight distance he preferred to keep. From that distance, he observed, critiqued, and offered hilarious commentary, the same process Fletcher had witnessed as they watched a mother whack her child over the head that hot summer day in New Orleans in 1960. It was this approach that characterized Toole's first interaction with David Kubach. Soon after Toole arrived, Kubach came down with tonsillitis. One night as the instructors slept in the Company A barracks, Kubach, overcome with the pain in his throat, periodically called out in raspy agony, "Oh my God!" Toole heard the suffering but remained silent. The next morning Toole asked what was wrong. When Kubach told him he had a sore throat, Toole appeared disappointed. "Oh, I thought you might be having a dark night of the soul." They both laughed heartily.

Toole and Kubach discovered that they shared an appreciation for satirical humor, a talent Toole had mastered at least in conversation. And Kubach appreciated Toole's talent for delivering acerbic one-liners. As Kubach remembers, "It seemed his range of satire had no limit." Tony Moore, a self-described third wheel to the Toole-Kubach relationship, made similar observations of Toole. "His satiric gifts were enormous . . . and he could be amazing in his observations." Moore recalls one evening after watching a Sofia Loren film and noticing her glistening plump lips, Toole commented, "She looked like she had been smacked in the mouth with a ripe tomato." It struck Moore as a unique way to express what he observed. On another occasion, Toole parodied a recently televised White House tour, impersonating Jacqueline Kennedy as if she were giving a tour of one of the Puerto Rican barracks. Pointing to grotesque graffiti of the male anatomy and using Puerto Rican slang, Toole said in the soft and dignified voice of the First Lady, "And here we see a picture of a *bicho*." He went on to describe the artistic merit of the image, much to the enjoyment of Company A.

Like his friends in Lafayette, his fellow instructors in Puerto Rico soon learned that his humor usually came at the expense of others in their circle. As Kubach remembers, "Everything was funny to John. We made fun of a lot of people. . . . He had a take-no-prisoners attitude when it came to humor." The other instructors recognized his uncanny ability to observe and comment on human behavior. But like several of his acquaintances in Louisiana, some instructors found his sharp wit worrisome; it seemed anyone could land in his crosshairs. Moore recalls Toole "wanted to poke fun at everybody." In retrospect, Toole reminded Moore of Thersites in *Troilus and Cressida*. Much like Thersites who mocks demi-god warriors and damns homosexuality, Toole's witticisms could sting, embarrass, and hurt. But his fellow instructors also recognized him as brilliantly perceptive and often considerate. He defended the instructors when they came under scrutiny, gaining their respect. Despite his tendency to make insensitive comments, they acknowledged his intelligence, his self-discipline and ability to mediate between them and Puerto Rican officers.

Of course, the social dynamic in Company A was only one aspect of Toole's life in Puerto Rico. Like the other instructors, he spent most of his days teaching phonetic English—for six hours a day, in seven-week intervals. He would dictate, and the Puerto Rican students would repeat simple English phrases. Eventually, he asked them basic questions, and they attempted to answer in English.

He humorously illustrates the maddening effects of the dull Fort Buchanan teaching method in a letter to his parents:

> As I was looking out of the office a few minutes
> ago, I saw an ambulance drive up to one of the Co. B
> classrooms. The instructor of the class, whom I know, is
> a very passive, scholarly Yale graduate, and I suspected

that he had finally passed out from asking, "What is this?"; "Who are you?" "Do you like to eat fried chicken?"

Much to the frustration of the highly educated instructors, the program offered no intellectual challenge. But the program was not developed around a liberal arts value of cultivating ideas or refining thought processes. It aimed at successful test scores. With tensions rising in Cuba and Vietnam, the U.S. Army wanted the recruits ready for the frontline. They needed to know how to follow orders on the battlefield, not weigh the ethics of war. But they first needed to pass the exam. Companies A, B, and C at Fort Buchanan efficiently achieved this goal. In March of 1962 an article in the *San Juan Star* describes the program: "Fort Buchanan crams 189 hours of English into an extensive seven-week instruction . . . that has no parallel elsewhere in the Army." The leadership at Fort Buchanan was quite proud of the program, as is evident when Toole's superior Captain Gil de LaMadrid, writes, "The English Language Program of the U.S. Army Training Center, Caribbean is the only program of its type in the worldwide scope of Army operations." But however unique or cutting edge they made it appear, at times it was despairingly oppressive for the instructors and the students. While several instructors, including Toole, could speak Spanish, which is likely one of the reasons they were assigned to Puerto Rico, they were not permitted to use that language in the classroom, although many of them did in secret. As the *San Juan Star* article describes,

> English instructors . . . do not teach English by comparing the language with Spanish. . . . The use of English is so stressed in Training Company "A" that no Spanish language magazines or newspapers are available for the recruits. . . . And "Think in English" signs have been conspicuously placed throughout the company buildings.

While Toole had felt elevated from Lafayette upon returning to Columbia and teaching at Hunter, he now taught in a situation that seemed far below his level, although present-day institutions would label what they were doing as teaching English as a second language, and would carry out instruction with far more cultural sensitivity. For Toole the whole experience must have taken some painful adjustment. And perhaps that is what Emilie Griffin saw troubling him when she came to Puerto Rico in January of 1962 and spent a day with Toole. They walked on the beach, ate lunch, and visited El Morro, where the waves of the Atlantic crashed below the walls of the old colonial fortress. She recalls seeing a "dark streak" that was "persistent" and "disabling" in her friend. It was the last time she ever saw him.

Eventually Toole found some degree of pleasure in his efforts at Fort Buchanan. Despite the intellectual sterility of his duties, he thrived as a teacher in Puerto Rico, as he did everyplace else he taught. In a commendation letter to Toole, Captain Gil de La Madrid writes, "Shortly after your assignment to this unit in November 1961 as an English Instructor, I observed that you would become one of the most outstanding men ever to serve in this program. This proved to be true." The *San Juan Star* article features a photograph of Toole in the classroom. He smiles as he paces with the gait of a lecturer, punctuating his annunciation with his baton; the students appear attentive and entertained. The caption reads, "Cpl. Toole's class is a top one at Ft. Buchanan." Somehow, Toole made the repetition of elementary English phrases engaging and innovative. His superiors took notice. They often exhibited Toole's classroom as an exemplar of the training program.

Unhampered by the shortcomings of the immersion-style instruction, Toole remained dedicated to his classes for the first six months of 1962. In one of several of his commendations, his superior observes that Toole exhibited "sincere and personal interest in the welfare and education of the Trainees." Toole always felt responsible for the success of his students. And occasionally he recognized the conditions from which they came and the adversity they faced. On May 22, 1962, he describes his students in a letter to his parents:

> We are in the middle (almost) of a cycle now.
> Fortunately, my current group of recruits is as pleasant
> as the others were. As I perhaps wrote before, these
> recruits are almost all volunteers, victims of
> unemployment in the mountains.

But as the rainy season took hold, Toole grew discontent. The cool sea breezes stilled, heat and humidity saturated the air, and "the red clay of the island . . . turned to paste." So, too, his classes became sluggish, and as a teacher he became tired of life on the island. On June 24 he writes home:

> Of the three cycles in which I have taught, this last was the most burdensome, for the recruits were almost all very young mountaineers with very limited education and backgrounds—generally—of almost abject poverty. I wonder whether they have absorbed any English; we certainly wrestled with that language six hours a day for seven weeks. After the last class, a recruit said to me of another, "El se va tan bruto como vino" ("He goes away as brutish as he came.").

With a tinge of humor, Toole begins to question the success of his classes. A few months later, after another cycle of recruits, he expresses utter exhaustion with teaching at Fort Buchanan. "I don't feel even vaguely like launching into teaching so soon again. . . . At the moment I don't think I could ask a class 'What is this?' and hear 'Ees a weendow!' without falling on my face. Dios Mio!" After four cycles of trainees, he had reached the end of his wits.

Fortunately, the summer months offered him a break from teaching. With the decline of incoming trainees, most of Company A, including Toole's close friend Kubach, was temporarily assigned to help prepare Salinas, a national guard training area on the southern coast. The remaining instructors taught under Company B. But having impressed his superior officers, Toole secured a clerical job within the Co. A office. Thus, he was free from the classroom, and he avoided the drudgery of clearing brush and living in tents during the summer months.

Initially, he considered himself lucky. His pursuit to excel secured him a privileged seat. He spent his days in the Company A office, performing the miscellany of office work, sometimes enjoying the luxury of cold grape juice with ice cubes. While never enduring the physical trials of Salinas, he missed the casual atmosphere of convivial evenings drinking rum and gin under the stars. Eventually, loneliness crept into his quiet office and a sadness cast its shadow over his days.

He had time and a typewriter at his disposal, so he turned to writing his parents more frequently. They replied with dire reports from New Orleans; once again the Tooles were in financial straits. As had happened throughout his life, lack of money loomed, and Thelma confided her anxieties to her son. Penury was a consistent specter; and while never destitute, the threat of such a condition darkened Toole's demeanor.

Had he been in New Orleans, he would have helped. In Puerto Rico, he had few options. Initially, his inability to aid his parents exempted him from his typical sense of obligation. He encouraged his mother's attempts to earn extra income. On June 24 he writes, "I hope that 'Operation Alert' at home is working. During the summer, I know one must be more alert to search for ways and means." As an independent elocutionist, piano teacher, and pageant director, Thelma's work tended to slow in the summer months. The schools were out of session, and many of her clients took holidays, fleeing the heat of the city. This dearth in employment coupled with her husband's wavering car sales apparently made the summer of 1962 especially difficult. "Operation Alert" was a call for "all hands on deck." In his absence, he offers her optimism and reassurance.

By July, the situation had worsened. With the memory of having to leave their home on Webster Street still fresh in their minds, his parents questioned the viability of staying in 390 Audubon Street—the apartment he had found and helped furnish. Still, Toole responds to his mother in platitudes. "Whatever its drawback, 390 is a 'good deal,'" he writes. "There's little sense in anticipating crises. 'We do the best we can.'" He offers one final consolation, "High hopes that 'peace and prosperity' exist for you during the summer," then abruptly shifts to personal hygiene. "The Thermodent seems to have no noticeable effects, but I use it regularly and realize that it is doing good for my *dientes*." He may have wanted to quell his mother's concerns. She could overdramatize at times. His own financial struggles had plagued him enough in New York, let alone the concerns of his parents' finances. And as an army private one thousand miles away from home, he must have felt helpless, perhaps fortunately so.

Ultimately, the desperate reports from home compelled him to take action. On July 13 Toole spoke to his mother on the phone and told her of his plan. He would claim his parents as dependents and establish an allotment, essentially garnishing his paycheck to support them. Their situation must have been so desperate that he felt the need to compensate them for the cost of the phone call during which he explained his plan:

> Whatever the long distance call last night cost you I
> hope to make up for it if my current plans for getting
> an allotment go through. When I spoke to the Personnel
> Center last week, they explained to me that I pay
> monthly $40 out of my $99/mo. salary; the government
> puts up $70 to make a total of $110 which you receive.
> I also understand that the government will pay more if
> the conditions seem to make greater payment
> necessary. . . . If I understand correctly, an Army
> investigator will call on you for an interview of some
> sort. I suggest that you make the case as financially
> clear as possible, for you should try to receive the
> maximum monthly payment. The payments depend (and
> this is important) on individual need, living conditions
> in the area. In your case, make the amount of recent
> monthly income clear.

Later in the letter he reiterates,

> Remember: $110/mo. is the minimum monthly payment
> to which you are entitled under this Class Q allotment.
> You may be able to receive more—and should be able to.
> Present a straightforward picture.

Toole's concern reflects his mother's two faces in regards to finances. She confided her financial woes to her son. But with friends and strangers, she did her best to convey a sense of financial security. After all, her Creole lineage—the aristocratic roots of New Orleans—influenced her sensibility of money and lifestyle. She was far too proud and too private to appear in need. Such behavior was not unusual, especially in Uptown New Orleans. But it puts in relief the discrepancy between their means and their persistence in living in Uptown, which created a recurring burden on Toole, both financially and psychologically. Toole pursued his own life goals, but his mother rang the fiscal alarm, and he felt compelled to aid his parents. And to an army investigator sent to verify income and living condition to determine government subsidy, their Uptown neighborhood would appear far from desperate. His mother would have to discard the mask of prosperity and be as honest with the investigator as she was with her son.

Whatever his parents received, it was much more than what Toole pocketed in Puerto Rico. And Thelma always delighted in windfall income. In an undated letter to her son, written sometime in the summer, Thelma exclaims, "Your check arrived and awaits you and me! Ah, delightful and sustainable income! Ah, boost to my economic status!" Such comments illustrate the emphasis, and thereby pressure on Toole to help the ailing family household. But for the time being, his contribution sustained them for another summer season. And while it took some maneuvering, it left him with enough money for his immediate needs in Puerto Rico. In the midst of this lonely summer, he may have seen the likely future now more clearly. This is the first documented instance where Toole, then only twenty-four years old, sent money home to help his parents who were well into their sixties.

Through a combination of factors—the weather, loneliness, and the financial struggles of his parents—his perception of Puerto Rico changed. He consistently offered despairing views on the people and culture of Puerto Rico, but in his letters from the summer of 1962, he becomes harshly critical and bigoted. He declared Puerto Ricans too salacious and too boisterous. Of course, these same characteristics intrigued him in the personalities of downtown New Orleanians. But Toole's heightened antipathy toward Puerto Rico in the summer of 1962 seems symptomatic of his loneliness. In a letter to his parents on July 5, he tells of his Independence Day celebration, one that highlights his deplorable characterization of Puerto Ricans, along with his own sense of alienation:

Yesterday, the Fourth of July, I went to the beach.
Because it was a holiday, all the Puerto Ricans were out,

creating the wild, motley appearance that they do en
masse. On the beach they scream, chatter, and giggle
continually, pushing each other in the water, throwing
sand at friends. And, as always, there are several fully
dressed people bobbing about in the surf. For a people
who allegedly suffer from nutritional deficiencies, these
[sic] are amazingly active . . . and the shouted, marathon
conversations that they maintain are admirable. What do
they have to talk about continually? Are they never
afraid of being overheard? I imagine that all the Latin
countries are this frenzied, volatile, and undisciplined.

Toole overlooks the beauty of the sea or the ease of a day at the
beach. Instead, he spends his time recounting the Puerto Ricans he
deemed unsophisticated and uncouth. Indeed, his sense of superiority
could lead him to some lamentable judgments. But tellingly, Toole
mentions no friends, no beach companion. It appears he is alone on the
Fourth of July, in a foreign place, watching families talking and playing
with one another as they enjoy their holiday. His disdain for them
cloaks his loneliness. From the perspective of the Puerto Ricans, Toole
must have seemed the odd character on the beach that day.

It might be easier to forgive Toole for his deplorable statements if
they came in an isolated incident. But throughout his letters in the summer of 1962, he consistently depicts Puerto Ricans as unintelligent and
uncivilized. Offering his parents "insight" into Puerto Rican life he
writes,

In Puerto Rican pueblos, the usual number of stonings,
incendiary suicides, and machete slayings are taking
place. The police are shooting innocent bystanders, and
the bleachers in the ball park collapsed Sunday. ¡Caray!
¡Que muchos accidentes hay! [Geez! There are so many
accidents!]

He snubs his nose at Puerto Ricans again five days later when he
writes, "Puerto Ricans often pass out or suffer from closed stomachs
whenever their diet is changed from rice and beans and dried salt

codfish." His cruel statements are difficult to justify, and seem pointless to defend. But they do not spring from hate.

By all accounts, Toole was courteous toward the people of Puerto Rico. In fact, he appears sympathetic to their plight when he writes in April of 1963 that the excessive money spent at Fort Buchanan would be better appropriated to "welfare programs here on the island." He also cared deeply for his students, who were all Puerto Rican. In his letter of commendation in February of 1963, his Puerto Rican commander writes, "Your success was due . . . to the interest which you took in individual students, the understanding and patience which you exercised." Such a description of Toole personally invested in the well being of the Puerto Rican trainees contradicts the supercilious posture he strikes in his letters.

Thus, his comments about Puerto Ricans seem less like intimate confidences to his parents and friends, and more like written performances. Toole adopts a narrative voice in the letters to his parents, not necessarily representative of his behavior or expression, but rather in the spirit of crafting an entertaining letter. He may have derived such a voice from his favorite writer Evelyn Waugh, who made famously racist remarks in his travel writings, which served as the workshop for his novels. In *Waugh in Abyssinia*, Waugh comments, "The essence of the offence was that the Abyssinians, in spite of being by any possible standard an inferior race, persisted in behaving as superiors." Replace "Abyssinians" with "Puerto Ricans" and the same statement would fit into any number of Toole's letters. Toole most likely encountered Waugh's sentiments on the native in the novel *Black Mischief*. Therein, a white Englishman aids the king of the small African nation of Azania. But he finds that the corrupt native conduct precludes them from any hope of progression. As he attempts to uplift the native race, the white "savior" is reduced to cannibalism. Similarly, Toole adopts the voice of a European colonizer, sometimes weary of "native nonsense" and sometimes amused by "native ways."

He reiterates this colonial perspective in late July when he took a three-day trip to Aruba. He won the all-expense paid trip with his recognition as Antilles Command Soldier of the Month, his first official honor in his military service. His superiors had noticed his remarkable talents as an instructor. Staying at Fort Buchanan and taking on an administrative role displayed his versatility. His superiors uplifted him, and continued to do so until his discharge.

While in Aruba, Toole explored the island, absorbed the culture, and enjoyed his air-conditioned room. He found it a Caribbean utopia. He writes, "Aruba's bone-white sands . . . and atmosphere of prosperity, cleanliness, and efficiency were a great contrast to Puerto Rico. . . . Every home sparkles; the native population is quiet, well-behaved, courteous, and likable." Recognizing Aruba as a well-managed Dutch colony, he seems to lament that Puerto Rico lacks an Anglo-hierarchy. After three days, he returned to Fort Buchanan.

And shortly after his return he received news that shocked him. In early August he wandered into the library base and there he saw the headline of a local newspaper: *Muere Actriz Marilyn Monroe.* Ever since high school, Toole had been captivated by Monroe, much like many men and women in the 1950s and early '60s. Before the age of countless sex symbols strewn about cable networks and reality television, she embodied a goddess-like status, garnering the affections and desires of her audiences. Toole's infatuation went far beyond an appreciation. "There was a time, I think, when my interest in her had reached the stage of obsession," he admits. "I don't imagine that anyone could understand my preoccupation with her." She was a figure that hypnotized many people, and because, as Toole explains, "Monroe and death are such incongruous partners," her suicide shook him to the core. He immediately wrote a letter to his parents, discarding wit and sarcasm, and expressing utmost sincerity. He is compelled, in essence, to write her a eulogy:

> On the screen she created the strangest and perhaps the most fascinating species of human being we will ever see. Her musical numbers had an entertainment value that few things in the world can equal. Will anyone ever be able to describe with justice—to a generation which will not know her—exactly what Marilyn Monroe was like in movies?
>
> Her life itself was a gruesome Evelyn Waugh view of American life. The illegitimate child of the strange Southern California society. An orphan in the

Depression. A defense plant worker during the war.
A movie star whose effect upon the public was
phenomenal even by Hollywood's standards. The wife
of an Italian baseball hero and a Jewish intellectual.
A suicide who could find no bearings in the society
which had formed her. Her life and death are both
very sobering—and even frightening.

In my own way I loved Marilyn Monroe very much.
Isn't it too bad that she never knew this.

Toole was not alone in his frightened reaction to her death. It appeared to the rest of the world she had everything one could ever want. She had achieved a dream life, so it seemed, far beyond what most people could imagine for themselves. To learn she took her own life didn't make sense to people at the time, which led many people, including her former husband Joe DiMaggio, to suspect she was actually murdered. By the end of the letter Toole appears to have reverted to his adolescent obsession. He usually signed his letters "Love, Ken"; this letter ends, "Love, Kenny."

In a rare moment where Toole gushes with heartfelt grief, it is tempting to overindulge in psychoanalysis. Perhaps Marilyn Monroe represented the voluptuous feminine tenderness absent from his mother's affections. Or perhaps he celebrated Monroe as an outlet for his inner femininity—as she is now recognized as an icon of the gay community. Perhaps her alleged suicide frightened him because he, too, entertained self-destruction. Or perhaps, she was only a boyhood fascination, an ideal that he had never overcome, until news of her untimely death forced him to do so. These are all possibilities, but Toole offers no answers. This letter is best understood within the context of his summer. It emerges from the malaise of June and July. It seems one of those personal moments when the trace comforts of adolescence wither under the sobering reality of adulthood and one's own mortality. He, too, was in his prime, yet found himself in stultifying circumstances: his parents were in need of support, and he was bound to an island he began to find repressive.

At last, mid-August brought relief. While the heat and humidity offered no pardon, the instructors returned from Salinas, enlivening the barracks once again. Toole was promoted to acting Sergeant and Head of Company A, which came with a salary increase of $20 a month and, more importantly, a private room, which he described as "bright, comfortable, airy." He shook off the melancholy of his summer and took pride in his promotion. He immediately writes to his parents, detailing his success. Now responsible for ensuring the English instructors passed regular inspections, he had the common frustration of middle management in that he now bridged two worlds, with one foot in Company A and the other foot in the world of his superior officers. While caught in the middle, he seemed uniquely adept to the challenges of this role. Company A saw him as competent and fair, someone who worked in their best interests. And his superior officers considered him an effective leader in motivating and coordinating the instructors.

This position also offered Toole a new perspective on Company A and its place in Fort Buchanan. He had regular interaction with his immediate superior Sergeant Jose Ortiz. A native of Puerto Rico, Ortiz had climbed the ranks of the army and showed devotion to his duties. He also displayed contempt for the English instructors. While Toole remained gracious to Ortiz in person, he could not resist detailing the eccentricities of Ortiz in letters to his parents, casting him as the most perverse personality at Fort Buchanan. He writes,

> Our First Sergeant is unpredictable and more
> temperamental than a prima donna. Now that my
> role in the company is principally disciplinary and
> supervisory, I have constant contact with him. Basically,
> he thinks a great deal of me ("You hahve eentelligence
> ahnd leadarsheep), but there are his transitory whims
> to contend with. And what strange ideas develop in
> his mind! Ideas that must be changed tactfully and
> carefully. His paranoiac suspicion of humanity is
> overwhelming.

Ortiz became the singular object of Toole's observations over the course of the next few months. And through these letters, he reconstructs Ortiz as a character who never failed to surprise Toole. When high-level inspections came in from the Antilles Command, many of the sergeants became nervous and unpredictable. When another Puerto Rican sergeant performed a pre-inspection, Toole tells, he "went into a hysterical fit . . . and began to throw tables around." Expecting a similar reaction from Sgt. Ortiz, Toole was amused by his surprisingly calm manner:

> Yesterday, when this First Sergeant came to inspect our barracks for the first time, I was expecting to see a few tables begin to fly in here. My room is furnished with two tables, a bookcase, an easy chair, and several plants—left by the previous occupant. I was sure that these would have to be discarded, for the appearance is not particularly barracks-like. Sgt. Ortiz looked at the chair, and said, "Ah, I see you hahve zees chari een here!" (Pause) "Well, poot a leetle vahrneesh oan eet." Then he noticed the plants—which I really don't care about particularly but would like to keep on principle— and said, "Tole (my name is pronounced by P.R.'s so that it rhymes with sole—they do not understand the oo sound in English), ahv you wahtering zees plahnts?" If you knew of the small world here you would comprehend the real humor of this situation.
>
> At any rate, our barracks in the inspection was far superior to the sergeants'—for the first time in Co. A history. Sgt. Ortiz was pleased in his curious way— and the English instructors (all of whom are terrified of him) were very excited in a remarkably juvenile way—for people who are all college products. Then Ortiz went off to harass the sergeants about their poor display, waving his swagger stick about like a demon. He even carries the swagger stick with him when he goes to the toilet.

While Toole reverts to his broad generalizations of the Puerto Rican disposition, he writes with interest, no longer snobbish disdain. Unlike his sharp jabs at Puerto Ricans in his July 5 letter, his descriptions take on a caricature quality. Ortiz wields his authority, but simultaneously exhibits his insecurities through the lengths he takes to please his superiors. In the letters he becomes a clown, reacting to situations with elaborate absurdity. On September 14 Toole writes,

> Sgt. Jose Ortiz, our ramrod-proud, swagger stick erect
> First Sergeant, whom I've described previously is intent
> upon beautifying our Co. A area. Huge urns filled with
> ferns and painted in the spectrum of colors line our
> road. Between the urns there is a heavy connecting
> chain painted yellow. Now there is a big blue sign in
> our parking lot that says "FIRST SARGEANT." Last
> week Ortiz sprayed all the leaves in front of the office
> silver . . . and they fell off and died the next day.

In October Toole offers a similar Ortiz anecdote of ridiculousness. When Tennessee senator Estes Kefauver visited Fort Buchanan, there was rumor he would visit Co. A. Upon hearing this rumor, Sgt. Ortiz issued orders for a reception.

> The closed mess hall was opened and our very
> confused mess sergeant cooked hundreds of doughnuts
> and cookies for Kefauver. The doughnuts would be taken
> to the orderly room for Sgt. Ortiz to sample them
> ("Thees doughnuts ahr too brown!"); then, when the
> perfect result was achieved they were set out on
> beautifully set tables on great trays. At noon it
> became clear that Kefauver was not going to show;
> Capt. Gil de la Madrid and Sgt. Ortiz sat disconsolately,
> viewing the piles of cookies and doughnuts as the mess
> Sgt. munched on the fruits of his labor. Finally Ortiz
> said to me, "Take thees to your people!"

Sgt. Ortiz captured Toole's interest as a uniquely conflicted character. Much like Ignatius Reilly with his plastic cutlass, Ortiz wields his swagger-stick authority to a futile end, where, despite his desperate attempts, he gains neither respect nor reward. In fact, Ortiz may be the most unsung hero of Toole's advent as a novelist. After his dealings with Ortiz, Toole's letters spark with narrative sensibility. He begins to focus on character development and situational humor. And while he did not begin to draft *Confederacy* until 1963, he clearly reveled in describing his commanding officer. Like Bobby Byrne, Ortiz was a bold literary character in the flesh, providing Toole with much material.

Ortiz also provided the pathway for Toole's shift in perception of Puerto Rico. With his promotion and his entertaining interactions with Ortiz, Toole looks about Puerto Rico and finds it charged with eccentricity, much like New Orleans:

> What a mad universe I am in at the moment. However, the politics and intrigue are fascinating in their way— and I have intelligent and very witty friends with whom the evening can often be spent savoring all of this.

For the first time in his letters from Puerto Rico, he references his friends. The loneliness of midsummer had lifted. He had earned a promotion, taken on new responsibilities, and assumed a position of leadership. "This is all very wild and strange and dreamlike," he writes.

Throughout September, he continued to document the hilarity of conflicts between Company A and the Puerto Rican officers:

> Our immediate superiors, all of whom are Puerto Rican, are wild and excitable and unpredictable and the combination of English instructors and Puerto Rican cadre is an uneasy alliance full of sound and fury and improbably funny happenings. The incident of the missing lawn mower wheel was magnified so greatly that it almost split Co. A asunder.

Indeed, Company A seemed to actualize the farces found in sitcoms like *Hogan's Heroes* or *Gomer Pyle, U.S.M.C.* The instructors followed peculiar orders from Puerto Rican officers concerned about the appearance of the base. They sanded the paint off the wood handles of trench tools and then repainted them light brown. They erected makeshift scaffolding to paint the ceilings of barracks. And when the instructors could not find a place to hide their contraband during high-level inspections, they filled army trucks with their bottles of liquor and highball glasses and drove them around base. But perhaps the most ridiculous of moments came during the somber procession of burial detail, when four soldiers would escort the deceased to the grave. Upon command, they were to turn right and shoot their rifles into the air. As Anthony Moore tells, "We botched up these routines so badly." On one occasion, one of the soldiers heard the command to turn right and, instead, turned left and knocked the rifle out of another soldier's hands. On another burial detail, an instructor from Company A accidentally knocked the helmet off the soldier next to him with his rifle as they turned. But these foibles pale in comparison to the time four soldiers, standing stoically over the fallen soldier, watched as a Puerto Rican wife, overcome with grief, jumped into her husband's grave and was then awkwardly pulled out from the earthen tomb.

Recognizing the wealth of comical situations, Toole used his letters as a narrative workshop, refining his comic timing and style in short accounts of life at Fort Buchanan. In one such story, Toole tells of a dance party organized for visiting sailors and airmen. Earlier that day, Toole had led the visiting officers on a tour of the base and San Juan. In the evening they attended a dance. Much like the episodic events in *Confederacy*, Toole's rendition of the story focuses on situational humor and escalating tensions between social classes:

> Friday night there was a dance for the guests at the pavilion of the Army-Navy beach—and toward the end of the dance a great wave crashed into the pavilion drenching everyone. Several people climbed trees when they saw the wave coming—and, as it washed back out to sea, it carried with it several shoes and caps. The girls for the dance were recruited from the San Juan YWCA—and a motley crowd they were. Several of the "girls" were near forty and some were extremely chocolate in "colour." Needless to say, the airmen and sailors were somewhat dismayed and many of them stayed in the men's room throughout the "dance." In addition to this, it seemed obvious that a few of the

YWCA girls were rather identifiably prostitutes. After
the wave struck, the outraged YWCA girls began to
scream volubly—and somewhat dangerously, I thought—
in Spanish, calling down the wrath of God upon the
Army for bringing them to this dance. It took almost
15 minutes for our Puerto Rican bus driver to get them
quiet, but not before one of the YWCA girls had tried to
strike him. The San Juan YWCA must be a very special
branch of that organization. At any rate it was an
evening that continually verged on the brink of hilarity.

Shades of this scene parallel the climax scene in *Confederacy* where
Ignatius, a veritable tsunami of flesh, strikes the Night of Joy club. In
the commotion the "fortyish latin" b-girl with halitosis demands payment for champagne. The tensions between her suggestive advances, her
grotesque physicality, and her demands mimic the YWCA women on
the beach.

Other glimmers of Ignatius also shine through some of his 1962 letters. When Toole informs his parents that he lost his Tulane ring, he
confides that his attachment to this token of his past affects him both
emotionally and physically. But instead of recognizing the lost ring as
misfortune, he points an Ignatian finger at Puerto Rico as a place of violence and disease that threatens his bowels and his life. "Actually, it's a
wonder I haven't been stabbed yet or paralyzed by intestinal diseases on
this insane little geological mountain top protruding from the
Caribbean." Of course, Ignatius would have never ended a letter as
Toole ended this one. "I love you both and miss you a great, great deal,"
he wrote. Then again, Ignatius had never been so far away from New
Orleans.

In the fall of 1962, Toole settled into his role as head of Company A
and became content with his place in the army. Markedly distinct from
his summer correspondence, in September he nonchalantly ends a letter
with, "I have no complaints." At the end of September, he writes to
Fletcher, who had gone to Florence, Italy, to run an English language
school. Toole still complains about the heat, but explains how the
shared boredom he and the instructors suffer bonds them closer together. Like a band of fraternity brothers, they plotted to disrupt a pro-

duction of *Macbeth* at El Morro in San Juan, in which one of the instructors was performing. "We are to begin with cocktails early in the afternoon," he writes, "and much later to proceed to the fort in a fleet of air-conditioned taxis. And so, with such plans, we pass the time. . . . " He later reports to his parents that he rather enjoyed the play. And for the first time since he arrived in Puerto Rico, the end of his service was in view.

He ends his letter to Fletcher expressing his hopes of leaving the army by the summer of 1963. But he also acknowledges that Fidel Castro, quite literally, loomed in the distance. Having recently toured the missile facilities armed with nuclear warheads at Ramey Air Force Base, Toole found the "terrifying" weapons and the "disquietingly spirited manner of the proprietors of the missiles and jet bombers gave him pause," even to his "desensitized tropical psyche." Assuming the country would not be throttled into nuclear war and "barring a complete paranoid breakdown on the part of Fidel Castro," he would be home in one year.

With his thoughts turned toward home he requested that his parents write him more frequently. He wrote letters to friends in Lafayette and New York. And as he felt the pangs of longing for New Orleans, he received word that his father was ill with shingles. In another rare moment of sentimentality, he writes home,

Dear Dad,

Mother wrote me that you are suffering from shingles, an infection which I know is extremely painful. Because you always enjoy such good health, I was especially surprised to hear of this. The illness is obviously the result of too much work, anxiety, and too little food and rest. Please take care of yourself for the sake of mother and me.

Mother, I know, will nurse you excellently. She seems quite distressed over the illness—as well she should be. I am only sorry that I am separated from you at so great a distance.

> Please rest. In your next letter I will hope to hear of
> some recovery.
>
> I love you very much, Dad, and I hope and pray that
> this painful infection passes. You have always been so
> good, so kind to me that it hurts me to know that you
> are in pain.

Most of his letters from Puerto Rico are addressed to both of his parents. This is the only letter in the Toole Papers addressed solely to his father. He clearly pitied him to the point of his own pain, as he states. The letter is touching and sincere but remarkably incongruent with the impressions he gave of his family and what others observed of them. He imagines a breadwinning father tragically fallen ill with his devoted wife tenderly caring for his every need. Thelma took care of her husband for many years. But Toole's heartwarming domestic image shares a closer semblance to the family dynamic of his friends from Lafayette, the Rickelses. Distance and longing has a strange ability to reconstruct the real into an ideal. In late October 1962, Toole decided he wanted to go home for Christmas.

In November his leave request was approved. And by then his parents had gained financial stability, whereas Toole lacked enough money for airfare. He repeatedly requested that they send money for the plane ticket, which after some delay, they eventually did. Once his tickets were booked, the cool weather approached, and he frequented the beach. This time he viewed his surroundings in a positive light, enjoying the clear water and interacting with fellow beach-goers. Perhaps calmed by the ideas of returning to New Orleans or the comforts of his home, he patiently waited for his leave.

In good spirits he writes to Fletcher on November 29, 1962, humorously depicting himself in the way that he so often characterized Sgt. Ortiz:

> Over my private telephone I contact headquarters,
> switching people here and there, waiting, listening,
> planning. I'm sure I will leave my duty here a

completely mad tyrant whose niche in civilian life will
be non-existant. In its own lunatic way, this is very
entertaining. I also enjoy posting edicts on bulletin
boards; the last paragraph of my most recent
proclamation reads:

"Further action will be taken against habitual violators
of these regulations."

But joking aside, he ends his letter with a sincere assessment of his
accomplishments in the army:

After a year in Puerto Rico (as of 25 Nov), I find that
the positive aspects of that year outweigh the
negative. Although this seems a great cliché, I can say
that I have learned a vast amount about humans and
their nature—information which I would have enjoyed
having earlier. In my own curious way I have risen
"meteorically" in the Army without having ever been
a decent prospect for the military life; but I feel that
my very peculiar assignment has been responsible.
The insanity and unreality of Puerto Rico itself has
been interesting at all times that it was not
overwhelming.

He would soon be back in New Orleans. It had been one year since
he arrived at Fort Buchanan. Within that time he continually grappled
with the "madness" of Puerto Rico. In the summer he found the island
loathsome, as he endured pangs of loneliness and reports of his parents'
financial woes. By the end of the year, he was confident in his place
within the army. He observed and commented on Puerto Rico with less
deplorable damnation, appreciating the characters and stories unfolding
every day at Fort Buchanan. And at the end of 1962, he beamed with
pride as he returned home. He had left New Orleans a draftee, unknown to anyone at Fort Buchanan. He returned, twelve months later,
Sergeant John Toole, U.S. Army.

* * *

Toole arrived in New Orleans on Saturday, December 22. The Christmas holiday was in full swing; carols played on the radio, families hung tinsel on their Christmas trees, and shoppers strolled along Canal Street marveling at the displays. But unlike the snowy scenes in the department store windows, New Orleans was no winter wonderland. As was typical for the winter months in southern Louisiana, cold rains drenched the city throughout the holiday season of 1962. But Toole had so yearned for his return home that even the winter rains may have signaled to him welcomed relief from army life.

For most of his vacation, he relaxed in his parents' apartment on Audubon Street, content with homemade meals and a comfortable bed. He received several invitations from friends in Lafayette, but, as he confessed to Fletcher, "Nothing would lodge me from the comforts of home." On a few occasions he ventured out to reconnect with his beloved city. Wandering about his hometown, reminiscing the past, and pleased with his year in the service, he likely grappled with a looming dilemma. In eight months he would be discharged. But the future was uncertain. He could teach or continue graduate studies, each option a worthy pursuit, although neither one closer to his dream of becoming a fiction writer. In the past his responsibilities of work and school, along with his own insecurities had stifled his muse. Since the age of sixteen when his novella *The Neon Bible* lost the writing contest, he mostly kept his attempts at fiction and poetry to himself, sharing occasionally with his mother. But his winter trip home may have reminded him of his ambition to write a true New Orleans novel. He was always intrigued by the stories taking place every day in New Orleans, with its panoply of characters much like the city: proud and desperate, opulent and decomposing, all at once. But no writer had yet captured its essence, at least not the New Orleans that he knew.

The few surviving letters that document his winter visit to New Orleans indicate an introspective journey, where Toole would once again find that spark of inspiration he'd found stargazing in Mississippi in 1954. He had never really recaptured that energetic spirit, despite his attempts at writing. This time his eye would turn toward his hometown in all its conflicted complexity. The accounts of his interactions with the few friends he visited suggest something was shifting in Toole. In a letter to Fletcher that recounts his visit home, Toole exhibits the sensibilities of a fiction writer, one who not only narrates an intriguing moment, but also explores the composition of the moment, such as characters and plot. His observations in this single letter indicate traces of material found in *Confederacy*.

Toole details a visit he made to Bobby Byrne, his unforgettable colleague from Southwestern Louisiana Institute, which was now University of Southwestern Louisiana. Welcoming Toole into his New Orleans home, Byrne stood dignified and sloppy, refined in elocution, and ridiculously dressed. Toole writes to Fletcher,

> I also paid the ritualistic visits to the Byrne home
> (coffee, Aunt May, Mama et al) where, of course, little
> has changed but the pot of fresh coffee and chicory.
> Bobby's worldview weathers humanity's derision and
> apathy. He does, however, begin to appear old. Both he
> and his brother received holiday visitors in long
> nightshirts and slippers with rather haughty formality,
> and Bobby was, as always good for a dogma or two.

Toole must have recalled this moment when he wrote the first chapter of *Confederacy*. Dressed in his "monstrous flannel nightshirt," Ignatius greets Patrolman Mancuso as he and Mrs. Reilly converse over coffee and chicory. Like Byrne, Ignatius prefers the comforts of his nightshirt, disregarding decorum in the presence of company. Ignatius also has a worldview that "weathers humanity's derision and apathy." And throughout the novel he offers countless dogmas, as he revolts against the Modern Age. While Toole had spent nearly a year observing Byrne at SLI, Toole's return to New Orleans may have reminded him of Byrne's potential to be made into a character for his novel.

Continuing his rounds of SLI faculty in New Orleans, he spent an afternoon with Nick Polites, who was home from Chicago to see his family. His aunt, the librarian at SLI, Mario Mamalakis, was also visiting for the holidays. In Toole's account of the visit, he observed the unique chemistry between the Polites family members:

> Polites is still spreading his own peculiar brand of
> fatalistic gloom as he continues to thrust upon the
> thorns of life and continues to bleed quite articulately.
> Although I saw him only briefly during the holidays, he
> quickly and efficiently categorized the horrors of
> Chicago, New Orleans, and life. The robust positivism of
> Mario and of his mother are hilarious counterparts to
> his breathy futility and negativism. And I was fortunate
> to visit with all three one Sunday afternoon.

Toole recognized the way in which the opposing personalities created humorous tension. He applied this rule of opposites to *Confederacy* as well. Every negative character has a positive counterpart, and while the negative characters (Lana Lee, Mrs. Levy, Ignatius Reilly) appear to be atop the wheel, even when they do not see themselves as such, by the end of the novel the positive characters (Burma Jones, Darlene, Miss Trixie, Mr. Levy, Irene Reilly) have ascended. And the tension between the character personalities generates the movement of the plot—just as it stirred the conversation in the Polites home, much to Toole's amusement.

Toole also reports to Fletcher a meeting he had with several other friends from SLI. In early January, he met with professors J. C. Broussard and Lottie Ziegler, along with Polites and a couple visiting from the Netherlands, whom he referred to as the Dutch Couple. The group gathered at the Sazerac Bar in the Roosevelt Hotel, the same establishment Huey Long favored for his favorite cocktail, Ramos Gin Fizz. They conversed over drinks as they sat under the vibrant Paul Ninas murals that adorned the walls, scenes of New Orleans life, depicting black laborers working fields of cotton and unloading cargo at the docks, while white proprietors watch and affluent tourists mill about Jackson Square.

Toole, Broussard, and Polites all wrote letters to Fletcher about the evening. Fletcher received the letters on the same day at his apartment in Florence, Italy. He refers to them as the Roosevelt Hotel Triptych—three varied depictions of the same event. In Toole's letter, he surveys the group and dishes slight jabs to both Broussard and Polites. He writes,

> I spent a few hours with [J. C. Broussard and Lottie
> Ziegler] and "the Dutch couple" at the Roosevelt. The
> Dutch were quite pleasant, wise, and politic in the

face of J. C.'s enthusiasms and Lottie's twitching.
Also present was N[ick] Polites who contributed a few
of the extravagances for which he is famous and which
effectively silence tables for a few minutes while
everyone stares at the floor. We must have appeared a
dubious group in the bar, and I'm afraid that I made my
departure rather rapidly . . . before the house detective
took us all away.

For Fletcher, who knew each member of this cast, from Ziegler's periodic tics to the unassuming Dutch couple visiting New Orleans, the group was certainly unique and, with the addition of a few potent cocktails, potentially hilarious. They formed a confederacy of sorts. And the meeting held true to a tenet of Toole's novel: where three or more characters convene, a rumpus will ensue.

Toole walked away from the evening, shrugging off Broussard and Polites with indifference. From all three letters it seems the old friends from Lafayette found little cheer in the reunion. But Broussard and Polites provide the other two pictures in this triptych, offering an insightful account of Toole's behavior that evening. Broussard describes Toole as

so enwrapped in his own ego, [he] responds and vibrates to one
string which an acquaintance must pluck continually—his almost
pathetic desire for being admired, his only conversation being his
award for "best soldier of the month," the letters that Wieler from
Hunter writes him imploring his return there, and the response I
wrung from him by telling of former colleagues' desires to see him.

Granted, Broussard tended to exaggerate. In his letters to Fletcher, everything from meals to personalities was either the best or the worst he had ever experienced. Unsurprisingly, a negative impression quickly escalated to an indictment. But Broussard's comments still hold significance. Toole often mentioned his achievements with a nonchalance that lacked humility, especially around Polites, whom he always seemed eager to impress. His inflated ego and nonchalant manner may have caused some eyes to roll; however, in the early days of 1963, it likely served as a veneer to his anxieties over the future. While he exhibited pride in his success in the army, he took little stock in it, as he had no intention of becoming a career soldier. Someone probably asked him about his plans after the army: the inevitable question that hung like fire over his head. If he gave the impression that Wieler begged for him to return to Hunter, then, like Broussard, he embellished the truth. Wieler eagerly offered Toole a position, but his letters do not suggest he was "imploring his return." In fact, it appears from Wieler's responses that Toole sent inquires to him about returning to Hunter. Here again, Toole distorted the truth for his own self-aggrandizement. Like any young man making his way into his unsure future, perhaps unnerved by the unknown, recognition, praise, and a sense of being desired soothed those anxieties.

Unlike Broussard, Polites was accustomed to Toole's occasional arrogance. In his letter to Fletcher, Polites observes, "The army is spoiling him, as all people and all institutions spoil him by flattery." From Tulane to SLI, Polites had watched institutions dole out accolades to his friend. However, Polites suspected Toole's swagger belied a less confident state of mind. He writes, "Ken looked healthy and tanned, but perhaps beneath the bronzed surface he is dissipated. I really don't know, except that perhaps he may be impervious to alcohol." While Polites detected the psychological toll of hedonism underneath Toole's exterior, he may have seen a man performing to his own social expectations, as an exemplar of accomplishment, but secretly struggling over the uncertainty of his future, what Toole would vaguely term months later in a letter to his parents, "the situation."

While on leave, Toole also intended to visit the Rickelses in Lafayette, but spent all his time in New Orleans instead. Once he was back in Puerto Rico, he felt compelled to write, especially after Byrne told him that Milton Rickels, whom Toole called Rick, had an accident, a particularly threatening event for his frail body. Toole writes to his surrogate Lafayette family,

Dear Pat, Rick and Gordon,

Unfortunately I did not see you during the holidays—although I doubt whether this greatly affected your Christmas either way. I had no access to an automobile.

The prospect of traveling via Greyhound stopped me in
the planning stage.

I am writing especially because Bobby Byrne
told me of Rick's accident—and I send my sincere
hopes for a quick and comfortable recuperation. The
three of you were extremely good to me during my year
in Lafayette; the thought of misfortune involving any
one of you is something that I would feel very
personally.

Rick, I hope that all goes well for you, that the new
year brings about a rapid convalescence. In a faculty
composed of "fiends and madmen," your presence—
as a stabilizing agent—is very necessary.

Sincerely,

Ken

In a self-conscious moment, he appears to believe the Rickelses
might be indifferent to his visits. Patricia maintained they always loved
his company, and they let him know it. Contrary to his performance at
the Sazerac Bar, this letter offers another rare moment of Toole with his
mask off, similar to the sincere letter to his father when he suffered
from shingles. He expresses concern for his friend with no need for wit
or reports of his accomplishments. Had he gone to Lafayette, he may
have been momentarily relieved from his compulsion toward an elevated status of success, perhaps reminded of what he saw in the Rickelses that gave him such comfort during his days at SLI. But he seemed
to be transfixed by a contemplation of what he would make of his future. His friend Nick Polites made an astute, albeit cynical, observation
of Toole during this winter holiday. Reporting to Fletcher, Polites suggests that Toole was "developing his tendency toward inertia to a point
of absolute self-realization." Indeed, the burgeoning author sat in stillness on the verge of becoming a novelist.

After twelve days of relaxation, Toole bid farewell to his parents and
reluctantly boarded a plane bound for Puerto Rico.

It happens ever so quietly. The caterpillar scuttles about here and there, eating and growing, until he can no longer bear the confines of his own skin. So he finds a place all his own. He cocoons himself in a protective sheath, suspended in stillness. And inside, where no one else can see, he undergoes a remarkable transformation.

Chapter 9

A Writer Emerges

At Fort Buchanan, Toole fell back into the lull of lazy afternoons. But the "inertia" of his holiday visit to New Orleans would give way to a tide of motivation. New Orleans would have its bard yet. He carried with him the seeds of inspiration; the essence of the Crescent City that he knew deserved expression. In late January, he writes to Fletcher,

> Back to the Caribbean again after New Orleans and all
> that it stands for. My holidays were very pleasant and
> very relaxing and, physically, New Orleans looked
> wonderful, as it always does. It is certainly one of the
> most beautiful cities in the world, although how the
> people who live there managed to make it so remains a
> mystery to me.

Toole was well aware that Fletcher lived within meters of countless Italian masterpieces of art. Certainly Florence was far more renowned for its beauty than was New Orleans. But for a New Orleanian, the majesty of Saint Louis Cathedral rivals *Il Duomo*, the intricacy of the ironwork in the French Quarter compares to the gilded Gates of Paradise on the Baptistery of St. John, and the estates of Uptown are the Medici palaces of the American South. For the native son, New Orleans is the center of the world.

Keeping one eye toward his city, Toole restarted the familiar routine in Puerto Rico of managing instructors and preparing for company inspections. In another letter to Fletcher dated February 9, Toole appears relaxed and contemplative:

```
A fairly cool period here seems to have succumbed to
Puerto Rico's traditional warmth. Today has been warm,
sunny, completely enervating. I ended the afternoon
with several rums with lemon and water and lay
beneath my mosquito net to contemplate the universe
and my position in it. The results of this contemplation
were negligible at best.
```

Emilie Dietrich Griffin detected such contemplation when she came to Puerto Rico in 1962 and spent a day with him. She deemed that he was "walking insanely along the far edges of experience not so much wanting to take reckless chances but wanting to confront the universe, to pierce through to the meaning of things." A year later, he returned to this meditation.

And one Sunday afternoon in 1963 he found the meaning for which he had searched for years. Sometime in late February or early March he realized he was in an ideal place for writing. He had a room of his own, substantial periods of free time, and a regular paycheck. Seizing the opportunity at hand, he decided to put his assets to good use and try once again to fulfill his dream of authorship. He lacked only the necessary accouterment of any serious novelist. But his good friend David Kubach was aptly equipped. Toole asked Kubach if he could borrow his typewriter, and Kubach agreed.

Toole placed the small portable typewriter on his desk. He rolled a piece of paper into position. His fingers settled into the shallow cups of the typewriter keys. With the first percussive smack of a keystroke, he broke the contemplative silence of his room. He recalled Humphrey Wildblood, the character he created while in New York, renamed him Ignatius Reilly, and set the beginning of his tale under the clock at the D. H. Holmes department store on Canal Street. And as his fingers started their fluttering dance across the keys, the world of Fort Buchanan and Puerto Rico, just outside his window, faded away. And from the recesses of memory, that immense catalog of personalities he had gathered over the past two decades opened. There Bobby Byrne preached the gospel of Boethius and psychoanalyzed his own obsession with hot dogs. Irene Reilly screamed and cursed, her voice carrying through the bathroom vents into the house next door, while the gum-smacking Irish Channel gal with large hoop earrings smiled coyly at her beefy Italian boyfriend. Hunter College girls scowled at those conservatives breeding in the vast lands west of Manhattan, while the poor mother on Elysian Fields whacked her son over the head with a plank. And sweaty, colored workers labored in the back of the suit factory, while flamboyant merrymakers exchanged witty flirtations at a party in the French Quarter. The sun was setting on the Mississippi River as the clock at D. H. Holmes neared the hour of five and a middle-aged son waited for his elderly mother with the wine cake she promised him before they headed home in their old Plymouth. From this vast parade, Toole selected, merged, refined, and wove characters together with all the absurdities that form the human condition. And there on the once blank sheet of paper in his private room in Puerto Rico emerged the city he had known all his life, his New Orleans.

It all sounds like a myth of the artist struck by genius one day, but for Toole this was the wave that had been building, and now it had unleashed with consuming urgency. For nearly ten years he had tried to muster his muse, ever since he wrote *The Neon Bible*. Since then, his attempted poems and short stories flopped. But this time everything aligned for him; he had an almost unwavering energy. Instructors in all three companies could hear the clacking of the typewriter at all hours of the day and night when they walked by his private room. Chatter circulated that he was writing a humorous novel about a fat medievalist in New Orleans. He shared bits and pieces to a select few, primarily his friend Kubach, and they praised his work.

Toole was well aware of the change that had come over him. He fancied himself in the midst of literary history when he writes in a letter to his parents, "In my private room with the fan, easy chair, book case and plant, I settle down with a borrowed typewriter . . . and grind out my deathless prose." Through his writing, he once again found purpose and place in his world; he had direction. On March 23 he writes home,

I am trying to leave this place with something to show
for the time I have vegetated here. Lately, I have been
doing a great deal of writing, and what I am working
on—one of my perennial "novels"—is very good—and
that criticism comes from a most reliable source whom
I permitted to read one (the first chapter). It is rolling
along smoothly and is giving me a maximum of
detachment and release from a routine which had long
ago become a somewhat stale second nature. I hope that
nothing develops which will slow my pace of writing or
turn me from the particular goal. The book is amusing
and well paced; however, it is unwise to make comments
upon a work which is so far from completion—and it is
not my duty to judge it.

He relinquishes his critical eye, dedicating his energies to the creative process, hoping his motivation would not wane. Almost two weeks
later, Toole writes home again reporting the value of his writing to his
own disposition.

I am writing with great regularity. It seems to be
the only thing that keeps my mind occupied; I have
never found writing to be so relaxing or so
tranquilizing, and I still like what I am working on.
Quite a bit has been completed already. Some of it,
I think is very funny.

The pace at which he wrote pleased and surprised him, although he
began to doubt the finished quality of the prose, recognizing the need
for revision. And he remained wary that his muse could desert him at
any moment, as it had in the past. On April 10 he writes,

Writing feverishly, I have completed three chapters and
am deep into the fourth. I only hope that my inspiration
and dedication last long enough to preclude
abandonment of the project. I want to come out of this
experience with something to show for my time. What I

am doing will require a great amount of revision,
editing, and rewriting, I imagine, but I should have a
basis at least.

For several weeks, occupied with his novel, Toole expressed pleasure
with his situation at Fort Buchanan. "All is still going very well . . . " he
writes, "and, surprisingly, for me, I am more or less content." The end of
April brought a potential threat to his progress. Kubach was again transferred to Salinas, taking his typewriter with him. Perhaps in private
Toole expressed disappointment about his closest friend moving miles
away, but to his parents he voiced his concerns about accessing a typewriter. He writes,

Unfortunately, PFC Kubach is being sent to the Salinas
Training Area for the summer this Sunday. Therefore, I
will have to find another typewriter on which to work,
for it is his which I have been using to type my writing.
The writing, incidentally, is now over 100 pages and is
still going strong.

His writing was paramount; it was worthy of a substantial investment. In early May he bought a new typewriter, which he would use to
finish his novel. He details this purchase to his parents:

This letter is written on the new Underwood-Olivetti
typewriter I bought yesterday. It is a rather large
portable that retails for something like $135.00.
However, I bought it in the PX for only $69.00; the
Olivetti name has become world famous, especially for
portables, and this seems to be a fine machine. It is
something that I have needed for some time, and I do
not regret the outlay of carefully saved dollars.

As he continued to write, he fixed his eye on the end of his service.
The uncertainty of life after the army, which had loomed in the distance
during his trip home in January, now pressed upon him. And his writing project was such that he prepared to dedicate the next step of his life

to its publication. Hunter had offered him an instructor position for the upcoming academic year, but he declined it. He informs his parents that

> At the moment, I want to spend some time in New
> Orleans, at least until I can decide or return to some
> semblance of civilian behavior . . . I am preoccupied
> with this writing project at the moment and feel that
> with some time in New Orleans, I might be able to wrap
> it up and polish it. Therefore, the plans [sic] to return to
> the city.

He requests his mother to send him contact information for private schools and colleges in New Orleans, as he planned to teach while finishing the novel. And despite all things going well for him, he ends the letter with a surprisingly spiteful description of an evening spent with the parents of fellow instructor Dave Farr. The disdainful voice of Ignatius shines through in this account. However funny, the humor came at the expense of two people who were welcoming and generous:

> I can not attempt to describe these people; it sounds
> unpleasant I know, to say that they are appalling, but
> I can say nothing else. They look like two skinny
> haystacks, burr-like r's rolling from their thin lips.
> About them there is no hint of social grace, civilization,
> etc. Hillbillies are bad, but these people were worse. The
> mother, emaciated to almost skeletal proportions wore a
> hair net, a house dress, and white Keds with socks,
> smoking continually and assuming frontiersman poses
> on chairs and tables. The father is indescribable simply
> because I doubt whether he exists. . . . For dinner I was
> served boiled chicken served in its own broth, a lettuce
> salad with Kraft French dressing, a slice of pineapple
> (fresh Puerto Rican variety, the tastiest thing on the
> menu), and pan bread and butter. That was it; however,
> as we were finishing our silent meal, a Tastee Freez
> truck jingled outside and the mother ran down in her
> keds to buy four sundaes for us. . . . I have never seen

such gray-white, sandy, freckled, powdery skins in my
life. These people were almost inhuman and gave me at
least a glimpse of what is lurking on the plains of the
great central area of our nation.

During dinner, Toole likely maintained his Southern charm and social graces in front of the parents of his friend. Even after their time in
the army, Dave Farr kept in contact with Toole, eagerly wishing to keep
his friendship. But Toole's comments speak to the razor-sharp cruelty of
which he was capable. The letter also illustrates the degree to which he
invested himself into his characters and the toll it took on him. Years
later, looking back on this time, he explained, "In the unreality of my
Puerto Rican experience, this book became more real to me than what
was happening around me; I was beginning to talk and act like Ignatius." At least in letters, this Ignatian voice was reserved for his
mother. In letters to friends like Fletcher, his witty remarks are far less
sharp and not nearly as mean.

However regretful his comments, his process worked. On May 15 he
documents his progression and begins to take stock in his accomplishment, recognizing both its personal and professional value.

The "creative writing" to which I turned about three
months ago in an attempt to seek some perspective upon
the situation has turned out to have been more than
simple psychic therapy. I am now well over one hundred
pages and feel that the story shows no signs of bogging
or faltering. . . . My most immediate hope is that I will
at least be able to complete the first draft before I am
released from the Army; at the rate of my current
progress, this may be possible. You both know that my
greatest desire is to be a writer and since I finally feel
that I am doing something that is more than barely
readable, I am very concerned about a civilian situation
which will make completion and revision of this
particular work possible. That is why I am planning on
New Orleans for a while at least . . . If this thing can be
worked upon, I am almost certain that a publisher would

accept it and so do one or two others to whom I have
shown excerpts.

Toole writes with confidence but tempers his arrogance when he
handwrites into the typed letter, "I must not set my hopes too high."
Throughout his letters during this period, he claims certainty of the
novel's success and then restrains his certitude with expressions of
doubt. Toole understood he was investing in a project that would make
him vulnerable to rejection. For a person whose natural talents propelled him to extraordinary heights, rejection would strike a devastating
blow. The failure of *The Neon Bible* to win the writing contest may have
cast a long shadow over his successive attempts to write fiction. Accord-
ingly, he may have taken measures to protect himself against the feelings
of failure.

But in Puerto Rico, his inner critic did not stifle his motivation. Day
by day, he progressed toward another completed chapter, another step
closer to his discharge. It was not until the tenor of Fort Buchanan
changed that his motivation lagged. As surprise inspections became
more common and the trainees far more disruptive, Toole found it difficult to write. At the end of May, he finished a training cycle that left
him exhausted. His one place of refuge was his private room:

Heat, wild trainees, and inspections combine to make
conditions more unpleasant than they have ever been
here; but I am still in my white room with my fan and
bookcase, having survived somehow through it all.
Writing comes only with great difficulty these days.

While Toole's writing had provided him relief, it also caused him to
retreat from the social atmosphere of Fort Buchanan. He became further detached from everything and everybody. He donned dark sunglasses when off duty and seemed to avoid the carousing at the officers'
club or the bars in San Juan. In pictures taken during a large picnic at
Fort Buchanan, he appears as a blurred, sunglassed figure, moving unnoticed through crowds of people, like Burma Jones in *Confederacy*.
Toole describes himself as a tragically humorous character in a picture
he sent to his parents:

Enclosed is a photograph of Sgt. Toole emerging from
the English Instructors' barracks; the window on the
right is my room; the people in the foreground are two
duds. The sunglasses and pith helmet add a tropical note
to Sgt. Toole's appearance . . . as he slouches off to new
triumphs.

By June he fell into a slump similar to the previous summer; however, his upcoming discharge offered him encouragement. And he still
took pride in the recognition the army continued to offer him: he was
promoted to Specialist Fifth Class. The army placed laurels upon his
brow every few months. But more importantly, the promotion may
have sustained him during a particularly bad cycle of trainees. With a
decrease in instructors, Toole returned to teaching, while maintaining
administrative duties. His writing suffered. And the trainees were more
colorful but also more brazen compared to the trainees a year prior. He
writes to his parents,

If only you knew how ludicrous this "Training Center"
is, a place where almost all the trainees this cycle are
wearing stocking caps. It is a general practice for Puerto
Rican men to use pancake make-up on their faces and to
use neutral polish on their fingernails, and it is not
unusual to see a trainee opening a compact during a
break in the English classes or working on his nails.

The image offers humor, but his jest clearly springs from frustration.
He had endured disrespect and insubordination, uncharacteristic of
army discipline and unusual for Toole who had enjoyed popularity as an
instructor. On one occasion during the cycle, "a ball of paper flew
through the air" and hit him on the head. Toole insists on the hilarity of
the situation but then, once again, generalizes the incident as representative of Puerto Rico. "What a frightening civilization exists on this island: ignorant, cruel, malicious, infantile, self-centered, undependable,
and very proud withal."
As he commanded less respect from the trainees, his relationship
with the instructors of Company A soured as well. Toole had earned

their trust as a superior who protected them from the authoritative whims of their commanders. They saw him as a fair and honest sergeant. But on one occasion his actions resulted in the downfall of his reputation. As Kubach recalls, one evening he and Toole walked into the Company A office and found Private First Class Bob Morter slumped over a desk with a large, empty bottle of pain killers next to him. All signs indicated Morter had tried to commit suicide.

Most of the instructors recognized Morter as a troubled individual. Some instructors in Company A recalled Morter drinking himself into oblivion all too often. And his mannerisms signaled to them that he was homosexual, a substantial personal challenge in both the military and civilian society of the early 1960s. While the instructors of Company A maintained a relaxed attitude toward Morter's behaviors, the group of young men periodically chided him, as he seemed marginal from the group, never quite fitting in. Whatever haunted Morter, his struggle culminated one evening as he sat alone in the Company A office.

As head of the company, Toole should have called an ambulance upon seeing Morter's limp body. While Toole was not particularly fond of Morter, he also knew that a suicide attempt would tarnish Morter in the eyes of the military and increase his suffering. He delayed calling the authorities, hoping Morter might revive on his own. After some time passed and Morter remained unresponsive, Toole called the ambulance. Morter survived, but the instructors questioned Toole's reason for delay.

Kubach maintains that Toole was trying to protect Morter from further embarrassment. But the rest of Company A found Toole's hesitation disturbing; they interpreted it as a chilling indifference to human life. According to Tony Moore, one instructor asked, "Why would Morter do something like this?" Toole dismissively and unsympathetically responded, "Why does Morter do anything?" Moore recalls a group of instructors in Company A convening one evening to decide if they should report Toole's delayed response. For many of the men, Toole had violated their trust and failed to fulfill his duty as a leader. But they also remembered that he had made their lives in Puerto Rico more pleasant than it might have been without his leadership; he often protected them from the tirades of their superiors. Moore suggests that their sense of appreciation prevented the group of instructors from pursuing official action, but they had lost respect for Toole. According to one account, to settle the score, several guys roughed up Toole one night outside his private room. But it resolved nothing. As Kubach recalls, "Everything really went downhill for him after that."

The incident prompted Toole to reflect over some hard-learned lessons. He writes a cryptic letter to his parents on June 30. Even his mother likely had difficulty making sense of what provoked such introspection.

> While I have had unusual success in the Army, I have
> also had unusual problems (This is a statement, not a
> complaint. I believe that I have matured sufficiently to
> avoid complaining—previously one of my more apparent
> characteristics.). Handling a contingent of English
> instructors trapped here together for almost two years
> and half-maddened by continual exposure to the
> trainees has not been easy. Some aspects of this have
> almost been tragic. I can sincerely say that nothing
> could phase [sic] me any more . . . and that nothing is
> all-inclusive."

As a leader, he had faltered. Once again, his daydreams of home offered consolation:

> If I am fortunate I will be able to forget many things
> that have happened in the last few months; however,
> this place is so far removed from reality that the
> happenings here tend to fade from your mind when you
> get away for only a day . . . I would like to sit in the
> living room and talk for hours and hours and hours . . .
> over black coffee, lemonade, bourbon or whatever you
> are willing to serve me.

In the summer heat, deviant trainees and military politics burdened him, but fortunately in late June his writing resurged. It was the glimmer of his future after the army. He reported this development to his parents and detailed his precise purpose in returning home:

> On the writing, I have experienced a "renaissance" and
> have been regularly adding to the manuscript page by
> page. My one hope in civilian life (in the immediate
> months following discharge) is that I will have
> conditions favorable to trying to complete this thing and
> to polish it. That is why I am planning to stay in New
> Orleans, for I feel that I should be able to do some work
> there while I am unburdened by having to shift for
> myself so far as housing and food are concerned. I must
> make one try at getting something published and I feel
> that this is the time. . . . One point should be made
> clear: I do not intend to go to Law School or to any
> other school at the present time. About the thing I am
> writing I have one conviction: it is entertaining and
> publishable, and I have more than a degree of faith in it.

He finally proclaims unrestrained belief in his talents and his creation. While returning to Columbia University was the more conventional road toward a life in academia, he chose an uncertain path, leading to either his dreams of authorship or nightmares of rejection. But in several letters, he returns to his reasons for moving back to New Orleans, as if he needed to repeatedly justify his decision, perhaps even to himself. Despite his attempts to idealize his visions of home, requesting gold-framed pictures of his mother and imagining quaint disagreements with neighbors, moving back to New Orleans came with substantial peril. After years of independence, two of which he had excelled in the military, he would once again live under his parents' roof, and once again he would answer to his mother. From his letters, he appears purely motivated by his literary aspirations, but his apparent need to validate his decision calls this premise into question.

The Tooles still struggled financially. Ever since he garnished his army paycheck for their benefit, he felt obligated to help them. If he negotiated between his sense of filial duty and his own desires, the publication of his novel offered him an exit plan and the possibility of financial security. His decision to move back home required both faith in his talents and faith in his plan to free himself from a life bound to his parents.

Thelma Toole in the year of her marriage, 1927. Her son requested she send this photo in a gold frame to him while stationed in Puerto Rico, where he wrote *A Confederacy of Dunces*. (Personal Collection of Joel Fletcher)

John Toole circa 1919. He enlisted in the Marines at the end of World War I, although he never left the country. (LaRC, Tulane University)

"The Beauteous Babe," as Toole's mother often referred to him. From the moment he was born, she noted how he was bright-eyed and observant. (LaRC, Tulane University)

From an early age, Toole took an interest in automobiles. His father was a car salesman, and his mother proudly claimed "Kenny Boy" could name the makes and models of cars at the age of two. When he was five, his father let him drive around the block with a friend, unattended. His mother was outraged. (LaRC, Tulane University)

A rare picture of father and son. John Toole lifts his "Kenny Boy" to the sky. (LaRC, Tulane University)

LEFT: One of the posed shots taken during the time Toole performed with youth theater troupes. (LaRC, Tulane University)

BELOW: The director at work. In addition to piano and elocution lessons, Thelma put together pageants and variety shows at local schools. In the late 1940s, she started a youth theater troupe that featured her son. Occasionally, she wrote parts specifically for him to perform. (LaRC, Tulane University)

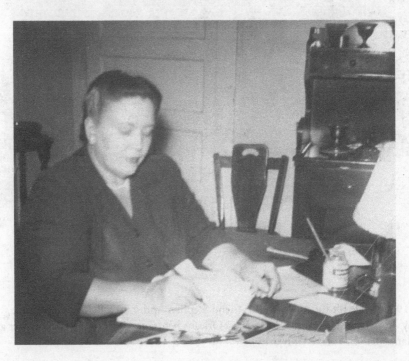

In McComb, Mississippi, Toole works the gears of a tractor while his high school friend Cary Laird smiles for the camera. Toole and Laird were the best of friends in high school. At the age of sixteen, he visited Laird's extended family in Mississippi. Toole was so inspired by this trip that he wrote his first novel, *The Neon Bible*, shortly after his return to New Orleans. (Personal collection of Myrna Swyers)

In 1955, Toole hit the road with his friend Stephen Andry. In a Bel-Air convertible, they drove from New York City to New Orleans before the start of the fall semester at Tulane. (LaRC, Tulane University)

The Hullabaloo, October 5, 1956. Toole was well aware of the politics of his age but usually searched for the absurdities in any situation. Here he depicts the tension between equally oblivious sides of academia and supporters of communism. (LaRC, Tulane University)

The Hullabaloo, November 9, 1956. This was part of a series of comics by Toole, inspired by the 1956 film *Bus Stop*, starring Marilyn Monroe. Toole was infatuated with Monroe and was devastated by her death in 1962. (LaRC, Tulane University)

A satire of the staff of *Carnival*, a student-run literary magazine at Tulane. In 1956, Toole contributed art and served as nonfiction editor. In this full-page comic, Toole depicts himself in the back, wearing sunglasses and holding a beer bottle. (LaRC, Tulane University)

"I don't care who you are, you'll have to see the manager for a free pass."

The Hullabaloo, February 22, 1957. Toole was an avid moviegoer. He shows humorous irreverence in this comic inspired by the 1956 epic film *The Ten Commandments*. (LaRC, Tulane University)

In the summer of 1958 before leaving for graduate school, Toole visited the beaches on the Gulf of Mexico just outside New Orleans. Throughout his life, he retreated to the Gulf Coast. In 1969 he returned to one of his favorite spots off the coast and committed suicide. (LaRC, Tulane University)

The view from Toole's dorm room on the top floor of Furnald Hall at Columbia University. Overlooking Broadway, the dorms for Barnard College are under construction and the bell tower of Riverside Church rises in the distance. (LaRC, Tulane University)

From Manhattan high-rises to Louisiana low-rises, Toole left New York and went to work at Southwestern Louisiana Institute in the capital of Cajun country—Lafayette, Louisiana. English classes were taught in "Little Abbeville," a group of old, termite-ridden buildings at the very back of the college. They were originally built as temporary structures by the U.S. Army to train troops during World War II. (University Archives, University of Louisiana at Lafayette)

The 1959–1960 English Department at Southwestern Louisiana Institute. Toole once playfully commented this was a "faculty composed of fiends and madmen." Department chair, Mary Dichmann, is in the far left of the front row. Nick Polites is in the front row to the far right. Moving to the left of Polites is Patricia Rickels, Muriel Price, Milton Rickels, and J. C. Broussard. Toole is in the top row to the far right. And Bobby Byrne, the most likely model for Ignatius Reilly, is the mustached man in the center of the top row. (*L'Acadien*, Southwestern Louisiana Institute, 1960)

In New York in February of 1961, Toole enjoys the mounds of snow in Central Park. He once observed that New Yorkers develop a "snowbound mentality" in the winter months. (LaRC, Tulane University)

Toole taught English to draftees in Puerto Rico. He was praised in the local newspaper for his engaging classes and remarkable success as a teacher. Toole was fluent in Spanish, although speaking Spanish was forbidden in the classrooms. (LaRC, Tulane University)

After being promoted to leader of Company A, Toole was given a private room. Here, one thousand miles away from New Orleans, he wrote *A Confederacy of Dunces*. (LaRC, Tulane University)

Toole enjoyed traveling while in the army. He visited Aruba, the Virgin Islands, and parts of Puerto Rico. Here he leans on a window sill confidently looking into the distance. (LaRC, Tulane University)

The English instructors enjoyed access to the officers' club where they would drink and socialize. With laughter in his eyes, Toole looks to Bob Young. Walter Carreiro prepares a smoke, and Toole's close friend Dave Kubach, whose typewriter he borrowed to begin *Confederacy*, digs into Christmas dinner. (Personal collection of Walter Carreiro)

RIGHT:
The original building of Dominican College facing St. Charles Avenue. Toole taught on the second floor. (Joseph Sanford)

BELOW:
Toole in his academic robes at a commencement ceremony at Dominican. This picture appeared on his memorial page in the 1969 yearbook. (St. Mary's Dominican College)

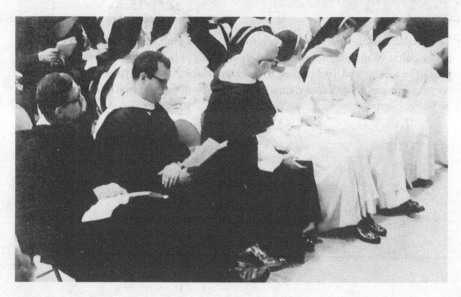

LEFT: Head of the English department at Dominican, Sister Beatrice was a close confidant to Toole. After the publication of *Confederacy*, she refused to grant interviews to reporters, vowing never to violate the trust Toole had in her. RIGHT: Sculptor Angela Gregory was another of Toole's confidants at Dominican. They would often walk to and from campus together. (St. Mary's Dominican College)

LEFT: Taken in the fall of 1968, this is the last picture of Toole before his death. He always prided himself on looking sharp, but in his Tulane library card photo he appears to have gained weight and looks unshaven. (LaRC, Tulane University)

RIGHT: Toole was laid to rest in the Ducoing tomb. Only three people attended his funeral: his mother, his father, and his childhood nanny, Beulah Mathews. (Joseph Sanford)

The "Queen Mother" in her glory. After *Confederacy* won the Pulitzer Prize, Thelma Toole became a local celebrity in New Orleans. Performing at events in her honor, she gave readings, played piano, and sang. She spent the last few years of her life relishing the attention, but she always gave her son credit and often ended an evening with the line, "I walk in the world for my son." (LaRC, Tulane University)

A picturesque view down Chartres Street leading to the iconic Saint Louis Cathedral on Jackson Square in the French Quarter. New Orleans was Toole's greatest source of inspiration. (Joseph Sanford)

As such, he welcomed his return to 390 Audubon Street as a temporary arrangement.

Content and focused on his life after the army, with his departure date set for August 6, Toole sought opportunities to escape Fort Buchanan. He visited Ponce, a fishing village on the coast of the Caribbean Sea in Puerto Rico. And he took a short leave to visit the Virgin Islands. He brought his typewriter along, but he rested much of the time. He splurged on hotel rooms equipped with air conditioning. And he observed scenes of island life he had not witnessed from the window of his barracks room.

He also received word that his best friend Cary Laird had become engaged. He writes to his parents, ribbing his old friend,

> The announcement of Cary's impending marriage came
> as no surprise. . . . However, the poor girl will have to
> adjust to a life free of the most sentimentally romantic
> notions along with a permanently bare coin purse. For
> all of Cary's sighs and valentines, I seriously doubt that
> he will ever permit his heart to govern his Hearty
> Green financial concepts.

Toole's droll response to his friend's nuptials may have come from his own loneliness. He continues,

> Sgt. Toole, alas, is rapidly approaching spinsterhood, it
> seems. I will have to cultivate a pet or two upon my
> return to civilian life.

By mid-July he prepared for his return to New Orleans. In his makeshift writer's studio, the sparse furnishings accented the seriousness of his artistic pursuit; he shipped his typewriter home, insuring it for two hundred dollars; it was his most valued possession. He asked his parents to make his car presentable as he planned to take some road trips, likely to visit Kubach in Wisconsin. And he accepted a teaching position at St. Mary's Dominican College, a small Catholic school in Uptown just a few blocks from his parents' house. He bragged and likely exaggerated to his mother that Dominican seemed to think it had a celebrity on its hands:

> The administration hired me with breathtaking dispatch.
> Later, they asked for a photo, and, after I had sent one,
> asked whether I would be willing to teach a course on
> WYES-TV also . . . I receive two page letters from
> Dominican almost daily; the nuns, apparently, are
> growing more and more excited as my date of arrival
> nears. Who knows? It might be a relatively pleasant
> experience . . . and will certainly provide me with the
> financial security for writing.

At $6,000 a year, his salary was a substantial increase from army pay. He would once again return to the task of teaching English; the job would serve his family's financial needs, as he worked to publish his novel. Ideally, once published, he would have the means to live and write independently. It seemed, in 1963, to be an exciting plan that would benefit everyone.

It is unclear how much of the novel he had completed by the time he sent his typewriter home, but it seems certain most of it was finished. What he had was enough to convince him of its imminent success. And by end of July it had become much more than a New Orleans story. He had developed a complex network of literary allusions, echoing the dark humor and sharp phrasing of Evelyn Waugh, employing insights from A. J. Liebling who concisely expressed the paradoxes of New Orleans from a New Yorker perspective, and perhaps gleaning lessons from Robert Gover, whose novel featuring a jive-talking black prostitute akin to Burma Jones, *One Hundred Dollar Misunderstanding*, Toole had acquired in Puerto Rico. And once people read Toole's novel, they would see in his characters hints of Miguel Cervantes, Geoffrey Chaucer, William Shakespeare, and Charles Dickens.

In addition to his wide-ranging inspirations from the canon of Western literature, Toole also applied the lesson he had expressed as an undergraduate at Tulane: every writer is "a mirror to the temper of his times." So as he drew upon his literary predecessors, he also satirized American society in the early 1960s, primarily through Ignatius Reilly.

The rotund medievalist sings in falsetto the wildly popular song "Big Girls Don't Cry" that played on radios all over the country. Ignatius becomes a ludicrous civil rights leader, seeking to spark the violent "Crusade for Moorish Dignity," at a time when the Civil Rights Movement reached a fever pitch. Ignatius also tries to form "The Army of Sodomites," as gay rights groups, taking cues from the Civil Rights Movement, gained traction in major cities. The absurdities of Ignatius's exploits are drawn from entrenched camps of the culture wars in American society of the early 1960s. But alas, Ignatius's plans are derailed when the black laborers are unmoved by his suggestive gyrations and he is pummeled by a gang of belligerent lesbians.

Toole had originally set out to write the quintessential New Orleans novel. His close friend Emilie Dietrich Griffin remembers that he felt New Orleans writers had operated under stereotypes of the city and "Out of the stereotypes . . . each writer had created some delusionary myth, missing the genuine texture of the place." His predecessors, such as William Faulkner and Tennessee Williams, had missed the greatest lesson of New Orleans: that its texture does not come from its gritty underbelly but rather from its centuries-long ability to enfold new voices, while never losing track of its elaborate roots, a cultural value that comes from living on the edge of existence. Toole not only understood this lesson, but in writing *Confederacy* he applied it, and in doing so he wrote a novel that did more than capture the essence of New Orleans; he struck a chord that would eventually reverberate through many countries and many languages.

Finally, his departure day arrived. On August 6 he awoke to his last morning in Puerto Rico. The sun shining through the louvered windows announced a day he had long awaited. He would no longer tread through the wet clay in the rainy season or retreat to his mosquito net in the evenings. He would no longer eat army-rationed meals or worry about surprise military inspections. But he would also surrender his private room, his creative sanctuary where he composed his literary masterpiece. In a letter to Fletcher, he reflected on his time in Puerto Rico:

> The two years in the Caribbean were, surprisingly worthwhile from several points of view. I at least completed the active military obligation, and the Army

treated me well (Remember that we are speaking here
in the context of military treatment.) and gave me the
leisure to accomplish several projects of my own. Puerto
Rico itself was worth experiencing: one can appreciate
Conrad much more deeply after having lived there for
two years.

In the afternoon, he boarded an Air Force plane bound for Fort
Jackson, South Carolina. Ascending over the Atlantic, the island gradually shrank behind him, a small green sentinel in the vast ocean. He was
free. And yet Puerto Rico would always be a part of him. In fact, it gave
him more than a room to write. It offered him distance and perspective.
It offered him a pace of life that allowed him to take stock of his dreams
and seize opportunities. But years would pass before he fully realized the
significance of his time in Puerto Rico. Stepping down from the plane,
he may have "kiss[ed] the ground in South Carolina," as he had said he
would. After two days of processing his discharge papers, Toole traded
in his army uniform for a gray suit. He returned to civilian life, he returned to New Orleans with his manuscript in hand.

Chapter 10

Back Home in New Orleans

Toole loved his city, and he undoubtedly loved his parents. But having held a teaching position at two colleges and earning a series of promotions and commendations in the army, he aspired to something more than a small apartment with two aging parents as roommates. He must have had some inclination that such a living condition would be difficult, although he may have underestimated the stress of it. Whatever the challenges, he could take solace in his master plan. So, like Theseus entering the Labyrinth, Toole held his novel as the string to lead him out of the maze that New Orleans and life at home would inevitably become.

In the year ahead he would use his spare time to refine his manuscript for submission to publishers. And in that year his mother, overjoyed to have him back home, encouraged his pursuit. She recalled the day he returned and presented her his manuscript. She read the first chapter and told him it was "promising." The next day she completed reading the whole thing. "It's a masterpiece, son," she told him. She was excited at the prospect of her son's work, but she noticed something different about him. He seemed quieter, as if completely absorbed by his book. She would eventually find his restraint and retreat worrisome, but for now he was to begin his teaching job, and the Toole household would enjoy a boon to its anemic coffers.

A few days after his return home, Toole visited Bobby Byrne. The two former officemates chatted over coffee. Never mentioning the novel, Toole told Byrne about his new job at Dominican. As a staunch devotee to the Franciscan order, Byrne was horrified. He found the Dominicans ridiculous and potentially dangerous. He cautioned Toole that "that Byzantine institution" would surely ruin him. Toole likely dismissed the comment with his trademark half smile. What an Ignatian thing to say. Despite Byrne's ill feelings toward the Dominicans, Toole had his plan that would ensure a short tenure at the college. And he retained his optimism as he began the school year.

In September Toole wrote to Fletcher, who was traveling across Europe,

> For now I have sought temporary shelter in New Orleans
> by teaching at Dominican College for the 1963–64
> academic year. Because I teach only 10 ½ hours a week,
> I will seem to have the same leisure I enjoyed in the
> Army. The college has been in session for about two
> weeks, and so far the routine there has been extremely
> pleasant. Barring some Inquisition, I should have a
> serene year, and, with the salary they've given me, a
> very financially solvent one, also.

The quaint college, a few blocks from Tulane and Loyola universities, offered him a warm welcome. While it did not hold the stature of its larger academic neighbors, the small school had a charming campus and rich traditions. Two towering palm trees marked the entryway to campus along St. Charles Avenue, and a brick pathway led to the main hall; a three-story building adorned with a cupola, onion-shaped dormers and a two-level arcade shading the huge sash windows. Toole taught in a classroom on the second floor. And among the faculty composed primarily of clergy, he quickly gained the adoration of his colleagues and students. The students were thrilled to have a smart, young scholar—who was also a New Orleanian—from the Ivy League teaching them. He left an impression of intelligence and gentility. In 1980 the Dominican alumni newsletter described him as

> The gentlemanly English teacher who asked for [student's] permission before removing his jacket on humid summer days in Dominican's fan cooled classrooms. . . . Students will remember his

polite Southern manners, his impeccably neat appearance, his dry humor, his insight into literature and his profound understanding of the absurdities of life in the 1960s.

His salient commentary in his lectures echoed aspects of the novel he labored over at home. Pam Guerin, who was an English major for a short time at Dominican, took many classes with Professor Toole. She recalls that his lectures

were mainly on issues from childhood or from New Orleans area situations. Not so different from his book. He made fun of the hot dog vendors in the city. And I did see a lot of his childhood in the lectures . . .

Of course, his students at the time were unaware of his novel writing. He kept his two roles as teacher and writer separate. And while he would later comment to his friends about the drudgery of teaching, once he was in the classroom it appeared to his students that he enjoyed it, and they enjoyed him. Perhaps his most lasting devotees to his memory at Dominican are the three Trader sisters. As they recalled, Toole routinely entered class at the last moment. And at times he could take on that supercilious tone so evident in Ignatius Reilly (as well as Toole's mother) that could be entertaining. He "ridiculed *Reader's Digest*" and occasionally spoke of "legitimate theater." He often commented on "the coming trend of making books into movies."

Toole left a lasting impression on Joan Trader Bowen, who took courses with him throughout her four years at Dominican. She identified a performance-like quality to his lectures. "He made the class interesting," she recalls, "how he said it was just as enjoyable as what he said." And Joan's sister Barbara Trader Howard observed that Toole was "subdued" but had "a spark underneath" it all.

In his courses he assigned authors such as J. D. Salinger and James Joyce, but also as an enthusiast of Southern literature, he often praised works such as *Lanterns on the Levee*—the autobiography of William Alexander Percy—who was the uncle and guardian of novelist Walker Percy. And somehow Toole seamlessly connected these works to life experiences to which his students could relate.

Among students and professors, he earned a reputation as a professor not to be missed. As Guerin confesses,

> I tried to take all my required English classes with him. . . . I found him to be very approachable but also very set in his opinions and grades. He had a dry wit about him that I enjoyed.

To this day his students and the Dominican sisters that once ran the college fondly remember Toole as one of the "most respected and well-liked faculty members."

He enjoyed the praise and attention at Dominican, but much like Hunter College, the job was a means to an end. And while most people had no idea he had written a novel, there were a few people that he trusted. In his first semester at Dominican, a senior named Candace de Russy caught his eye. And his mother, concerned about her son's introverted behavior, encouraged him to invite friends to their home. Whether by chance or design, Toole and de Russy kept running into each other on campus, although it seemed to her that the young professor sought her out. Over lunch or coffee they would talk about literature. He was undeniably smart, but de Russy thought he "projected a kind of loneliness, even timidity," even though he was always "proper and appropriate." As their conversations became more frequent de Russy noticed there was a "remoteness" about him, as if he had difficulty sustaining a conversation. He would listen, and he could tell a great story, but engaging in an exchange of ideas became awkward and clumsy for him. For a moment, she thought he might be depressed.

One autumn afternoon Toole invited her back to his house to meet his parents. They strolled down St. Charles Avenue to Audubon Street. Thelma Toole greeted de Russy at the door and eagerly welcomed her into their home. She was introduced to his father, as he sat in a darkened room. He kindly waved but did not join them for tea. Over the course of the afternoon, it seemed to de Russy that Thelma was careful to create a pleasurable experience. It occurred to her that her invitation might have stemmed from Toole's interests in dating her or from a mother's hope for her son "to gain a more normal life." It must have taken substantial trust on Toole's part for him to invite home a student at the college where he taught. But de Russy, perhaps through her empathy for him, had gained his confidence, so much so that he talked to her about his novel.

What she previously identified as depression, she now recognized as an astoundingly deep immersion in his manuscript. She noticed that Toole acted as if his mind was split between reality and his book, not as if he couldn't distinguish between the two, but because he had poured his soul into the novel. "The center of his existence had become his book," she observed. "When he walked on campus, he looked straight forward, not making eye contact, and every once in a while he would kind of chuckle to himself as if something just struck him as absurd." He discussed characters and scenes with de Russy, but sensing that more lay underneath his plot summaries, she attempted to draw out what troubled him. She gleaned from their conversations that he had "a consuming desire to have the book acknowledged and recognized. He was not egotistical, but it was something deeper. He believed in the exceptionalism of the book, but he had anxiety about it. It had very much to do with his identity and profound sense of self."

It seemed he had given himself over to his creation, as if the actual people surrounding him were shadows and the truth lie in the pages that he continued to edit. But this was not a thesis or dissertation he had written. It was not a task to display his literary prowess. He was an artist, and he had created something far more alive than an academic argument. And this creation was the pathway to his dreams of authorship.

So Toole continued editing for a few months after his return, until a guillotine that had been rising, slowly and silently for months, finally dropped. Back when Toole was settling into his home, editing his novel, and drinking coffee with Bobby Byrne, another man who was about to make the history books walked about the Crescent City. Another New Orleanian, Lee Harvey Oswald, was living in Uptown in the summer of 1963, two miles away from the Toole home. Oswald spent his days organizing a New Orleans chapter of the Fair Play for Cuba Committee and passing out pro-Castro propaganda along Canal Street. By November of 1963, Oswald had moved to Dallas, Texas, where he worked at the public school book depository. And on a sunny day in Dallas, as John F. Kennedy's motorcade slowly rolled down the street with the president and First Lady waving to crowds from the back seat of a convertible, two bullets ripped through the president's skull. Oswald was charged with the assassination. Three days later, as he was transported to the county jail, nightclub owner Jack Ruby sent a bullet of his own into Oswald's abdomen. The shots echoed throughout the country. America stood paralyzed, just before hurling itself into the most turbulent decade of the twentieth century. And as Toole watched this tragedy unfold from his home in New Orleans, his months of editing and rewriting came to a halt. His fingers rested still on the keys of his Olivetti-Underwood typewriter, and all was silent. He later confessed, "The book went along until President Kennedy's assassination. Then I couldn't write anything more. Nothing seemed funny to me."

By the beginning of 1964, Toole decided to submit his novel to a publisher. While most writers and agents would have sent a manuscript to several publishers, he selected one: Simon and Schuster. It was a house undergoing a transformation, in large part due to its star editor Robert Gottlieb. While Simon and Schuster had once focused on nonfiction and self-help books, Gottlieb ushered in fiction titles such as *Catch-22* and the novels of Bruce Jay Friedman. Toole had an especially "intense personal reaction" to Friedman's *Stern*. And when his mother later asked why he submitted the manuscript to only one publisher, Toole explained that Simon and Schuster was reputable and prestigious. He deemed that their books sold, while others collected dust on bookstore shelves. Toole wanted more than publication; he had an intense yearning to reach as many readers as possible.

Today, most large publishing houses acquire works through literary agents. But in the early 1960s Simon and Schuster not only accepted unsolicited manuscripts, it also meticulously documented submissions, considered the work, and then responded to authors. So the novel that carried the weight of Toole's future traveled from the small apartment in New Orleans to New York, and it landed on the desk of Robert Gottlieb. In many ways, Toole could not have been more fortunate. Michael Korda, an editor under Gottlieb who eventually rose to editor-in-chief at Simon and Schuster, recalled Gottlieb's fierce dedication to the art of literature. In *Another Life* Korda explains that Gottlieb approached his role as an editor like a midwife in the creative process—he could see both the big picture of the book and "how intricate changes might bring out the best in it." And he was surpassingly industrious. He labored for years over *Catch-22* with Joseph Heller. Even as the advent of the literary agent emerged among trade presses, he avoided schmoozing at martini-filled business lunches in midtown Manhattan restaurants, preferring that anyone interested in having lunch with him bring a sandwich to his office. In fact, the first time Bruce Jay Friedman arrived at Simon and Schuster to have a working lunch with Gottlieb, he was surprised to find the rising star of Midtown offering him a plate of raw vegetables to munch on while they went over the manuscript for *Stern*. And of the voluminous number of manuscripts that flooded Simon and Schuster every week, piling up on Gottlieb's desk, a new humorous writer from New Orleans stood apart from the rest. Gottlieb's assistant, Jean Ann Jollett, loved Toole's manuscript and recommended it to Gottlieb. After he read it, Gottlieb wrote encouragingly to Toole.

In just over a year, Toole had gone from staring at a blank sheet of paper in a borrowed typewriter in Puerto Rico to catching the interests of the most dynamic editor in New York. Things were proceeding according to his plan. Next, editor and writer had to figure out their delicate dance. As Gottlieb knew, every writer is different, and Toole had no experience in publishing a book. Toole had been praised for his writing abilities all his life. When he was sixteen his college professor said he was ready to submit to an academic journal. And his professors at Columbia had little to critique about his writing. But New York publishers did not operate in the realm of grades or degrees. Toole was entering a world of both art and business, subject to market forces, although not driven by that measure alone. However noble the pursuit of publishing literature, at the end of the day it is a business. His novel not only had to be good, it had to sell.

In June of 1964 Toole made arrangements to go to New York and visit with Gottlieb, so author and editor could work together, presumably to address some issues in the manuscript. But Toole could make it only near the end of June when Gottlieb would be in Europe. It was the first misstep in this dance that would become increasingly awkward. Jollett wrote to Toole to warn him of the situation, hoping that he could make his trip earlier in order to meet with Gottlieb. She ended that letter asking Toole, "Is now the time for me to tell you that I laughed, chortled, collapsed my way through *Confederacy*? I did."

Unfortunately, Toole and Gottlieb could not coordinate their schedules, so Gottlieb sent some of his editorial comments in a letter. His critique was direct. He took issue with Toole's plot structure, particularly at the end of the novel. He admitted that Toole had created brilliant scenes and "wittily tied them together at the end." But the "threads must be strong and meaningful all the way through." His comments echoed Emilie Dietrich Griffin's advice when she wrote to Toole in 1961 saying, "You have to be saying something that you really mean . . . not just dredging characters and situations up because they are charming." Gottlieb reiterates, "There must be a point to everything you have in the book, a real point, not just amusingness forced to figure itself out." After his criticism, he encourages Toole to keep working on the book, while suggesting some time away from the manuscript might be helpful. But he clearly states, "Please, no matter what, let me see the book again when you have worked on it again."

Toole still took his trip to New York. Jollett, a Southerner herself, welcomed him. She was eager to see "what the author of the book looked like." The trip was an opportunity for Toole to gain some insight into the publishing world. But she gave Toole fair warning that she would be unable to offer any more editorial advice. It must have been quite disappointing if Toole earnestly sought clear direction from Gottlieb, as he was navigating a world that was quite foreign to him.

While in New York, Toole visited Joe Hines, an English instructor he had met in Puerto Rico who lived on the West Side of Manhattan. They spoke of Toole's venture into publishing that was now in limbo. Once Toole returned to New Orleans, Hines wrote to him,

Dear John,

It has now been some time since you returned to the land of the night-blooming jasmine. I wonder how your meisterwork is progressing. Have you finished and presented it for re-examination to Miss Jollett? I take a rather selfish interest in the book, since, upon its completion and publication, I will have some contact, however slight, with fame and notoriety; one needs a touch of megalomania to get by.

Hines spends the rest of the letter discussing a trip to New Orleans to visit Toole, who had told him of the "interesting and unusual" city. Later that summer, Hines had the benefit of having Toole as his New Orleans tour guide. During the visit, they took in the film *Becket*, the story of the thirteenth-century Saint Thomas à Becket, which left Toole questioning the reasons behind the saint's "sudden conversion to goodness, religion, selflessness." At a time when Toole was urged to think most deliberately about the reasons for his characters and their behaviors, he found the about-face of a famous religious figure puzzling. While the audience liked to see characters transform, rarely do people change so drastically. Toole posed the question to Hines, who responded that it must have been "the grace of God," a response that Toole likely found unhelpful. Hines provided Toole a break from edits and rewrites, allowing time to talk to a friend and showcase his city.

In many ways New Orleans still gave Toole a sense of wonder as he spoke with his army friend and showed him around. After nearly a year back at home, preparing the revised manuscript to send back to Gottlieb for review, he still relished the quirkiness of his hometown. One evening in the summer of 1964 he met with Byrne and Fletcher at the Napoleon House. Fletcher had recently returned from Europe and like any globetrotter back in his provincial home, Fletcher was eager to share with his friends stories of his adventures. But he was "disappointed to discover that all they seemed to want to do was gossip about their uptown New Orleans neighborhood." Toole was deeply invested in his city at the time, rewriting a novel about the people of New Orleans, the very people Byrne and he discussed. Let alone, Ignatius Reilly had nearly consumed his mind for well over a year, and here sat across the table one of the major inspirations of that character. Fletcher felt snubbed by his friends, but it must have been a productive evening for Toole.

In the fall of 1964, as Toole started his second year of teaching at Dominican, he sent the revised manuscript to Gottlieb and awaited his response. Still troubled by some parts of it, Gottlieb asked his close friend and literary agent Candida Donadio to read it. While Gottlieb was not trying to impose an agent on Toole, he knew that if he were to get an agent, Donadio, who represented Joseph Heller and Bruce Jay Friedman, would be the one for him. Both agent and editor agreed on some significant changes that needed to be made to *Confederacy*. In mid-December Gottlieb writes to Toole, summarizing their suggestions. They agreed Toole was "wildly funny, funnier than anyone around, and our kind of funny." They praised almost every character in the story with the exception of Myrna Minkoff and the Levys. They concurred, "Ignatius is in trouble." With directness, Gottlieb critiqued the character Toole had been developing for years, "He is not as good as you think he is. There is much too much of him." Donadio and Gottlieb also agreed the book was too long. But the area that they found most disconcerting was its lack of "meaning." Gottlieb writes, "With all its wonderfulness . . . the book does not have a reason . . . it is a wonderful exercise in invention, but . . . it isn't really about *anything*." Gottlieb seems at a loss as to how to direct Toole, at least through the medium of a letter. But, yet, he restates his dedication to him, claiming, "We can't abandon it or you (I will never abandon Mr. Micawber)." While Gottlieb admits that the book could be "improved upon," he also says it would never sell. He continues on a rather confusing explanation, "When Candida and I know something is basically for us, but not right, it is very difficult to have it right for other people in town on our wavelength; and the others are out of the question." So what was Toole to do? He could try another publishing house, but Gottlieb, who had already dedicated much time to the novel, told him it needed a particular kind of editor. And Gottlieb was right. Publishing houses were not clamoring to release comic novels in the mid-1960s. They have always been difficult to place, but Gottlieb had edited some of the best in American fiction. From Toole's perspective, this letter must have been difficult to swallow, as well as somewhat disorienting. Where did he stand in the midst of these messages? Gottlieb tells him that he could give up on the book but then tells him that is not a good idea. And yet the book was not really marketable; however, Toole shouldn't despair. The letter fluctuates with Gottlieb's stream of thoughts. And in the end it reads more like a personal letter than business correspondence. Having typed it himself, Gottlieb confessed he could not "dictate this kind of letter," a letter from an editor searching for a balance between honesty and encouragement to help a young writer.

Recognizing letters were not the best way to communicate these messages, Gottlieb asks if Toole could come to New York and they could sit down to talk, with intent to discuss "specific editorial suggestions." That may have been the best course of action. But it didn't happen. Toole brooded over the letter, then replied in thanks for his honesty.

That same month, Toole received a letter from his friend Joe Hines. Having spent some time with Toole in New Orleans, Hines now addressed him as Kenny, instead of John. He discusses the works of Evelyn Waugh, Toole's favorite writer, and then asks about the status of the book, the project that dominated Toole's life:

> One wonders how your masterwork is doing. When last
> I saw you, you expected to have the revision completed
> before the beginning of this semester and sent winging
> on its way to Jean [Jollett] so that she might laugh and
> chortle on every reading of each page. I wonder if it has
> been sent to "your publisher" and when it may see the
> light of day and the book store's shelf.

But with the latest of Gottlieb's letters, Toole must have doubted if his novel would ever sit upon a bookshelf, let alone be read. He came to the maze of New Orleans, and now it seemed his work had entered into the labyrinth of New York publishing. The way toward publication must have appeared far more daunting then he imagined it would be. Still, he retained the face of optimism at least. He writes to Gottlieb on December 16, 1964, stating that he found Gottlieb's letter "encouraging" and requests that Gottlieb call him collect.

But something seems to have changed for Toole over the holiday season. In late December of 1964, Toole retreated to Lafayette and met with his friend J. C. Broussard. Broussard saw a man drastically altered from the inflated ego he witnessed in the Sazerac Bar two years prior. Reporting the sad episode to Fletcher, Broussard writes,

> Ken came for two days at Christmas and, under the
> influence, confided in me his deplorable state—a virtual
> incarceration (entre nous) with parents prematurely
> senile and giving full vent to a latent possessiveness.
> My advice to him, who is too young for such, was to

escape after this year. One can tolerate the aged when
they are really old and when the disparity in the age of
parents and children is not so great.

Over the course of the evening, Toole did not discuss his correspondence with Gottlieb. He must have labored over the words of the man
who held the key to his escape from his current situation, but instead
with his guard down after a few drinks he spoke to Broussard about his
parents. It is possible that the words of his mother lay heavy on his mind
as well. According to Nick Polites, Gottlieb's fluctuations between praise
and critique drove Toole's mother wild. During this period, Polites remembers making several visits to the Toole house, where he sat in audience to her rants. He recalls,

> Whenever I visited, Ken's mother would sit with us, and Ken would
> tell me of another letter from the publisher requesting more changes,
> and Ken's mother would take over and rail in the most sweeping
> terms of "art" and "beauty" and "genius" and how publishers didn't
> understand anything at all. And Ken would sit silent as his mother
> would swell with scorn. It was quite a performance.

From such testimony, one wonders whose work Gottlieb had criti-
cized. Surely the editor discussed the novel, but by extension of the
mother-son relationship, in criticizing her son's genius, he berated her,
as well. Thelma may have believed her tirades in the parlor defended her
son's honor. She likely detected that Gottlieb's words fell hard on him,
but her theatrics may have exacerbated the issue. Had Toole been receiving these letters away from home, in his own apartment, he may have
been spared the protective tirades of his mother. Then again, he may
have felt even more detached and lonesome if he had not had Thelma to
share in his disappointment. And one can only imagine if Thelma performed with such vehemence in front of a guest, how she would have
carried on when they were alone. Byrne sensed this startling disconnect
between Thelma's public praise of her son and their one-on-one interactions. In the 1995 interview with Carmine Palumbo, Byrne recounts
how his aunt, who taught Toole in grade school, used to talk about
Thelma bragging about her genius son. When Byrne told Toole of this,

he looked puzzled, saying, "My mother spends all her time telling me how stupid I am." Toole received sharp criticism from both Gottlieb and his mother, as he struggled to determine how to edit his novel. And from what Polites witnessed, Thelma amplified Gottlieb's criticism, stirring a toxic mix. Some part of Toole must have wanted it all to end.

Toole decided to request Gottlieb return the manuscript. He was almost ready to give up. In January of 1965 he writes to Gottlieb, "The only sensible thing to do, it seems to me, is to ask for the manuscript. Aside from some deletions, I don't think I could really do much to the book now—and, of course, even with revisions you might not be satisfied. I can't even *think* of much I could do to the book." Clearly, Toole was demoralized. And a worsening situation at home did not help matters. Yet, he had come too far in a remarkably short time just to walk away from it. His mother, who never settled for retreat, would not approve of him giving up. And perhaps Toole recognized that if he gave up on the book, any hope of changing his situation at home was impossible. Toole couldn't hold his "stiff upper lip" for long. Without an appointment or a call announcing his intentions, Toole went to New York to speak to Gottlieb face to face.

His mind must have reeled during the long trip north. He had restrained himself in his replies, trying to maintain his composure. What would he say when he stood in front of the man who had called his work "meaningless"? But when he arrived at Simon and Schuster, he found Gottlieb was once again out of town. For the second time, he stood in the office of his would-be publisher after a full day's travel, only to find Gottlieb away. As he spoke to Miss Jollett, a tide of emotion overwhelmed him. As he later explained, he was "bent with obsequiousness" as he "almost sank through the floor in between . . . silences, cryptic comments and occasional mindless (for it had left me) absurdities." Then he blacked out. Moments later, returning to consciousness, he left a request for Gottlieb to call him, and he returned to New Orleans. He had suffered a nervous breakdown in the offices of Simon and Schuster.

Toole knew he had embarrassed himself. To Gottlieb in 1965, Toole was one of the hundreds of talented young writers with manuscripts that would pass by his desk in any given month. And the busy editor could carry on a conversation through letters without it intruding on his daily work. But now Toole had come to his place of business unannounced and created a disturbing scene. As a potential partner in an artistic endeavor, Toole had presented troubling, unstable behavior. The whole fiasco even took Toole by surprise. What had caused him to act so irrationally? What compelled him to lash out at the one person he had identified as his lifeline? It was the first incident indicating the paranoia and the despair that would consume him.

After such an episode, many editors would have justifiably walked away, cutting off all communication. But in late February or early March Gottlieb called, and Toole asked him to clarify some of his statements made in the December letter. During that conversation, Gottlieb made the suggestion that it might be time for Toole to work on another novel, which Toole interpreted as "an opening to withdraw with at least a little grace." By this point, Gottlieb knew he was dealing with an incredibly sensitive, possibly disturbed writer, and he opened all possibilities to Toole. Perhaps a rejection letter would have made a clean break between editor and writer. But something about Toole kept Gottlieb's interests. Perhaps recognizing Gottlieb's willingness to overlook the episode in New York, Toole let his guard down. He wrote Gottlieb a letter detailing the story of his life and the story behind *Confederacy*. It was rare for Toole to be so open and candid about his personal affairs. He confesses, "I've been trying to think straight since speaking to you on the telephone, but confusion and depression have immobilized my mind. I have to come out of this though, or I'll never do anything." He also recognized that his own relationship with his work was confining him. The intensity that he felt toward his novel, which de Russy noted in 1963, had increased. He writes to Gottlieb, "Whenever I attempt to talk in connection with *Confederacy of Dunces* I become anxious and inarticulate. I feel very paternal about the book; the feeling is actually androgynous because I feel as if I gave birth to it too."

Toole goes on to explain his experiences in New York, Lafayette, and Puerto Rico, and then refocuses on the book:

> The book is not autobiography; neither is it altogether
> invention. While the plot is manipulation and
> juxtaposition of characters, with one or two exceptions
> the people and places in the book are drawn from
> observation and experience. I am not in the book;

I've never pretended to be. But I am writing about things that I know, and in recounting these, it's difficult not to feel them.

And while he draws a distinction between himself and his creation, he writes later in the letter that in some ways Ignatius became part of him:

> No doubt this is why there's so much of [Ignatius] and why his verbosity becomes tiring. It's really not his verbosity but mine. And the book, begun one Sunday afternoon, became a way of life. With Ignatius as an agent, my New Orleans experiences began to fit in, one after the other, and then I was simply observing and not inventing . . .

In a twist of roles, Toole, who had spent so much time observing people around him, had placed himself into his character he created to re-envision his world.

He goes on to address Gottlieb's critique of the novel. He fully acknowledges, "I know that it has flaws, yet I am afraid that some stranger will bring them to my attention." He admitted that the Levys were "the book's worst flaw" and Myrna Minkoff may be "a debacle." But he holds fast to Irene Reilly, Santa Battaglia, Patrolman Mancuso, and Burma Jones because "these people say something about New Orleans. They're as real as individuals and also as representative of a group." Clarifying his point, he states,

> One night recently I watched again as Santa bumped around while Irene sat on a couch guffawing into a drink. And how many times have I seen Santa kissing her mother's picture. Burma Jones is not a fantasy, and neither is Miss Trixie and her job, the Night of Joy Club, and so on.

Gottlieb had suggested the novel had no point. Here Toole explains, at the very least, the novel makes a statement about New Orleans, because it offers the real New Orleans. Toole understood that Gottlieb meant it needed more universal significance. But his "doubts [turned] into despair" when one of Gottlieb's comments struck hard. Echoing the editorial criticism that haunted him most, Toole writes, "The book seemed to become about nothing." Toole's frustration seems rooted in his confusion over how to change the novel. He confesses he felt "somewhat like a bouncing ball," never finding a clear path to gain Gottlieb's approval. Still, he determines to continue on with the revisions, accepting some of the editorial suggestions:

> This book is what I know, what I've seen and experienced. I can't throw these people away. No one has ever done much insofar as writing about this milieu is concerned, I don't think. Myrna and the Levys may only serve to hinder the book, especially in their being extraneous. If the Levys cause me such problems, they don't belong. . . . What was very accurate in your commentary about the revision was your separating real and unreal characters.
>
> In other words, I'm going to work on the book again. I haven't even been able to look at the manuscript since I got it back, but since something like 50 percent of my soul is in the thing, I can't let it rot without trying. And I don't think I could write anything else until this is given at least another chance.

After this confession to a person he had spoken with on the phone a few times, but had never met, a version of *Confederacy* without the Levys or Myrna Minkoff and perhaps significantly less Ignatius was in the works.

With a decade of editorial experience, Gottlieb understood the diverse nature of writers. They can be sensitive creatures, and the editor must tread softly at times. He usually appeared sympathetic to Toole's frustrations, although he rarely sugarcoated his points. But there were moments when Gottlieb must have become fatigued with the indulgences writers afforded themselves as they operated in a creative pursuit initially outside the marketplace. One could imagine that, as Gottlieb responded to such writers, at times he must have grumbled to himself.

In fact, George Deaux—who taught at University of Southwestern Louisiana, formerly Southwestern Louisiana Institute, the year after Toole left, and who also worked with Robert Gottlieb throughout the 1960s when Simon and Schuster published his three novels—recalls a moment when Gottlieb appeared exhausted with a writer, perhaps after reading a confession like the one that Toole sent him. In passing, Deaux mentioned to Gottlieb that he enjoyed Fellini's *8 1/2* in part because he "identified with the Mastroianni character." Gottlieb's response was "uncharacteristically irritable, almost angry. . . . He denounced Fellini for his neurotic self-pity and went on to rail against artists generally for their self-indulgence." Deaux initially thought that the criticism was aimed at him, but he realized Gottlieb was too polite and too direct "to make gratuitous comments about my personality . . . through the vehicle of an Italian movie. I concluded that he must have had a bad day with a self-indulgent author other than me."

Gottlieb took a few weeks to reply to Toole's letter. He wrote a cordial response, thanking him for the personal history. It still rings with slight derision as Gottlieb attempts to describe why Toole has been unable to produce satisfactory revisions:

> When someone like yourself is living off from the center
> of cultural-business activities, with only a thin lifeline
> to that center, through vague and solitary contacts,
> everything gets disproportionate, difficult to analyze,
> to give proper weight to.
>
> It is like those odd people who turn up in New Zealand
> or Tanganyika or Finland, writing or painting
> masterpieces. They have their own power, but they read
> or look as if the artist has had to discover the forms for
> himself. They don't have the assurance of worldliness
> and mutual interest and energy with others. So I can
> see that to you I (or Jean) is not merely a person, but a
> voice with more authority than it could possibly
> deserve. Not that I'm not good at my job, because I am
> and no one is better; but that I'm just someone, and a
> good deal less talented than you.

Much has been made of this passage as an indication of Gottlieb's Manhattan condescension. And while there is some value in that interpretation, it also stands true that Gottlieb refers to himself when he writes "the thin lifeline." Whatever he thought about an artist rooted to New Orleans, his main point is true to an editorial philosophy that he had long held and expressed forty years later in an interview with Charlie Rose when he states, "I think the cult of editing is far overblown." Gottlieb seems to suggest that Toole might be trying too hard to please his editor, instead of receiving the comments and figuring out how to apply them to benefit the novel.

In closing the letter, Gottlieb leaves the door wide open for Toole:

> You are a good writer and a serious person and are
> doing your job seriously and modestly and of course it
> isn't easy. . . . A writer's decisions are his own, not his
> editor's. If you know you have to continue with
> Ignatius, that is of course what you should do. I will
> read, reread, edit, perhaps publish, generally cope,
> until you are fed up with me.
>
> Please write me short or long at any time, if only to
> say that you're working (or not). Or if you like, show
> me bits of what you've done. Or don't; whichever
> would be more useful. Cheer up. Work. We are
> overcoming.

Toole found Gottlieb's letter "calming." And he wrote back to him with renewed vigor for the novel. He reasoned that the decade between writing *The Neon Bible* and starting *Confederacy* he had pent up "unused energies" that "came flooding into this book and created too great a concentration of emotion." But now he recognized that editing a manuscript so bound up in passion sometimes requires some bloodletting:

> What is most apparent is the need for a red pencil
> through a lot of it. There are hints in the book of
> developing themes and ideas, but they seem to be

abandoned before they become consistent statements.
I see a possibility of having the book say something that
will be real, that will develop out of the characters
themselves and what I know of them, that will not
simply be a superficial imposition of "purpose." The
book as it is evades certain logical consequences of the
nature of the characters themselves, and in this way
wastes a character or two. But I do have ideas for the
book, and I am beginning to work on it. I hope that I'll
be able to send you a re-working of the thing in the not
too distant future; since I am able to "see" and "hear"
these characters, I can always work with them . . .

I have rallied, have begun to work. And spring is here.

As the academic year of 1965 came to a close, nearly completing his
second year at Dominican, Toole reflected on his progress, although
surely disappointed that his plan was not coming together as quickly as
he originally thought it would. He writes a letter on May 4 to both
Fletcher and Polites,

Since both of you know my writing project, I must say
that eight air mail letters and one hour-long distance call
from Simon and Schuster later, I am still faced with
revisions. Although I am "wildly funny often, funnier than
almost anyone else around," the book is too "intelligent to
be only a farce." It must have "purpose and meaning."
However, it is full of "wonderfulnesses" and "excitements"
and "glories." But they worked "more than three years on
Catch-22." If and when it does appear, it will be
unbearably "significant," I imagine. Also, I am like "one of
those geniuses who turn up in Tanganyika or New
Zealand." Poor New Orleans. Suppose I had sent the thing
in from Breaux Bridge . . . or Parks. Broken and
leering toothlessly, I may yet be on some book jacket.
Looking at this more constructively, I have been

```
(and am) fortunate in having the book reach so
quickly people who have given me a degree of
confidence in what I'm trying to do; goodness
knows they've extended much time and interest.
```

Toole still maintained his sense of humor, and he certainly recognized his remarkable advances in his pursuit of publication. But getting a book published was clearly more difficult for him than being in graduate school or in the army. And for someone to whom success came relatively easy, this challenge took an emotional and psychological toll. It seems the revisions wore on his spirit to the point they began to change his outlook on life. Somehow, in his mind, what he calls his "pretentious rambling" connected to the Gulf Coast. He continues,

```
All of which leads to something else, I guess. The
Gulf Coast looks better when you're not there. I was
there recently; it looked much more appealing in
undergraduate days.
```

Even his notions of New York had shifted. He once dreamt of that city as an exciting cultural mecca. After all, it was at the center of "cultural-business" affairs as Gottlieb had written. But Toole writes,

```
Although you may not agree, life here is certainly
better than the masochism of living in New York,
which has become the Inferno of America the
American Dream as Apocalypse. And I'd never be
able to try to write anything if I were caught up
in the Columbia-Hunter axis.
```

Fletcher always sensed that his friend would have liked to live the literary life in New York. Expressing such spite toward the city, and such disappointment in the surrounding region of New Orleans, suggests Toole's possible routes of escape were becoming limited. The passages were narrowing, and he was losing grip on the thread that would lead him out. When his New York friend Clayelle Dalferes visited him in

New Orleans, he told her he never had intentions to leave New Orleans again. "It was the only place he felt comfortable." And yet, in that same conversation when she asked how his job at Dominican was going, he dryly replied, "Teaching smells."

As Toole began his third year at Dominican in 1965, Hurricane Betsy slammed into New Orleans. On the evening of September 9 the water and winds broke levees, floodwaters reached thirteen feet high in some neighborhoods like Chalmette and the Lower Ninth Ward, and many people drowned in their attics. President Lyndon Johnson flew in on a helicopter to offer his support. Uptown was spared the worst of the damage; however, much of New Orleans was under water. But as New Orleanians have always done since the founding of their city, they slowly rebuilt their neighborhoods out of the rubble.

And as the city put itself back together, it seems Toole renewed his hope for publication. He sent a letter to Gottlieb in early January of 1966. The letter no longer exists, but from Gottlieb's response, Toole wanted only to maintain connection with him. Nine months had passed since Toole's last letter, but he still had no revised manuscript to submit. Gottlieb replied,

Dear Mr. Toole,

I was glad to hear from you, particularly since a week or two ago—when the year changed—I had wondered how you were coming along. My interest in the book remains what it was. I liked a lot of it a lot; thought it needed much work; and have a small doubt that something so long agonized over is ever going to live up to (at least) your own expectations. I certainly want to read it again, when you're through doing what you're doing.

I don't think your purpose in writing me was vague. Everyone needs to feel outside, professional interest in what he's doing; we live on it. But you are not working in a void, even as far as New York publishing is

concerned: at least this one editor is interested. And
hoping that you've made the right choice in continuing
with this book rather than starting something new. But
that decision has been made; now to see what you do
with it. Onwards. Best, Bob Gottlieb.

It had been more than two years since Gottlieb first read the manuscript, and he still remained open to it. Over the course of their correspondence, Toole received more compliments and criticism, more attention from a New York editor than many writers will ever receive. But Gottlieb never offered pure praise. He was known for being courteous and direct. And while Gottlieb has long been vilified as the one that ruined Toole, there was no way for him to understand the pressure building inside the Toole home. As evident in his replies, Toole was deeply impacted by Gottlieb's criticisms. But it may have been difficult for Toole to keep a clear perspective on that criticism if boundaries between work and family, between his professional writing career and his relationship with his mother were not upheld. From what Polites witnessed on several occasions, Thelma ranted and raged but did not comfort her son with sympathy at a moment he may have needed it most.

The publication ordeal had been a difficult saga. It was becoming clearer to Toole that his stay in New Orleans was not temporary. With many congratulations, he was promoted to assistant professor at Dominican. And with an increased salary, his family could afford to rent a nicer home. Toole found a duplex in Uptown on Hampson Street, a short distance to Dominican. A step up from their apartment on Audubon Street, it had a lovely garden. And at the end of the street, on the corner of Hampson and Pine, lived Dominican College art professor Angela Gregory.

Toole and Gregory became good friends, enjoying morning and afternoon walks to and from campus together. Gregory had lived in Paris where she studied sculpture under Antoine Bourdelle and befriended mythologist Joseph Campbell. Her artwork adorns buildings and public spaces throughout Louisiana. Her statue of Jean Baptiste de Bienville, the founder of New Orleans, stands proudly in the French Quarter. Nearing her mid-sixties, she had already led an exciting and successful career as a sculptor. And so the two artists, one famously trained by a master and recognized in her own day and the other a bright scholar and writer who suffered the woes of dejection all too common in the arts, must have had riveting conversations strolling under the live oaks of Uptown. In the afternoon they would stand at the corner of Hampson and Pine, talking for what seemed to be hours. They may have discussed her recent projects working toward a Louisiana statue at Gettysburg, or perhaps his attempts at publication. Or it might have become more personal, perhaps about his struggles at home. Whatever they discussed, Toole had found a friend with whom he could share the final moments of the day before returning to his parents for the evening.

But for all the niceties the move to Hampson Street provided, Toole had driven deeper into the labyrinth. Seemingly at a loss as to how to edit his novel without destroying it, unable to spill the blood of his creation, his master plan now lay unraveled in his hands. Just as he did with *The Neon Bible*, he put away his manuscript in a box. He cut the string and gave himself over to the trappings of his own condition.

Chapter 11

Decline and Fall

Much of Toole's life had been a continual progression toward achieving some stature of greatness, either in academics or fiction writing. And many of his accomplishments had come easy to him. But the novel had posed the most formidable challenge; it also held the greatest potential to elevate him and his parents out of their financial state. The fact that he could not revise it to the satisfaction of a New York editor must have been a devastating blow to his pride. What would his life become now that the path leading out of the drudgery of working to merely sustain his family seemed inaccessible? Many of his friends had left New Orleans: Emilie Dietrich had married William Griffin in 1963 and was living and writing in New York City. Nick Polites was writing and publishing articles on design and architecture while working at a prestigious design firm in Manhattan. Cary Laird was living in Miami and working for an insurance company. Joel Fletcher was living in Paris. And each day Toole walked to the small Catholic college a few blocks away to teach, and then walked home at night, living with his parents in the same neighborhood that he had known all his life. But there was something at play more sinister than personal failures or a sense of confining filial duty. Toole's brilliant mind was falling under the grasp of mental illness.

His family history had more than its fair share of mental health issues. His father slowly deteriorated into senility. Thelma's uncle, James Ducoing, committed suicide a few months before Toole was born. In December of 1941, several years after Thelma's sister died of an illness, her surviving husband threw himself off a high-rise building on Canal Street. And in 1966 one of Thelma's brothers, George Ducoing, exhibited a full-blown mental illness that was getting out of control. Excluding Thelma, the Ducoing siblings lived in a small home on Elysian Fields, two doors down from the home where they had grown up. In a letter to the coroner dated February 28, 1966, Arthur Ducoing sought to have his brother committed:

> My brother's nervousness is apparent by his incessant loud talking at home. A source of great annoyance to three other people in the house, ranging in age from sixty-six to eighty. Placing him in the House of Detention—his last stay of three weeks—doesn't seem to accomplish much good.
>
> His need for institutional treatment is most urgent at this time. I would certainly like to see him placed in the Psychiatric Department at Charity Hospital, and would appreciate your helping the family as we really need it.

The elderly siblings had requested the white Cadillac ambulance to come for their brother, just as it had for Ignatius Reilly. And now the seeds of psychosis germinated in the mind of Thelma's genius son.

It is difficult to determine when Toole started suffering from his illness. It appears the letters from Gottlieb, especially in their encouraging moments, sustained him in some ways. But Toole had embarrassed himself in New York with an uncharacteristic outburst, perhaps the first sign of his decline. One year later, Gottlieb still encouraged Toole to keep working at his revisions. But Toole tried to justify his decision to stop working on the novel when he told his army friend David Kubach that "if his book were published it was such a scathing satire of New Orleans that he wouldn't be able to live there, but he couldn't live anywhere else." Kubach had read enough of the manuscript "to know it was fairly tame as far as satires go." Toole's conviction seemed to offer him some comfort, so Kubach did not challenge his friend's reasoning. But packing up his novel must have put his life in terrifying perspective. As Kubach observed, "I think he thought his life was going to get long."

In 1963 Toole had arrived in New Orleans, sensing his own ascent; now he found himself at the bottom of Fortuna's wheel. And, at the bottom, the world looks different, as if the top seems unreachable. Toole succumbed to an inner force as he gradually lost grasp on reality. At first there came isolated incidents of strange behavior that his friends dismissed as anomalies. In retrospect, these episodes offer glimpses into the complex distortions of a brilliant mind suffering from paranoia; some people have conjectured paranoid schizophrenia. Whatever his diagnosis would have been, these episodes now appear as signposts pointing to a tragic end.

In 1966 Toole was still teaching at Dominican with no pervasive signs of illness. His students still enjoyed his lectures. However, Pam Guerin recalls that during this period he spoke frequently about "the Mother," not *his* mother, specifically, but rather a caricature of a mother dragging her child to dance lessons and other performances, instilling in her offspring all the crucial social graces to be expected but also living vicariously through her child. Many of his students, having experienced the upbringing of a "proper lady," could relate to such a figure. But his insightful description of this mother and child dynamic suggested "he was part of it." Guerin and other students could tell that he had intimate knowledge of the very character he mocked.

As he explored this notion of the mother figure, he began having long conversations outside of class with his department chair, Sister Beatrice. She was described as "a master listener" because people often started conversations with her about literature and minutes later found themselves pouring out their souls. Sister Beatrice became one of Toole's closest confidants. And as their friendship matured, as he opened up to her, she recognized his suffering. On at least one occasion, she visited the Toole home for dinner, a visit that would take special approval for a nun at the time. While Toole often seemed indifferent about his faith, it is ironic that in his descent into illness one of his closest confidants was a nun. Despite many attempts by journalists and writers to interview her, she took his confidences to her grave in 2004.

Kubach, who had lent Toole his typewriter in Puerto Rico, also witnessed moments in his tragic decline. In the summer of 1967 Toole visited Kubach in Madison, Wisconsin. It had been years since they had seen each other in Puerto Rico, and Kubach was eager to show Toole his city. But he was not prepared for some of Toole's odd behaviors. One day, as the two were walking in downtown Madison, Kubach spotted a friend approaching. Toole suddenly dove into a store, leaving Kubach awkwardly alone as he greeted his friend who had seen him walking with a companion. As Kubach recalls, "John was in fairly good spirits, so the action caught my attention." He was puzzled as to why his affable friend had behaved so strangely to avoid meeting a new acquaintance.

During that trip, Toole sent two postcards on July 20. He wrote to his parents, "The weather is clear, pleasant; the air is very fresh and clean. I'm having a very interesting time and will see you sometime next week." His language seems forced and trite. He also sent a postcard to his friend Angela Gregory with a simple message on the back: "Wish you were here." While a cliché script for a postcard, he may have desired her company. He had spent many hours with Gregory, as they slowly walked home after classes, pausing at the corner of Hampson and Pine, continuing on with their conversation. Perhaps if she had been there in Wisconsin, he could tell her his thoughts, why he had suddenly fled to avoid meeting someone new.

The trip ended without further incident. Months later, Kubach visited Toole in New Orleans. Taking an overnight train from Madison, Wisconsin, he fell asleep in the northern reaches of the United States and awoke to "beautiful pastoral images of Northern Louisiana." Toole met him at the train depot, and within a few turns they were in downtown New Orleans. As Kubach recalls, "He showed me right away the place that he would eventually be buried, those above ground mausoleums." Often called "cities of dead," the above-ground graves necessitated by the frequent floods are a popular tourist attraction in New Orleans. But it was certainly a morbid way to start his tour.

They continued on to the French Quarter where Toole "had a number of quips to say" about the "exotic looking people walking around." Passing old colonial structures, such as the Old Absinthe House and Jean Lafitte's Blacksmith Shop, Toole bragged to Kubach that the famed pirate Lafitte, who had inspired Lord Byron's poem "The Corsair," was his ancestor. But then, as they drove through the historic city center, the paranoia that Kubach had seen in Wisconsin appeared once again. Toole became increasingly nervous. Looking in his rearview mirror, he explained to Kubach that his students from Dominican were following him, again. Determined to lose them, he started taking "evasive maneuvers" through the tight, cramped streets. Kubach saw no suspicious cars filled with deranged Catholic schoolgirls behind him. But since Toole was his guide, Kubach respectfully kept quiet. Eventually they slowed down, turned toward Uptown, and headed back home to Hampson Street. Kubach presumed they had successfully eluded the stalker students.

While Toole played tour guide for part of the trip, he appeared generally uninterested in showing off his unique city. After the long journey south, Kubach wanted to experience New Orleans. But Toole just wanted to talk. "John never wanted to be out," Kubach remembers. "His favorite scenario with me was drinks and talk. And he did most of the talking. I sometimes feel like I disappeared entirely in our friendship. I was just an audience really." Eager to connect with his friend, perhaps Toole wanted to recapture some of the spirit of his army days. Kubach even suspected that Toole warned his mother not to interfere with their conversations. Thelma seemed to go out of her way to keep her distance. And somehow Kubach never met Toole's father during their many hours spent in the small home. As the main breadwinner of the family, Toole had grounds to request his parents stay out of the way. He would need to make the inside of the home comfortable for him and his friend, especially if the outside world stoked his anxieties.

Eventually, Toole and Kubach left the house to see the environs of New Orleans. They crossed Lake Pontchartrain, traveling the long twenty-three-mile bridge to Mandeville, and then returned. They headed west to Lafayette, although they did not stop to see the Rickelses or other friends. They also drove east to Biloxi, Mississippi. And after seeing the waterfront town, they headed back to New Orleans. But there was one more place Toole wanted to show Kubach. As they drove along the Gulf, Toole suddenly turned off the road. He drove north for a short distance and then pulled over onto the shoulder. They looked out to a nondescript field with a few pine trees. Toole seemed to think that this was a beautiful, peaceful place, a special spot that he wanted to share with his friend. But Kubach, accustomed to the majestic vistas of the upper-Midwestern states, found it unimpressive. "I suppose I wouldn't have brought someone to that place," Kubach comments, "unless something had happened there, or in this case something was about to happen." Slightly puzzled by the trip, Kubach said goodbye to Toole and returned to Wisconsin.

Granted, it would be unfair to cast Toole as a perpetually brooding, melancholy soul. Despite the episodes of odd behavior, he still had moments where his personality shined. Charlotte Powell enjoyed his company at several of her parties in 1967. Her apartment on Decatur Street in the French Quarter was a popular gathering place, in part because she had the luxury of a spacious kitchen. They would boil shrimp and crawfish, spread the feast on newspaper-covered tables, and a full array of French Quarter characters from hippies to professors would dig in. While some guests railed against the Vietnam War, Toole preferred more convivial conversation, playing off puns, discussing the current state of literature, bemoaning the popularity of *Valley of the Dolls*, and of course talking about New Orleans. Powell marveled at how Toole "brought the city to life" whenever he talked about it. She told him about a time she asked a lady for directions and couldn't understand a word the lady said. She struggled to mimic the lady's accent. Without skipping a beat, Toole went into an interpretation of a New Orleans woman giving directions. To Powell's amazement, he sounded exactly like her. His humor, his intellect, and his quick wit, Powell recalls, made him "a most amazing person." And despite some of the stories about Toole's mental illness, Powell has no recollection of him appearing uneasy or behaving strangely. In fact, she marveled at how he "would walk into a room not knowing a single person and within twenty seconds be at ease, comfortable, and chatting with someone."

Toole also appeared cheerful during the Christmas of 1967, according to Thelma. Enjoying the extra income from his promotion at Dominican, they purchased a large Christmas tree and took out those fine European ornaments that they had bought just after Toole was born. They reminisced about their early days as a family. Thelma Toole would remember that holiday season as their finest Christmas in their new home.

Unfortunately, the yuletide cheer could not dispel the clouds that gathered over the charming house on Hampson Street. Polites had been to the Toole home many times since his friend had returned from Puerto Rico, and he witnessed the storm building. Usually, Polites visited several times with Toole when he was in town, but the last time he saw him in 1968 the weight of depression pervading the house nearly chased him away. Polites recalls,

> After a dreary session I took my departure saying something like, "I'll call and hope to see you once more before I leave." But being with the Tooles had been such a downer that I couldn't bring myself to call again, except when leaving from the airport. I said to Ken that I was sorry not to have seen him again before leaving, but that I became tied up and was busy for the rest of my visit and hadn't had a chance to call. I felt guilty saying it. It wasn't true. Maybe Ken recognized it. Certainly, his response literally shocked me. "That's okay," he said, "we saw each other just the right amount of time." There was bitterness in his voice.

Shortly after Polites's return to New York, Fletcher called to ask about their friend whom he had not heard from for some time. Polites recounts,

> I told him about Ken and his parting line and said, "Ken's not with us anymore." I sensed Ken's deep depression but I'm not certain whether I really articulated it to myself. I had no conscious notion of what I was saying to Joel. I never saw Ken again. I wish I'd known of the danger to come, though I doubt I could have done much.

As Toole descended into depths his friends could not follow, everything seemed to be changing around him. The student body at Dominican, which had been previously required to wear high heels to dinners and prohibited from wearing pants to class during Toole's first years at the school, was coming under the influence of the hippie generation. One of the three Trader sisters, Elise Trader Diament, sensed that Toole was baffled by these students who sat in class in raincoats and hair rollers and just stared at him, not engaging in discussion. He talked to them about authors one would expect the youth of the late 1960s to embrace—the predecessors of the hippie movement, the Beats. Elise recalled how he admired the Beat Generation and how he "thought Jack Kerouac was wonderful." Yet the students in hair rollers remained unresponsive. And perhaps this silence represented the chasm that was growing between the way he saw the world and the way the world seemed to be headed. It was painfully clear that Dominican could never serve as the peak of his literary life. As Elise explained, he was "a very deep person—too deep for Dominican."

By the fall of 1968, the students at Dominican started to notice that Professor Toole was not acting like his usual self. He was humorless, serious, and bitter—some students described him as "caustic." He made snide remarks to girls who had received flowers during the holiday season. "How ridiculous," he muttered. Chatter started to circulate about Professor Toole's odd behavior. As Elise admits, "He had a few dark days."

Eventually his visions of Dominican students chasing him through the Quarter landed on his doorstep. One weekend over coffee, Toole told Bobby Byrne that students were driving by his house at night and honking the horn to taunt him. Even though Byrne had predicted the Dominicans would surely ruin him, he recognized that Toole was not well. While the threat of students may have been hallucinated, according to one Dominican student, some girls did honk their horns as they drove by his house at night. It was likely youthful teasing and some degree of flirtation. Clearly Toole's state of mind misinterpreted their behavior as hostile. But these occurrences were irritants atop the far more disturbing confession he made to Byrne. He confessed he believed that the government had implanted a device into his brain. "Do you think I am imagining these things?" he asked his friend. Byrne recognized the telltale signs of paranoid schizophrenia. He replied, "Yes," and advised him to get help. Unbeknownst to Byrne, Toole had gone to his family practitioner about debilitating headaches he was suffering. Of course any physician requires openness from a patient in order to achieve an accurate diagnosis. And while the conversations between doctor and patient remain confidential, his friends acknowledge Toole, even in his darkest moments, held a fierce dedication to his own perception. "He was so convinced of his own mind," Kubach recalls, "you couldn't change it." In a rare moment he had opened up to Byrne, acknowledging the possibility that his perception might be distorted. But he had refined his mind over the years to be acute, sharp, quick, and accurate. He trusted it. Barring rarely seen moments of self-doubt, it appeared he would have faith in his own delusions. Then, as they sipped coffee, it seemed as if Toole flipped a switch somewhere in his mind; he returned to his usual self, making small talk about mutual friends in Lafayette and New Orleans.

Perhaps in an attempt to re-center himself on a track toward the prestigious and gratifying future he so deserved, Toole once again took up the pursuit of his PhD. But his condition and commitment to his parents left Tulane the only viable option for graduate studies. Between Dominican and Tulane he walked in two different worlds, a professor by day and a student by night, just as he had done at Hunter and Columbia. He took only two courses: a seminar on Dreiser and an Old English course with Professor Huling Ussery. His classmates remember him as intelligent and well prepared. His class notes demonstrate clear thinking and the ability to reason. These were not the scribblings of a madman, but rather notes from a mind that could parse out academic pursuits and the unnerving anxiety that something was not right in his world. Toole often visited Professor Ussery during office hours and after class. They began frequent and long one-on-one discussions, conversations that convinced Ussery his student was not well. Ussery could tell Toole was suffering. Just as Toole had done with Sister Beatrice and Angela Gregory, he confided in Ussery. When asked about the nature of their discussion, Ussery declined to comment. But he admits they did not discuss Old English or the PhD program. They were delving deeper and more personal than two professors talking shop. With growing concern for his student's well being, Ussery went to his department chair to suggest they recommend Toole for psychological evaluation. The chair decided that the department would not get involved in the personal matters of a student.

Toole's paranoia came to a head one day in Ussery's class. Thomas Bonner was in the course with Toole and remembers him as "competent in his preparations and quiet in demeanor." Having taught at University of Southwestern Louisiana (formerly SLI), Bonner knew Toole's old Lafayette circle. But after acknowledging their common acquaintances, such as the Rickelses, Byrne, and Broussard, their communication ceased. It appeared Toole kept to himself, not socializing with other graduate students. One day in the basement classroom in Gibson Hall, as Toole sat in his regular seat by a pillar in the middle of the room, he stood up during the class session. As Bonner recalls, Toole announced

"There's a plot against me here." There was sudden quiet. Professor Ussery asked him to point out the plotters. Toole said nothing. Then Professor Ussery asked those who had nothing to do with this situation to leave the room. Everyone left but Toole. My last sight of him was his standing silently facing Professor Ussery, who was partially sitting on the edge of his desk.

The students were clearly unaware of any event in class that might have prompted such a reaction. Toole never returned to class. Obviously, he sensed that forces beyond his control confined him. He had become suspicious of his students at Dominican, and he determined some contingent at Tulane worked against him.

But, these neuroses were minor compared to his most horrifying realization that he shared with Patricia and Milton Rickels. Since returning from Puerto Rico, he often spent an overnight in Lafayette visiting the Rickelses. Typically he would make the drive on a Saturday afternoon; they would have dinner and drinks, talking into the evening, then enjoy a relaxing breakfast the next morning before he returned to New Orleans. But on one of his weekend visits in 1968, he pulled into the Rickelses driveway after the two-hour trip and remained in the car. Noticing he was not moving, Patricia went out to greet him. "What are you doing, Ken? Come on inside." He looked at her and said, "No. I don't think you want me." Patricia dismissed his self-pity. "Oh don't be an ass!" she replied. "Come on inside." Ken nodded, "Ok. But I am going to leave my bags in here, because I don't think you want me." He came into the home, and they enjoyed a pleasant meal. After dinner they sat around the table, talking as usual, but Toole's conversation surprised them. For the first time, he told them that he had written a novel and that it had been under consideration at Simon and Schuster. They praised his worthy accomplishment. But then Toole shared his shocking insight: *A Confederacy of Dunces* had been stolen and given to another author at Simon and Schuster.

In what sounded like an elaborate conspiracy theory, Toole explained that George Deaux, the writer who came to teach at SLI a few weeks after Toole left for Columbia University, had gained access to *A Confederacy of Dunces* and Simon and Schuster published it under a different title. Indeed, during the time Toole and Gottlieb exchanged letters and the manuscript, Simon and Schuster had published three of Deaux's novels, and Robert Gottlieb had worked as an editor on them all. Deaux's second wife worked in the publishing industry, as well, and Toole somehow connected her to Simon and Schuster. According to Toole, Deaux had gained access to the manuscript through his wife and Robert Gottlieb.

Patricia listened to her dear friend explain how the work that was supposed to save him from the rigors of teaching and the pressures of living with his parents, had been unjustly taken from him. Sympathetic to his distress, Patricia assumed him correct. While there was no evidence to support his claim, she had an unfavorable view of Deaux from his days at SLI. But Milton Rickels placed the story in context with Toole's odd behavior in the driveway. Much like Byrne, Milton recognized his symptoms of paranoia and his increasing detachment from reality. That night, as Toole rested in the guest room across the hall, Milton explained to his wife that her dear friend was losing his mind. "No. No, it can't be true," Patricia muttered, as she lay on her pillow in disbelief.

While Toole's faculties of reason might have made emotional leaps of logic, perhaps spurred by jealousy of Deaux's success as a novelist at Simon and Schuster, his suspicions were not entirely unfounded. Toole never mentioned any specific titles by Deaux, but there are some remarkable similarities between *A Confederacy of Dunces* and Deaux's third novel, *Superworm*, which was published in 1968 just before Gottlieb left Simon and Schuster to become editor-in-chief at Knopf. Considering Toole's theory sprang from a troubled mind, it should be stressed that a comparison between the two novels serves only to offer insight into how Toole may have come to believe his work was stolen from him, not to legitimize his claims.

Toole owned Deaux's first novel, *The Humanization of Eddie Cement*, which had been published in 1964, but that novel as well as Deaux's second book, *Exit*, are nothing like *Confederacy*. Toole must have read *Superworm* to conclude that his novel had been stolen. In *Superworm*, history professor Claude Flowers can no longer stand the villainies of modern times. Taking to task adversaries that represent modernity, Claude dons a self-made superhero costume and plots to undermine the grand inequities in "the system." The dust jacket commentary describes Claude as an American Don Quixote. In the foreword of *Confederacy*, Walker Percy defines Ignatius as "a fat Don Quixote." And while Toole was not alive to read Percy's commentary, he was certainly well aware of the quixotic nature of his main character.

Both Ignatius Reilly and Claude Flowers are self-marginalized intellectuals. They bite their thumb at the modern world through their actions, comments, and dress. Claude "wears Clark's desert boots and Rooster ties, and shirts with button-down collars." Most days his jacket and trousers are mismatched. Ignatius wears a hunting cap, a plaid flannel shirt, "voluminous tweed trousers," and "suede desert boots." Through their misadventures, both characters modify their apparel. Claude becomes Superworm, dressed in long underwear dyed black. And Ignatius becomes a piratical hot dog vendor, complete with eye patch, plastic cutlass, and hot dog cart. They both disregard social standards of dress, and both characters find costumes that empower them to revolt boldly against society.

Claude is much more proactive than Ignatius in his attack on the Modern Age. He is highly attuned to the places of the worst offense with a "nose, sensitive to evil" and the "fetid wave of wrong thought." He searches for the perfect opportunity to "leap" into his superhero role. His lectures in history classes bore his students, but his subversive actions inspire them. The laziness of Ignatius prohibits such zest, although his physique certainly gains destructive momentum. While Claude aims to embody the revolutionary spirit, Ignatius aims to incite revolution.

And through their social activism, they develop a savior complex, wherein they continually speak and act for the disenfranchised populations of society. But in both books their schemes to save the world are more about legitimizing their own place in society, rather than a sincere attempt at social reform. In *Confederacy* Ignatius feels compelled to impress the radical activist Myrna Minkoff, his epistolary love. From his Crusade for Moorish Dignity to the Army of Sodomites, he fantasizes about Myrna's amazed reaction. And Claude's subversive heroism offers him an avenue of personal expression, where he can render the paradox of lecturing students on the glories of revolution from the bourgeois comforts of a university professorship; he can operate in mainstream society but take on a persona to become the revolutionary. But the villains they take on—a polluting pizza factory, a billboard sign, and an old custodian in the Smithsonian in the case of Claude, and a pants factory in the case of Ignatius—convey the absurdity of their revolutionary spirit.

So the noble ambitions in both Ignatius and Claude are skin deep; they are both incredibly selfish men. While they claim to fight for justice, they mistreat the people that they depend upon most. Ignatius constantly insults his mother, while Claude verbally and at times physically assaults his wife. And yet the most abused characters remain surprisingly devoted to their abuser.

And in the end Ignatius and Claude must leave their home. Ignatius narrowly escapes the Cadillac ambulance coming to take him to the psychiatric ward in Charity Hospital, as he heads to New York City with Myrna Minkoff. Claude is not so lucky; the men "in immaculate white suites" place him in the "padded compartment" of a police wagon. While they meet different fates, both characters are purged from the community; their psychotic self-indulgence had become a consuming vortex. And despite the pleading of their loved ones to change, they could not. The only way to deal with Ignatius and Claude is to get rid of them.

Of course, despite their numerous similarities, one glaring difference between these two novels remains. Under the auspices of Robert Gottlieb, *Superworm* was published; *Confederacy* was not. Toole must have asked, "Why Deaux and not me?" Some key aesthetic differences between the two novels offers insight into Gottlieb's decision against *Confederacy*. *Superworm* has a focused plot, closely following the protagonist and not wandering into the lives of other characters. In essence, the plot drives the characters. But the plot of *Confederacy* is the medium providing opportunity for the humorous expression of the characters. Indeed, Toole had spent his life observing and mimicking characteristics of personalities, and his characters take a primary role in the book. In this regard *Confederacy* is quite Dickensian: the seemingly disparate yarns of various characters strewn about the city weave together to form the narrative. But this approach requires time, space, and patience from the reader—and perhaps a willingness to lose oneself in a character. But unlike Dickens, Toole avoids sentimentality and agendas of social reform.

Furthermore, *Superworm* offers a pointed commentary on society in the 1960s. Its message was quite clear. The final words of the novel cast

Claude, the radical activist, as "just another naked nut." Through satire, it critiques the tide of social activism in the late 1960s. Thomas Lask of the *New York Times* explains, "Mr. Deaux makes a few sharp comments on the do-gooders who are more concerned with action than with results. . . . He is also acute in showing how often personal drives are elevated to crusades." Clearly Gottlieb's final criticism of *Confederacy* was not only an expression of his opinion, but a valid observation from the standpoint of an editor with the responsibility of finding sellable material in a particular market. In *Superworm*, Gottlieb may have seen marketability; it must have had that "meaning" that he deemed missing in *Confederacy*.

And yet *Superworm* received similar criticism to that of *Confederacy*, even though a decade separated the publication of the novels. Reviewers said of both writers they were "trying too hard." Lask observed that Deaux's "humor was too mechanical. . . . You can feel him cranking the machine up. But there are scenes of genuine hilarity." Lask sees the meaningful commentary in the novel but finds the point and humor forced at times.

In his belief that *Confederacy* had been stolen, Toole had created a compelling and elaborate narrative of Gottlieb and Deaux conspiring against him. Deaux points out that Gottlieb actually had very little to do with *Superworm*. And it would be remarkably out of character for Gottlieb, who had behaved with so much compassion and took two years to help a writer with whom Simon and Schuster had no contract, only to lift the ideas and hand them to another writer in their house that had proved a moderate success. But to a powerless and once aspiring writer now defeated, the publishing world could be enigmatic. Writers on the margins have used all kinds of methods to understand the road to publication, looking for clues at the bottom of teacups, hoping to make sense out of the exclusive and seemingly insurmountable stratosphere in those high-rise buildings of midtown Manhattan.

If Toole kept up with the *New York Times*, then he may have seen in March of 1968 the profile detailing the sweeping changes in the publication world, including Gottlieb's transition to Knopf. As Henry Raymont reported, "Possibly the most striking change was that of Mr. Gottlieb, who took with him Simon and Schuster's top editorial production team." Raymont acknowledges that in the midst of this consolidation and emergence of multimillion-dollar publishing houses, a shift from family-owned businesses to huge corporations, publishing houses would be less likely to take risks on writers. Ultimately, the publishing world was getting bigger, stronger, more concentrated, and far more difficult to navigate, and the media cast Gottlieb's move to Knopf as a key indicator of this dramatic change. In this context the exchange Toole had with Gottlieb appears remarkably rare. And if Toole read the newspaper article, it may have put a final end to any thoughts of resubmitting the novel. The editor who once said he would never abandon Mr. Micawber likely seemed unreachable now. Gottlieb finished up his spring 1968 list for Simon and Schuster. *Superworm* was one of the last novels under his wing. From Toole's perspective, Gottlieb had thrown his creative work to another writer as he jumped ship, and there was nothing Toole could do about it.

But even in the midst of his outrage, Toole never lost his capacity for wit. When Patricia Rickels asked about his plans for the novel, now that it had been stolen, Toole replied dismissively that he had given up on it. He had begun writing another novel. The working title of his new novel, he said, was *The Conqueror Worm*. He would outdo Deaux; he would conquer *Superworm*.

Patricia and Milton caught the allusion to the poem with the same title by Edgar Allan Poe. Poe's poem is an allegorical tragedy of Man, who succumbs to the all-consuming worm. Over the breakfast table at the Rickelses house, Toole cited the horrific futility of life. He determined the world had entered into a confederacy against him. And it seems he began to see his life as if he were sitting in the theater of Poe's mind:

> *Lo! 'tis a gala night*
> *Within the lonesome latter years!*
> *A mystic throng, bewinged, bedight*
> *In veils, and drowned in tears,*
> *Sit in a theatre, to see*
> *A play of hopes and fears,*
> *While the orchestra breathes fitfully*
> *The music of the spheres.*

Mimes, in the form of God on high,
  Mutter and mumble low,
And hither and thither fly—
  Mere puppets they, who come and go
At bidding of vast shadowy things
  That shift the scenery to and fro,
Flapping from out their Condor wings
  Invisible Woe!

That motley drama—oh, be sure
  It shall not be forgot!
With its Phantom chased for evermore,
  By a crowd that seize it not,
Through a circle that ever returneth in
  To the self-same spot,
And much of Madness, and more of Sin,
  And Horror the soul of the plot.

But see, amid the mimic rout
  A crawling shape intrude!
A blood-red thing that writhes from out
  The scenic solitude!
It writhes!—it writhes!—with mortal pangs
  The mimes become its food,
And angels sob at vermin fangs
  In human gore imbued.

Out—out are the lights—out all!
  And, over each dying form,
The curtain, a funeral pall,
  Comes down with the rush of a storm,
While the seraphs, all haggard and wan,
  Uprising, unveiling, affirm
That the play is the tragedy, "Man,"
  And its hero the Conqueror Worm.

Poe was an artist who explored the darkest aspects of the human mind. And Toole could find many relatable traits to the Gothic poet. Poe had an actress mother. He had lived a life of financial struggle. As a Southern writer, he had faced a literary field dominated by figures in New England. His most famous poem "The Raven" was essentially stolen from him, widely published without his permission or benefit. And it has been theorized that Poe also grappled with mental illness. Of course there were few options for treatment, let alone diagnosis in his day. In the end, Poe ended up unconscious in a ditch. A few days later, deranged and muttering nonsense in a hospital in Baltimore, he died.

Over a hundred years of medical advances separated Poe's death from Toole's descent into mental illness. And yet the therapy for severe mental disorders was a grim prospect in Toole's day. Plenty of writers in the mid-twentieth century illustrate this point. When Ernest Hemingway fell into debilitating depression and displayed suicidal tendencies, doctors administered electroshock therapy, sending a current of electricity coursing through his body. In July of 1961 Hemingway decided only the blast from his shotgun could cease his suffering. And when Allen Ginsberg "saw the best minds of [his] generation destroyed by madness," he had in mind his friend Carl Solomon in Rockland Psychiatric Center, who was undergoing insulin-shock therapy—repeatedly induced into a convulsive coma through massive injections of insulin. Fortunately, Solomon survived. But poet and novelist Sylvia Plath did not. She had undergone both insulin and electroshock therapy in her periodic stints in mental hospitals. In February of 1963, at the age of thirty, she laid her head down in her gas oven and the hissing fumes filled her lungs. And in 1966 Toole's Uncle George had reached the point to where his own siblings made a plea to the coroner to commit him to the psychiatric ward at Charity Hospital, a place that was described in the 1950s by one doctor as "a giant cage" where "most patients were strapped to the beds, and they had to be untied in order to examine them." Had Toole's illness been delayed a few more years, he might have had the benefit of advances in drug therapy and humanitarian laws implemented within the field of mental health. But that was not to be the case.

Having completed the fall semester at Dominican, the winter holidays of 1968 offered Toole a reprieve from teaching as well as several weeks at home with his parents. He weathered Christmas and New Year's Eve. But after the holiday season, the blinking lights, pine trees propped in living rooms shedding dry needles on the floor, smiling plastic Santa Clauses on lawns, and giant wreaths on department store windows, always seem sad and surreal in the bleakness of January. From the windy snows of New York to the chilling rains in New Orleans, winter usually dampened Toole's spirits. This melancholy season was worse than others. As the holidays concluded, and with Mardi Gras on the horizon, Toole decided he could not return to his position at Dominican. He was absent the first day of class, and he never came back. In this decision, he compromised the family's livelihood. The illness that plagued his mind now threatened to consume the whole family.

On January 19, the bough snapped. Toole and his mother had a disagreement that erupted into a devastating fight. Thelma never confessed to the cause of the argument. Whatever the tipping point, the dispute escalated beyond reason. Bitterness, resentment, and a mind riddled with paranoia exploded in their house on Hampson Street. Toole stormed out. The next day he returned while his mother was away. He packed some of his belongings and went to the bank to withdraw his money. He quit his job, and he quit his parents. In his blue Chevy Chevelle he left New Orleans and took to the road embarking on his final journey.

Every spring a special generation of the Monarch butterfly travels thousands of miles north, across America to return to its ancestral home. Its route was once veiled in mystery, but eyewitnesses have seen the Monarch in the middle of the Gulf of Mexico. Whatever its path, shortly after it reaches home, the delicate creature will die.

Chapter 12

Final Journey

On the day Toole left New Orleans, Richard Nixon ascended to the office of president to take the helm of a country mired in the Vietnam Conflict and countless Cold War fronts. In his inaugural address, Nixon spoke of peace and love and of the world as God sees it, "Beautiful in that eternal silence where it floats." Just as the pristine blue-and-white marble spinning in space belies the heartache of its inhabitants, the silent passing of days tormented Thelma as she waited to hear from her son. He was out in the world somewhere. He could have gone in any direction.

She suspected he would head to Lafayette to the home of the Rickelses. In his moment of crisis, it would make sense to seek refuge in the warm embrace of the family that always appeared to him stable and lovely. The next day Thelma called Patricia Rickels to make sure her son had arrived. Patricia told her that she had not seen him. Thelma did not believe her. "Please, Please!" she begged, "From one mother to another, just tell me he is there. I won't even ask to speak with him. Just tell me he is safe." Hearing the guilt-racked pleas, Patricia wanted to tell her that her son was okay, but she could not. "I am sorry, Mrs. Toole," she said. "I have not seen him." "How could you be so cruel?" Thelma turned on her. "Why would you torment me so?"

Days turned into weeks. Thelma called anyone she could think of who might know where he was. No one in Lafayette had seen him, so they told her. She called Cary Laird, who was now living in Florida. Laird had not seen him. "How long has he been gone?" he asked. "For several weeks," she responded. He could sense her distress, and he reassured her that Toole would never do anything to harm himself. He would certainly come back.

By mid-February, Mardi Gras celebrations were in full swing. Streets echoed with the sounds of marching bands and laughter. The Mardi Gras Indians danced in their costumes of vibrant feathers and beads. And yet her son never broke the aching silence in their home. Her boy with those "dark, luminous eyes" who once doted on her, praised her piano playing, and requested gold-framed pictures of her, never relieved her pain.

But this wasn't about Thelma. Toole had unbound himself from his roles as professor, writer, and son. With money in his pocket, throwing care out the window, he roamed the country. North, south, east, or west, he was on a journey, looking for something he had not yet found, perhaps something more to life than the confinement of his dutiful expectations. He spent two months on the road. The details of his trip remain largely a mystery. But one certainty lay in the distance: every journey must come to an end. After such a long period, perhaps the challenges of home weren't as bad as he thought. Perhaps he just needed some time away from it all, a little room to breathe. It seems he turned back toward New Orleans.

It was nearing the end of March, when the warm sun chases away the cold rainy days of winter, when the irises bloom in the bayou. But as he headed west toward New Orleans, the road signs, the landscape, the smells must have grown familiar. And perhaps those sights, no longer recollections softened by the sepia tones of memory, cut with the sharpness of reality. He turned off the main route onto Popps Ferry, an inconspicuous road just outside Biloxi. He parked his car under the shade of pine trees, the same area he took his friend Dave Kubach years before.

In those woods, removed from the beaches, it seems he found some peace. He placed a final letter to his parents atop the pile of papers in the passenger seat. He unwound a garden hose, inserted one end into the exhaust pipe and propped the other end in the window crevice. Returning to the driver's side seat, he shut the door. He had followed the ritual: a final word in writing, a method of his choosing, and now to follow through with the design. He placed his fingers to the keys in the ignition. In New Orleans his mother waited for a sign, the phone to ring, a note in the mail, anything. At Dominican, whispered rumors circled among students as to what had become of Mr. Toole. In New York, Gottlieb had moved on to his new job at Knopf, never hearing again from the young, talented writer from New Orleans. Somewhere over the Gulf, a brown pelican flew low over the water, the tips of its wings nearly grazing the dark, glassy surface. The novelist, the poet, the scholar, the professor, the man who brought so much laughter to his friends, turned his wrist. The engine roared, and the noxious fumes billowed into the cabin. John Kennedy Toole faded from this world, alone in the woods on a balmy spring day, as the Monarch butterflies fluttered across the Gulf of Mexico, dancing on air, returning home.

His journey was over. His body lay lifeless in the car. It was March 26, 1969. He was thirty-one years old.

Hours later, the Biloxi police department received a call about a suspicious car on the side of the road—likely a suicide. They dispatched an officer to the scene. Shortly thereafter, Thelma Toole received the sign she had awaited and most feared. Within twenty-four hours the car was towed, the papers in the passenger seat collected, and his body returned to New Orleans. At 3:30 the next day, services were held at a funeral home on Elysian Fields and a religious service at St. Peter and Paul church a few blocks away. There were only three people in attendance: his mother, his father, and Beulah Mathews, his childhood nanny. It was an unusually quiet end to a life that held such promise, a life that had been tailored for brilliance. In a city that never shied away from death, where people sing dirges to the grave and celebratory songs after burial, where they once held picnics in graveyards and whitewashed family tombs on All Saint's Day, Toole had no litany of eulogies recalling his better days when his mind was sharp, his smile bright, and his laughter infectious—no such graces for a man who had committed the sinful act of self-destruction. In fact, he was fortunate to have a service at all, considering the stigma the church placed on suicides, even though the second Vatican council softened its stance on the issue. Fortunately, the church that the Ducoings had attended for generations agreed to hold the funeral. Born and baptized in Uptown, his final rites were performed in the church where his parents had married, in that same working-class section of the city they sought to escape, the Faubourg Marigny. And after the service, the elderly parents escorted their son's body to the Ducoing tomb in Greenwood Cemetery.

The next day his obituary was published in the *Times Picayune*. It was the shortest entry on the page. The "beloved son of Thelma Ducoing and John Toole" and a "native of New Orleans" had died. The implicit understanding of his actions needed no publication. In taking his own life, he had shamed the family and left his parents devastated.

* * *

Thelma now had years to ponder the haunting questions that remained. She started to piece together where her son had spent the last sixty-four days of his life. She still believed he had gone to Lafayette. And perhaps she was right. But if he had gone to the Rickels house on January 20, he would have found their driveway full with cars; they were hosting a book club party. As his world came undone, he would have found his sanctuary overrun with a convivial sort, strangers talking about literature. In such a fragile state of mind, he likely continued down the road.

From his receipts and remaining belongings, it seemed her son headed west to San Simeon, California, and visited the Hearst Castle, an icon of American excess and the inspiration for Xanadu in *Citizen Kane*. California was the land of stars, the land of Marilyn Monroe. And Alvin Foote, his mentor from his early college days, who had believed in Toole's gifts as a writer, had once lived an hour away from San Simeon. But when Toole needed saving from the "bottom of Morro Bay," as Foote had written to him in 1957, no voice from afar came to save him.

From California it appears he headed east, driving across the country to visit Andalusia, the home of Flannery O'Connor, in Milledgeville, Georgia. In a taped interview, when Thelma was asked how she knew he visited O'Connor's home, she emphatically responded, "He did . . . we saw the STUB . . . IN . . . HIS . . . POCKET!" It is unclear what ticket stub she references. While O'Connor died in 1964, her home was not open to the public in 1969. He could have made prior arrangements to visit the home, but there was no ticketed entry. Perhaps he just drove by to see the house where the frail Georgian Catholic once fed her brightly colored peafowls when she wasn't writing her stories of violence and re-demption.

Between California and Georgia, he could have visited any number of places. And aside from a possible attempt to visit the Rickelses, it seems he did not attempt to reach out to friends. He knew people in Wisconsin, Chicago, New York, Colorado, and Florida, but perhaps he did not search for company or counsel. While we may never know for sure what route he took, his journey stands as a powerful metaphor for his experience. From the opulence of the west to the tempered graces of the east, he had traveled to the edges and determined he could carry on no longer.

Of course, difficult and haunting questions come with every suicide. Why did he do it? What drove him to follow through with such a heinous act? What was the breaking point that determined his actions? Perhaps the letter he had written to his parents and placed upon the pile of papers contained some insight to his reasons. When asked about its contents, Thelma varied in her responses. Sometimes she would say it was filled with "insane ravings." Other times she would say that he apologized for what he did and that he loved them. But we will never know for sure. Thelma destroyed the letter. And the other documents found in the car were placed in a box in the Biloxi police department. In August of 1969, five months after Toole committed suicide, Hurricane Camille slammed into the Gulf Coast, and the waters carried away those papers. The beginnings of his third novel, *The Conqueror Worm*, may have dissolved into the Gulf of Mexico. Much like the details of his journey, the true contents of his suicide note and his other effects with him at the time of his death will remain a mystery.

Regardless of those documents, Thelma supplied an answer to the question of why. She unequivocally blamed Robert Gottlieb. As she saw it, the editor from Simon and Schuster had singlehandedly lifted her son's hopes to unrivalled heights, only to dash them upon the jagged rocks of his "vitriolic attacks." She never suggested that her son mentioned Gottlieb in his final letter. Nonetheless, she determined the New York editor had tortured her son into his psychosis. But Gottlieb proved a convenient scapegoat, especially after the publication of the novel.

Perhaps Thelma was unaware, or chose to ignore, the degree to which her son confided in Gottlieb, confessing aspects of his life that he rarely shared with others. In fact, when George Deaux read the letters from Gottlieb to Toole, he observed that the letters "sound more like the responses of a therapist to his patient than an editor to a professional writer." Deaux found a stark difference between his own interactions with Gottlieb and Toole's correspondence with him. "I always found him to be kind and supportive, but I would not have expected him to be so indulgent in dealing with a writer's personal problems and sensibilities." While Thelma saw Gottlieb as a tyrannous tormenter, his letters demonstrated that he recognized and praised the talents of her son. Ultimately, as an editor, he had to think about the interests of the publishing house and the literary market. Initially, Toole did not weather Gottlieb's call for revisions well. But to suggest Gottlieb singlehandedly destroyed her son's otherwise stable mental state may have been a way for her to displace her own feelings of guilt.

Other claims have been made as to the roots of his psychological crisis, some of the most onerous coming from the biography *Ignatius Rising*. Biographers René Pol Nevils and Deborah George Hardy intended to write a book on the making of the movie *A Confederacy of Dunces*, but their project became a biography of Toole once the movie deal fell through. Their narrative repeatedly suggests that Toole suffered from latent homosexuality. They interviewed a man who claimed to have had a strictly sexual relationship with Toole in the late 1960s. However, as Fletcher has pointed out, the authors of *Ignatius Rising* offer this man's testimony, even as he admits those years in New Orleans were a drunken blur to him.

A tale of conflicted sexuality may have made a scintillating story for Hollywood at one time, as was evident when Fletcher was interviewed by a producer wanting to do a biopic of Toole. Determined to depict the author in the dark corners of French Quarter gay bars, the producer grew frustrated when Fletcher maintained he never thought his friend gay. He always found Toole to be rather asexual. Granted, some of Toole's friends held suspicions that he harbored unrealized homosexual inclinations. Polites sensed it, especially considering Toole's awkward reaction at the gay party they went to together. Although, Polites admits his interpretation was not based on a confession or evidence. And Toole's high school and college friends recall his friendship with the rather attractive and effeminate young man named Doonie Guibet. On one occasion, they went to see Mae West together, delighted by her sexual euphuisms. Cary Laird and his sister, Lynda, knew that Toole was socializing with Guibet. Lynda observes, "I always thought Ken was so interested in people that he wanted to befriend all walks of life." To the Lairds, Guibet was another color in the spectrum of humanity that Toole sought to understand, not a reflection of an unrealized aspect of his identity. According to Thelma, when Toole paid a visit to Guibet at his New York apartment years later, he found a questionable picture hanging on the wall. He "didn't like what Doonie was doing with his life, and eventually he broke with him." Guibet was later accused and arrested for the murder of his roommate in the early 1980s.

The women Toole dated may also contest suggestions of Toole being latently homosexual as well. Most likely Ruth Lafranz would not have carried on their relationship so long had she thought him gay. The mysterious "Ellen" repeatedly declared her love for him in a letter from New York. And Patricia Rickels, while never dating him, always felt he was attracted to women, especially considering his flirtations with her in front of her husband, as well as flirting with some of the wives of other faculty members. "A lot of people say he was homosexual," Patricia says, "but I never thought that. He liked women. . . . He liked me, very much. He took a fancy to me." And one of his final confidants, Professor Ussery, who was sensitive to Toole's mental anguish, never detected that his sexuality had any bearing on the illness that consumed him.

It is possible, as it is for any human being, that Toole had desires other than heterosexual ones, but there is no firsthand evidence and no credible testimony to the fact. It is possible that he suffered from a conflicted sense of sexuality. But to date there is no love letter confession or secret declaration scribbled in a journal. And without such evidence, it is unwise to suggest the impact this mere possibility had on him. Delving into such murky waters offers little more than sensationalism to the story of his life. And as discussed later, because it is mere conjecture, the suggestion has no bearing on the merit of his artistic work. In the end, Toole's sexuality remains his own.

There have also been questions that Toole had an unhealthy relationship with alcohol. Biographers Nevils and Hardy document several stories of Toole drinking. But he rarely appears drunk in any of these tales. Nonetheless, they suggest when speaking with his family doctor about his headaches that Toole downplayed the "the sexual problems he may have had" and his drinking. But New Orleanians tend to have a more casual relationship with alcohol than much of the country. So infused in the culture, alcohol has a virtually unavoidable presence in the city. Unlike most cities in the United States, the culture of New Orleans was shaped in part by the Catholic Church, an institution that has long celebrated alcohol, not demonized it. After all, wine is sanctified in the Catholic Mass, Trappist monks have perfected beer making, and Benedictine monks discovered how to make champagne. In present day New Orleans, frozen daiquiri stands may be more common than Starbucks. Toole scoffed at the puritanical notions prevalent in the Southern United States that saw devils in the rum bottle. Granted, if he struggled with depression, drinking would have worsened his condition. But from all accounts, he held his composure, never suggesting to anyone on record that drinking hindered his daily life. His behavior at Dominican was odd near the end, but not drunken.

One reviewer of *Ignatius Rising* praised the work, stating, "The authors present considerable evidence that Toole was alcoholic, gay and closeted." But the authors don't offer any substantive evidence to support those conclusions. It is tempting to fit Toole into the trope of the fatally troubled artist, his genius unrecognized, sinking into an abyss of vices. This narrative is so commonplace that we seem willing to overlook a lack of evidence to believe it. After all, we have grown to expect the artistic genius to descend into a dark world of indulgence, perhaps searching for some sensation to once again find himself or seeking a sedative to dull the pain. But such a naïve approach to a man's crisis tragically oversimplifies the complexity of a mental illness.

Feelings of dejection from the failure to publish his novel, conflicted sexual identity, alcohol addiction, a narcissistic mother, and an insufferable home life, all provide convenient answers to the question of why he committed suicide. And while they may or may not be true, they ultimately fail as reasons for his suicide. When using such measures, the result, as Thelma Toole once said of her son's final decision to take his own life, appears "insupportable." Suicide is not simple. Despite our best efforts to understand the ghastly human potential for self-destruction, it cannot be explained by a series of events like some kind of formula. And yet we tend to approach the question of suicide from this insupportable angle, seeking the single, loosened lynchpin that caused a mind to come undone.

Foremost suicidologist Edwin Shneidman described suicide as an incredibly complex event. He coined the term "psychache" to express the intricate and complicated condition leading up to suicide. After years of studying suicides and interviewing people with suicidal tendencies, some of whom ultimately carried out the act despite his efforts to help them, Shneidman determined that suicide is not reactive, but rather "purposive." In his definition it is a "concatenated, complicated, multidimensional, conscious, and unconscious 'choice' of the best possible practical solution to a perceived problem, dilemma, impasse, crisis or desperation." And before arriving at the decision to kill oneself, Shneidman argues, the person is in excruciating pain; the pain may have no physical manifestation but still relentlessly tortures the subject. To the person suffering from this "psychache," the pain is just as potent and troubling as the ghost pain riddling the body of an amputee. They cannot point to the wound they feel, but they feel it intensely. In this context, suicide is not a moment of weakness, but rather a final attempt to take control of the pain, regardless of its origin. Understandably, Thelma and many people who have pondered his life want to name a single source of that pain. However, Shneidman's research indicates that a single event or a single person is rarely the cause of suicide. Gottlieb, his mother, or his sexuality ultimately falter as isolated reasons for his final actions.

Perhaps the most arresting insight into Toole's mind in regards to suicide comes from his own hand. In his papers at Tulane, there is an undated short story he wrote titled "Disillusionment." It is an experimental piece, a fairly chaotic story with flashes of characters in New Orleans at different time periods, its earliest moment beginning in 1937, the year of Toole's birth. In the rough of this story, there are some gems. It opens with a boy, Samuel, looking for a home. We discover that his love died in a boat accident and, determined a coward for not saving her, he was driven from his town in shame. Searching for a place to lay his weary head, he comes to a house on the outskirts of the French Quarter, owned by a lonely woman. Samuel approaches the middle-aged homeowner, and Toole offers his most poetic description of New Orleans that he ever composed. At twilight in the Crescent City,

Someone was calling her child to come for dinner. A dog barked at a moving shadow. A car moved down the street. The city was preparing for night. By this time Canal Street was aglow with flashing lights, people walked its ways. There were no-goods, lost women, dandies, young and old, rich and poor, artists, the strippers from Bourbon Street; they were all part of a last scene. The curtain would never come down on these actors, the scene would never change. Those who were down to their last dime, some who never knew money at all, others who kept trying to get to the top, forever slipping back down. Here was a living panorama. All existing, not really living. The woman took the boy's hand and led him into the house.

Unlike the absurd carnival of *Confederacy*, which also begins as day turns into night, here the narrator sees the city filled with the walking dead. And like Poe in "The Conqueror Worm," Toole uses the theater metaphor, albeit far less emphatic, to approach the existential problem at the heart of the story. The woman realizes that life is "a parade, filled with all the characters in the world. Not one of them caring about the other. Even if you fell out of step it would keep moving." In response to this dilemma, Samuel offers a solution. At first it seems these two characters of the world, trampled upon by the unstoppable parade, could take solace in each other. But Samuel has another intention. Once alone in his room, he slits his wrists. The description casts the moment of death as a passageway to serenity, where Samuel's lost love beckons him:

The boy watched as the blood ran down his arm. It didn't hurt too much, of course the razor felt kind of bad, but that part was over. His bed was sopped with blood, it was making criss-cross pattern [*sic*] on the sheet, and that somehow added to his fascination. His mind was now spinning, like a deep, dark, whirlpool.

"See Sameul [*sic*], you and I are together again. I promised you didn't I? Come with me, hold my hand. You'll see things that you never dreamed could happen. Of gods and devils, poets and lovers, you and I. Come Sameul [*sic*], peace at last. Follow me."

There was his Cathy, running across a field of beautiful flowers. Her blue dress was blowing in the wind, her long black hair streamed behind her. She was smiling, just for him. He had tried, but lost. Life had been a heartache. But he was happy now. After all, all he ever needed was love, and he had now found it.

"Do not be afraid Samuel, do not be afraid." Samuel closed his eyes and died.

We will never know what Toole experienced in his final moments. Naturally his friends and family wondered if there was something more they could have done for him, if they could have somehow saved him. Cary Laird thought if he had stayed in New Orleans perhaps he could have helped his friend. David Kubach wondered if he should have paid another visit to Toole. And staring out the large windows of her home, looking over the land that her dear friend helped clear, Patricia Rickels wondered if they had just planned the book club meeting for another night, maybe he would have gotten out of his car and knocked on their door, and they could have diverted him from the path he ultimately took. But his friends also recognized with a mind as intense as his that there was little they could do. Perhaps that is what a small group of his confidants realized early on: all they could really do was listen. Toole chose to confide in a select few as he descended into his illness. Despite attempts by critics and scholars to find answers to the questions of Toole's demise, there are those who promised and kept his secrets. Sister Beatrice at Dominican, his artist friend Angela Gregory, and Tulane professor Huling Ussery, had no connections to his family or other friends, and Toole chose to open up to them. Even Ruth Lafranz Kathmann, the woman he dated at Tulane and Columbia, expressed regret over a single interview she once offered a reporter in 1981. She remarks, "What Ken and I shared was special, and it was between us." These confidants carry his confessions in their hearts. But they keep them sacred, not out of selfishness, but out of respect, out of honor, out of love for their friend.

Whatever path he took to arrive on that road outside Biloxi, he had determined his own end, likely seeing no other way out. He had mired under the binds of filial duty. He had two failed novels tucked away in his house. In some ways he became what he must have feared most: a so-called scholar who lectured to undergraduates with nothing of note to his name, no legacy to leave behind, and an endless pursuit to keep his parents afloat as they deteriorated into old age. He left New Orleans but seems to have been compelled to return. In the end, like Boethius trapped in a cell, Toole resolved that this earthly prison had just one escape. Fortuna had pushed him to the bottom of his existence, and there she held him down. But just as Boethius learns before his execution, Fortuna only holds physical bonds over a person. The soul is free. In answer to his own existential dilemma, Toole designed a solution and freed himself of his body.

Coincidentally, on the day of Toole's disappearance, a poet living in New Orleans going by the name Mallord sent Toole a book of self-published poems titled *Love Alone Finds Cold*. Toole must have left before he had a chance to read it. But perhaps his mother perused the pages as she waited for her son to call or as she tried to make sense of his end. One untitled poem reads

> *The closet slams shut*
> *filled up with yesterday,*
> *Catching a dandelion*
> *In its hinge.*
> *The dandelion bows,*
> *Having lived in hope of its seed.*

Chapter 13

Publication

W hile the weight of unknowing had been lifted from the Toole home, it was replaced by the terrifying silence of solitude. As the news of Toole's demise sent a shockwave through the lives of his friends and family, the closed doors of the Hampson Street house concealed two aging parents who suffered the wrenching heartache of their son's damnable death. One by one, his friends, students, and classmates received word, and the awkwardness of the death made it difficult for people to know how to respond. The obligatory sympathy cards must have come in the mail. But just as Thelma destroyed the suicide note, she also must have discarded such expressions of condolence. In the Toole Papers—a collection that holds everything from letters to financial statements—the absence of these initial reactions to his death creates an eerie silence, as if his end, and in part his life, could be edited somehow.

Thelma kept only one letter of condolence sent a few weeks after the suicide. His devoted student, Joan Trader Bowen, aimed to honor him. In 1969 she writes,

Dear Mrs. Toole,

As all of Dominican feels, I am very saddened by the death of your son, who was not only my teacher but someone whom I respected and liked a great deal. His death has left an emptiness on our campus which will not easily be filled.

> We the students of Dominican, would like Mr. Toole to
> be remembered by future students in a tangible way.
> Therefore we want to start a scholarship fund in Mr.
> Toole's name. I hope you will recognize this gesture as
> a manifestation of the love we all had for Mr. Toole. We
> hope it will be a perpetual memorial to a good person
> and a dedicated teacher.

Bowen felt that she had come to know Toole "as a person, more than just a teacher." She counted herself "fortunate to have been his student." So impacted by his teaching, for decades she cherished her notes she took in his classes, which she would occasionally consult in developing her own lessons during her career as a high school English teacher in Alabama. Despite her best intentions in 1969, there was never a Toole scholarship established at Dominican.

The college did, however, hold a memorial service for him. Thelma served as the sole representative for the family. Her husband's physical and mental health had so declined that he rarely left the house. The students also dedicated a memorial page to Toole in their yearbook. Therein, he appears professorial in his academic robes at the 1968 graduation ceremony. In their tribute, the yearbook staff writes,

> All of Mr. Toole's students will remember his barbed wit and his daily commentaries on modern society as well as his knowledge of all facets of English. But more important than the knowledge of the subject he taught, was the fine example he set as a mature, responsible, conscientious adult for both his fellow faculty members and his students. Mr. Toole will always be remembered fondly by all who knew him. . . .

Once the belated eulogies were made, the pragmatic consequences of his absence had to be addressed. As the breadwinner in the home, Toole's death created momentary financial turbulence for his parents. Fortunately, he had a life insurance policy. And with that payment, Thelma invested in bonds, aiming to derive some interest income. By 1971 their financial affairs settled into a position comfortable enough that they decided to contribute fifty dollars to the Columbia University capital campaign. In a reply letter addressed to John Toole, Columbia acknowledged the generosity of their charitable alumnus. Clearly, they were unaware their high honors graduate was dead.

Several years passed, during which his parents seemed to live a quiet existence in their home on Hampson Street. But inside the home, John Toole was suffering from his own health complications, both mental and physical. Thelma tended to his needs, keeping him inside the house as much as possible. The shame she suffered from her son's suicide was enough; a senile husband need not add insult to injury. Harold Toole recalls his father, who was the brother of John Toole, one day going to the house on Hampson Street and demanding entry into the back room to see his ailing brother. By then the relationship between Thelma and the Tooles was deeply embittered for reasons that remain unclear other than a long-standing disdain for each other. Harold's father nearly broke down the door to find his brother diminished by the cruelty of dementia. "Near the end," Harold Toole recalls, "he didn't even recognize anyone." While his son was a flash of brilliance gone too soon, John Toole eroded slowly. On December 28, 1972, having lived a life that seemed a colossal disappointment to his wife, having suffered from an illness that estranged him from everyone he knew, and having buried his "Kenny boy," John Toole died of a stroke and heart attack.

Thelma was now alone in the house on Hampson Street. She had a modest income from investments, life insurance, and her husband's veteran's benefits. She had stayed busy all her life, taking on project after project. But her days of directing variety shows were long gone, and her decreased mobility made teaching classes difficult. One day she opened the box on top of the cedar armoire that contained her son's manuscript. It occurred to her that there might be hope for him, yet. She held in her hand the testimony of his genius. He had submitted it to only one publisher. Certainly someone else out there would recognize the brilliance of her son's novel.

In the spring of 1973 she gathered the names and addresses of editors at New York publishing houses and started submitting the only copy of the manuscript she had. She typically attached a cover letter explaining Toole's many accomplishments. In essence, she became her son's post-mortem literary agent.

In March of 1973 she sent the manuscript to Knopf, perhaps un-aware that Gottlieb, whom she blamed for her son's death, presided as editor-in-chief there. She would find Knopf's seeming indifference to-ward *Confederacy* just as intolerable as Simon and Schuster's response years prior. Indignant when they failed to acknowledge receipt of the manuscript or respond with a decision after a month had passed, she wrote Knopf requesting that they send the manuscript back if they had no intention of publishing it. By May she still had received no word. Who knew where the manuscript was sitting or if anyone had read it? So Thelma tried another angle. She contacted literary agents M. P. Matson and Harold Matson to act on her behalf and inquire if Knopf would publish the novel. She requested the agency provide her an ac-count of how much such a service would cost. Rarely do literary agen-cies have an à la carte menu of services, not to mention they had no idea if this novel was worth representing. A week later she wrote to Knopf again expressing frustration that they had not even the decency to send her a receipt of the manuscript. She informed them of their responsibilities:

> With the lack of a response from you I have come to the
> conclusion you are not interested. If such is the case
> this will be your authority to place subject manuscript
> in the custody of Random House, Inc.

A week later Knopf expressed no desire to publish the novel and re-turned it to Thelma.

She then sent the manuscript to W. W. Norton. They acknowledged the merits of the novel, but declined in straightforward language. Nor-ton's response burned into Thelma's memory, words she would fre-quently recall years later. "It has literary style, but comic novels don't sell." It struck Thelma as odd. She could name many comic novels that had sold very well. But the comment rang true to some of the remarks Gottlieb articulated to Toole in 1965, regarding the difficulty of placing his novel.

Perhaps feeling rebuffed from the New York publishing world, she turned to Pelican Publishing, based in Louisiana, which also declined. In July she sent it back to New York to Harcourt Brace Jovanovich.

They were kind enough to send an acknowledgment, explaining the industry standard of six to eight weeks for a reply (a standard that Knopf had upheld). They ultimately declined the novel.

Thelma grew frustrated. It seemed the novel's prospect of publication had worsened over the years. In 1964 her son was revising it for a New York editor, and in 1973 she could barely find a publisher with an interest in it. "Each time I sent it off first class and it came back bulk rate," she remembered bitterly. From New York to Louisiana, it seemed to her the whole publishing industry was populated by dunces set on muting her son's last letter to the world. When asked why she thought so many publishers rejected it, she answered, "Stupidity."

To make matters worse, her health started to decline, forcing her to take a break from submitting the manuscript. Her weakened state rendered her situation in Uptown impossible. Reluctantly, she made the decision to move back to Elysian Fields with her brother, Arthur. They had a strained relationship at times, although he seems to have been the closest uncle to her son. She referred to him as "the poet laureate of the Standard Fruit Company," a sneering chide for the poor verse he would occasionally write for coworkers and friends. But there was nowhere else for her to go. Thelma and Arthur were the only living Ducoing siblings, and he was alone in his house. She packed up her belongings, all the memorabilia of her son and family history—from his birth certificate to his high school math homework—and left behind their Uptown home. By August of 1975 Thelma was living with her meager but devoted brother in the small house on Elysian Fields, the same house in which her brother George went certifiably insane. It was a few doors down from the much larger house in which she grew up.

She spent much of her time indoors, claiming in 1976 that she was a "shut-in" with "failing health." Her brother did her errands around town and helped her with her finances. And despite health complications, she became determined to go through another round of submissions. She made an odd choice in sending it to the Third Press, a small house in New York that primarily published books with a specific African American interest, although in 1971 the owner of the press declared he had no "ideological axe to grind." The Third Press released a few titles that veered from its original focus on racial issues, but they were popularly billed as a black publisher. Perhaps Thelma thought the justice that *Confederacy* offers Burma Jones might be attractive to them. They declined.

Thelma sent the manuscript to eight publishers; she received eight rejections. And like her son, she took the responses to heart. With each rejection, she "died a little," she said. But she showed initiative and endurance in submitting the manuscript. From Thelma's perspective she offered a publisher a rare gem. From a publisher's perspective, Thelma was trying to sell a one-hit wonder. She presented a high-risk investment from a publishing standpoint. First novels that reach only moderate success could usually be followed up by a second novel. She chose not to tell them about his other novel that she had found, *The Neon Bible*. And then there was the question of how to edit such a manuscript, especially if it needed substantial revision. In addition to all of these challenges, Thelma's posturing and outright demands likely deterred publishers. In New Orleans her vibrato might be heard, but through letters sent to New York she was easily dismissed, drowned out by the thousands of other represented writers vying for publication.

Regardless, Thelma was not one to take "no" for an answer. One day in the fall of 1976 she read in the *Times Picayune* that Walker Percy, whose first novel, the *Moviegoer*, which had won the National Book Award, was teaching a writing seminar at Loyola University. Thelma saw an opportunity. If letters and a manuscript could not entice publishers, then perhaps she could gain a champion with connections in the publishing world. She first reached out to Percy by phone, making calls to his office at Loyola. Percy resisted her with gentlemanly manners, which was more than what some editors offered her. So she decided the days of patient letter writing and polite phone calls were over. With sixteen years of training in the dramatic arts, certainly she could persuade a fellow artist to consider her son's novel. It was time for some theater.

She told Arthur to prepare himself for a drive to Loyola. He obediently put on his suit and cap. Thelma dressed in her finest attire, dousing herself in talcum powder as a finishing touch. She grabbed the box containing the manuscript, determined this would be the day her son would be recognized. As the elderly brother and sister made their way

Uptown, Walker Percy had no idea that he would stand as an audience to Thelma Ducoing Toole.

Percy's class concluded around five o'clock, after which he would make his drive out of New Orleans, across Lake Pontchartrain, to Covington, where he and his family lived. As he left his office one fall day, an old woman in a fine dress, a pillbox hat, and lace with white gloves holding a white box tied with a string approached him. Clearly this was some aged daisy of an old Southern line, somehow still benefitting from profits made in the family business of cotton or coffee or some other commodity traded at the port of New Orleans. Her driver in the suit and cap maintained a respectful distance. The old lady told Percy of her son, how he had committed suicide but left behind a novel. She wanted him to read it. "But you are biased," he said. She explained that she was an avid reader, and what she offered him was a great novel. As a Southern gentleman, he could not in good conscience reject the pleas of a mother who endured the grief of her son's suicide. He was cornered. He took the box from her and offered his condolences.

Driving across the twenty-three-mile bridge to the Northshore, the skyline of New Orleans silently sank into the horizon behind him. The manuscript that Toole had labored over for months in Puerto Rico and sent back and forth to New York City, lay in the passenger seat of Walker Percy's car. Like most novelists, the idea of peddling a manuscript not his own, in essence becoming a *pro bono* literary agent, was the farthest thing from his mind. He had a class to teach and his own writing to do. He walked into his home holding the white box in his hand and greeted his wife, Bunt Percy. He told her of the Uptown lady with the driver and the tragic story. But he was hungry and tired and had no energy to read a questionable manuscript unfairly thrust upon him. He said to Bunt, "You read it. Tell me what to do with it." She agreed to take a look at it later, and the two sat down for a late dinner.

Originally from a small town in Mississippi and now living in a small town in Louisiana, Bunt was intrigued by the ways of New Orleans. That city across the lake that rises out of the water like an island metropolis held a mysterious lore, a place and people of vast eccentricities. She was "eager to hear how they talked" and eager to understand their customs. So the next day she untied the string, removed the loose leaf, unedited manuscript and entered into Toole's New Orleans, which some would argue is the most accurate portrayal of the Crescent City ever cast into fiction.

A few days later, Walker asked Bunt what she thought of the novel. She understood the fate of the book largely lay in her hands. If she deemed it unworthy, then he could simply return the manuscript and be relieved of the burden of an unpublished novel from a dead writer. "It's ready for you," Bunt replied. "I think you should read it." He knew that she approved of the book. Holding respect for her judgment, he was obliged to give Toole a chance.

Walker sat down to read the tattered pages. He prided himself on being able to determine the quality of writing after reading only the first paragraph. Immediately, he recognized Toole's keen talent for observation. In a single paragraph through setting, character, and description, he masterfully captured that ineffable texture of New Orleans. Walker was hooked. In December of 1976 he wrote to Thelma with a positive response, but he also saw some problems in the novel. He suggested the dialogue was too long in places. But it was too early to discuss editorial decisions in detail. Percy was unsure if a publisher would accept it. So he began asking people around town to read it. They came back with mixed reviews. Some people liked it; others did not. He lent a copy to Garic Barranger, who was enthusiastic, but also felt the manuscript needed to be trimmed. Percy read a few chapters to his class at Loyola, and they recognized Toole's unprecedented and accurate portrayal of New Orleans. But when he asked his own publisher, Farrar, Straus and Giroux, to consider the manuscript, they declined. The *Chicago Tribune* later reported they "seemed to applaud its quality but turned it down nonetheless because its author being deceased could neither help to promote it or help to follow it up with another book." At the very least, Percy knew he had a work that elicited response. No one seemed indifferent to the novel.

It just needed some traction, a way for publishers to see the vision of its publication and readers' reactions. Percy sent the manuscript to Marcus Smith, a professor of English at Loyola and editor of the *New Orleans Review*. In spring of 1978 the first two chapters of *Confederacy* were published in the review, followed by several favorable critiques that acknowledged the brilliance of the book and Thelma's challenges in getting the novel published.

Although the *New Orleans Review* was far from Simon and Schuster or Random House, Thelma was pleased. In March she requested several copies of the periodical be sent to select faculty members at University of Southwestern Louisiana, including Pat Rickels. And she instructed one copy should be sent to John Wieler, her son's helpful professor at Columbia and department chair at Hunter College. The *New Orleans Review* was the first step in garnering public recognition, providing the footholds to capture the interest of a publisher.

Percy was determined to see the manuscript through to full publication, even as he worked on his novel *The Second Coming*. He recognized the humor and the tragedy in *Confederacy*. And as someone who suffered with depression throughout his life, Percy must have sympathized with Toole as a writer. In one of his last notes to Thelma, he referred to himself as an "admirer" of her son. But Thelma, for all her admirable tenacity, could be a nuisance. He wanted the novel to succeed, but after two years of promoting it, Percy was eager to put the project to rest. He saw an opportunity in Rhoda Faust, a family friend who owned Maple Street Books, a small bookstore in Uptown.

After being in the bookselling business for years, and at the encouragement of several local writers, Faust aimed to establish a publishing house in New Orleans. One afternoon she called Percy to ask if he had any unpublished writings lying around that she could use to jumpstart her company. He suggested she read the recent edition of the *New Orleans Review* to see what she thought about the beginning of *Confederacy*. After acquiring a copy and reading the chapters, Faust found it breathtakingly brilliant. She immediately contacted Thelma to meet with her. Thelma, of course, was thrilled to have someone interested in the novel and more so when Faust told her she wanted to publish the book. Even the daunting pragmatic details of starting a publishing house could not quell the excitement Faust and Thelma felt about the future of Toole's novel.

Meanwhile, Percy got word that a friend in Covington knew an editor at Louisiana State University Press. At that time it was unusual for a university press to publish novels. However, LSU Press had recently started a fiction program, intended to nab talented writers who had been cast to the margins of the megalithic publishing industry. The manuscript made its way west to Baton Rouge and landed on the desk of editor Martha Hall. Like Bunt Percy, Hall immediately loved *Confederacy*. She encouraged Les Phillabaum, the director of LSU Press, to publish it. Phillabaum later claimed that he never doubted they would publish the book. However, Bunt recalls that Martha had to repeatedly prod Phillabaum to go through with it. The novel was sure to lose money, but eventually the risk Phillabaum took on *Confederacy* paid off more than he ever imagined.

Still, Phillabaum took six months to make the decision—a review time common among academic presses. Thelma had grown impatient with New York publishers when they did not respond in a few weeks; six months must have seemed unending. Yet LSU Press was really the end of the road, and a longshot at that. If they declined the novel, Thelma had few options left. Rhoda Faust remained dedicated to publishing it, although ahead of her still lay the long process of establishing a publishing house, which could take more time than Thelma had left to live. Thelma entertained self-publication, but that lacked credibility and required more money than she had. So she urged Percy to contact Phillabaum and ask for his intentions. On April 19, 1979, just over ten years after her son's death, Phillabaum wrote to Thelma,

We have at long last completed our review of "A Confederacy of Dunces," and our reading has been favorable in the extreme. The novel has been approved for publication. . . . We are very surprised that the book has not long since been published, but we are indeed pleased that we will be the ones able to do it.

Respectfully, Thelma called Faust to see where she stood with the upstart publishing house. Faust could not offer what LSU offered. So she called Percy to ask his advice. "Don't make the Pullman wait any longer," he responded. Not wanting to stand in the way of the novel, Faust encouraged Thelma to accept the contract—a decision Thelma had likely already made.

Perhaps feeling some pangs of guilt and wanting to reward Faust for her dedication, Thelma later gave Faust her son's collection of books to sell in her store and to collectors. Faust cataloged each one—from *The Poetical Works* by Geoffrey Chaucer to a first edition of Walker Percy's

The Moviegoer. The books that he studied, enjoyed, and used in the creation of his own novel were sold in the little store on Maple Street in Uptown after the publication of *Confederacy*. The gift certainly helped Faust's cash-strapped store. But then, according to Faust, Thelma offered a prize of far greater value than Toole's old books; she promised her the rights to publish her son's first novel, *The Neon Bible*.

Thelma would eventually deny ever making that promise, but at that point, she wanted to keep Faust's friendship. Both women would benefit from an agreeable relationship. And Thelma would need an advocate for the last unforeseen hurdle between her son's genius and the world's recognition of it: the Toole Family.

While Thelma possessed the manuscript and held the copyright to the novel, she did not hold exclusive rights to the work. Both her son and her husband died without a will. And under Louisiana law, based on the Napoleonic Code, her husband's surviving relatives had claim to a portion of the rights to *Confederacy*, as lawful heirs to John Dewey Toole's estate. Thelma was outraged. At first, she maintained a degree of decorum, but for some reason she abandoned diplomacy. The thought of the Tooles profiting from her son's work incensed her. She claimed the Tooles had a long history of exploiting her for money—something she called "The Old Toole money squeeze." While Thelma had two lawyers to work on the case, Faust found herself going back and forth between Thelma's rants and Marion Toole Hosli—Thelma's niece to whom she taught piano as a young girl—trying to figure out a way for them to agree. The Tooles wanted to read the manuscript to ensure that it did not reflect poorly on the family. But Thelma refused to give them a copy of it. Recognizing a stalemate was forming that would prevent the publication of the book, Faust went against the wishes of Thelma and lent the Tooles her copy. Once ensured it would have no impact on them, the Tooles signed over their rights to *Confederacy*. They had no way of knowing the value that those rights would carry.

At that point LSU Press took *Confederacy* fully under its wing, from resetting the type to the cover design. Walker Percy authored the foreword to the novel. Thelma sent a picture of her beloved son, with the anticipation that it might adorn the dustcover. She selected a photo from his senior year of high school, sixteen years old, casting him in his infinite youth.

It was a project more than twenty years in the making, and it passed through countless hands before reaching publication. And history, as it so often does, has tended to shine a light on the integral male figures in this saga. Aside from Thelma, people like Robert Gottlieb, Walker Percy, and Les Phillabaum are the ones seen shaping the story. And while these figures performed major roles, they tended to overshadow the women that recognized Toole's talent before their male counterparts did. Jean Ann Jollett was the first to see the novel's greatness and suggested Gottlieb read it. Bunt Percy gave it her approval before passing it along to her husband. Martha Hall championed the book at LSU, pressing Phillabaum to publish it. And Rhoda Faust eased the concerns of the Toole family, which helped clear the legal pathway for its publication. From his honors thesis to his lectures on "The Mother," Toole had spent many hours pondering the female role in literature and life. It is fitting then that at every major impasse there was a woman who proclaimed faith in his work and encouraged its progression. And yet these women would recede to the backstage, as Thelma prepared for her debut.

With her son's novel passing through copy editors and running through presses, Thelma frequently invited the Percys to her home in New Orleans. It was upon their first visit to the modest house on Elysian Fields that it became quite clear Thelma was no Uptown daisy with a personal driver. They saw the working-class neighborhood, and Walker recognized the individual he had originally thought to be her driver: her brother, Arthur. Thelma preferred to keep her guests to herself, so Arthur knew to keep his distance. And she also preferred Walker visit without his wife, confessing years later how she had an innocent crush on him—"the guardian spirit" of her son's novel.

Before the release of the book, Thelma arranged her finances for the change she anticipated. She removed Arthur from all of her accounts, requesting that he sign an agreement to "no longer associate . . . with Mrs. Thelma D. Toole in money matters of any kind." It was perhaps for the best, considering the financial boon she was about to receive.

LSU Press printed three thousand copies of the first edition. And as it circulated among reviewers, it quickly gained attention, in part because of its merits as a novel, but also because of the remarkable story of its publication. From its first moments in the public, the novel became indelibly linked to the story of Toole's death and the resilience of his mother to ensure his dream came true. In March 1980, *Kirkus Reviews*, a first-stop reviewer for book critics, billed it as "a masterpiece of character comedy" with its "mix of high and low comedy," making it "almost stroboscopic: brilliant, relentless, delicious, perhaps even classic." But the review ended with regret that having committed suicide, Toole left "only one astounding book." A month later *Publisher's Weekly* released a glowing review, claiming of the author, "The way he crams invention and exuberance into a perversely logical plot and molds his Pandora's box of ills into a comic novel which rings with laughter is something of a miracle." LSU Press had added a "classic" and a "miracle" of fiction to its list. But it was quickly apparent the small academic press would never be able to meet public demand for the book. In April, Grove Press bought subsidiary rights to publish *Confederacy* in paperback, which would allow it to meet the market demand. It had taken fifteen years for the manuscript to find its way to publication, but the success that followed happened at breakneck speed. Editions of *Confederacy* flew off the shelves. And as a Cinderella story of the publishing world, large newspapers and magazines took interest in both the novel and the tale of its publication.

In the summer and fall of 1980, reviews came in overwhelmingly positive. From small town papers to big-city book reviews, from novelists to professional critics, it seemed almost every week somewhere in the country a paper published a review of *A Confederacy of Dunces*. Several of these echoed *Kirkus*, claiming it an immediate classic, an original masterpiece, and one of the few books that made austere reviewers laugh until tears welled in their eyes and their bellies hurt. They compared the novel to the works of Dickens, Joyce, Rabelais, Waugh, Chaucer, Cervantes, Shakespeare, and T. S. Eliot. It seemed every reviewer strived to compare Toole's sense of comedy, his use of plot, and his characters to one of his literary predecessors. But they still acknowledged that Toole was no mimic of other novelists. Most agreed, his work was highly original.

As reviewers celebrated the achievement of the novel, they were bound to discuss its remarkable path to publication. Prior to the commercial success of the book, they knew far less about Toole than most readers do today. Initially limited to Percy's foreword, the unanswered questions surrounding Toole's tragic end haunts these reviews. Desperate to understand the author, at times reviewers had difficulty distinguishing Toole from Ignatius. In 1980 in the *Bloomsbury Review*, Michael O'Connel merges the author and protagonist into a single entity, claiming, "Toole-Ignatius despises living in the world, inveighs and scolds; Ignatius in his Big Chief diary and Toole in his fiction." Even the *Chicago Tribune Review of Books*, after declaring the novel was not a good book, suggested that it was "an exorcism, a cry nobody heard." Seeing his novel as a call for help offers a poignant and rich answer to the mysteries surrounding Toole. But such an interpretation served the reader's curiosity about the author at a time when little was known, more so than offering insight into his life. From the earliest discussions of his life, there have been misgivings in approach, people looking for answers in places without considering who he was or from what circumstances he had come.

Gradually, interviews and reporters discovered more information about Toole's sense of dejection. Writers sympathized with his struggle with the publishing industry, expressing heartfelt indignation as they imagined Toole suffering rejection after rejection. But this sympathy seems to veil their own incredulity. David Shields barely restrained himself from a tirade against the monstrosity of New York publishing when he wrote, "One has to believe there was a deliberate effort somewhere in those ivory towers along the northeastern seaboard to keep this book from the reading public. Why? Well, the answer to that would overrun this space and wouldn't be very pretty to boot." His suspicions seem to stem from his own frustration with publishers.

Jonathan Yardley, in a review reprinted in several papers across the country, proclaimed the utter fallibility of New York editors, and in doing so expressed the underlying issue that threads many of the positive reviews: the system of book publishing may serve the interests of a company more so than the interests of readers and the art of literature. The meeting point between art and business has never been easy. Writers such as Toole watched, in the late 1960s, as publishers grew into multimillion-dollar corporations and agents became facilitators between writers and editors. And while the filtering process became more rigorous, there emerged an uneasy sense that it didn't produce higher-quality work. Writers and readers grumbled that the publishing industry, in its shift toward big business, might be rejecting works that deserved publication as a valuable, cultural product, not just a sellable item created to attract the whims of the mass market. Yes, *Confederacy* had its problems, reviewers admitted, but so did the last five books from Random House or Knopf or Simon and Schuster. And those books, they seemed to say, didn't give me half the enjoyment *Confederacy* did.

This silencing is part of why the story of its publication held such interest to readers. It suggests that the presumed cultural role of publishers to deliver quality literature may be compromised by motives of profit and marketability. Ironically, as this story validates a critique of the commercialism of the publishing industry, it simultaneously made the novel more marketable. Toole didn't have this story to reference in 1963. A solitary writer complaining about publishers, convinced no one appreciates his genius, has few sympathizers. Toole's heartbreaking life story disables dismissal of those complaints, allowing many readers and writers to feel vindicated in their frustrations and suspicions of the publishing world.

Of course, the history of Toole that emerged in the popular media did not take into full context his circumstances. Thelma did not want to talk about her son's death, especially the notion that he suffered from mental illness. She all but rejected that possibility by blaming Gottlieb. And Toole's struggle and his mystery spurred reviewers to engage in mythmaking. Anthony Burgess imagined Toole "hawking [the manuscript] around the publishing houses of New York" and after receiving the final rejection from "the biggest of the publishing mavens" committed suicide. And one reviewer in the *San Francisco Review of Books* imagined that Toole likely killed himself directly following his completion of the final page of the novel, as if the labor pains of his glorious creation were so taxing he could live no longer. The critics were unaware that Toole sent it to only one editor, an editor that sustained a lengthy correspondence for more than two years and never closed off the possibility of publication to him. He could have sought publication through another press, perhaps a smaller one. And reviewers seem to overlook the risky territory of publishing a manuscript of a dead, unknown writer. After all, if the novel had been poorly received by readers and reviewers, the question would have gone the other way: Why would they publish a dead author's work when there were plenty of talented writers still living?

A few reviews maintained sympathy for the tragic end of the writer but were not ready to offer the book accolades that pervaded media discussion. Negative reviews tended to fault Toole for not following the rule of creating a dynamic main character. They argue that no one changes in the book. Such reviewers saw no hope in this world that Toole created and therefore despaired in the creation of it. And the most damning reviews cast doubt on the novel's ability to stand had the author not committed suicide. Such sharply critical responses mostly came from media venues with small, local readerships, not a national audience.

By and large reviewers acknowledged some faults of the novel. Granted, had Simon and Schuster published *Confederacy* it would have been a very different book. Toole made changes, but Thelma destroyed the "Gottlieb revisions." She instructed LSU Press not to edit a word, "not even a preposition." So it appears the version of *Confederacy* we have today is the first version, the one that Thelma deemed pure, even though Toole may have believed that the novel was getting better with those edits. There was another version of *Confederacy* in the making, but Thelma determined that anything to do with Gottlieb would taint the genius of her son. And while critics identified technical flaws in the novel, most reviewers resisted literary pretentiousness. They recognized that the joy to be garnered from the reading of the book might be as valuable a literary contribution as a political or social message.

But perhaps such issues stem from our awkward cultural relationship with comedy, especially when it strives to be high art. America has long seen comedy as a genre for the masses, unsophisticated and often adolescent. It is a sideshow to more serious endeavors, like tragedies or histories. But Toole did not see comedy as an afterthought. The humor in a story, ironies, and contradictions were emblematic of real life. David Evanier, fiction editor of the *Paris Review*, may have offered the most perceptive comment regarding the way to understand the humor of this novel when he wrote, "*A Confederacy of Dunces* transcends the suffering of life through laughter." Evanier echoes literary critic, historicist, and philosopher Mikhail Bakhtin who, in analyzing Rabelais, recognizes that in the culture of carnival, the culture from which *Confederacy* springs, laughter is not a veiled cry for help or a reminder of tragedy, but rather the sound of victory.

Indeed, the triumph of Toole's novel seemed unstoppable. It was one of five books nominated for the PEN Faulkner Award in 1981. It made best-seller lists in the *New York Times*, the *Chicago Tribune*, and the *Los Angeles Times*. Translated versions of the book were printed in nearly every European country. But the greatest recognition came when a select group of representatives from the publishing world gathered together at the Graduate School of Journalism at Columbia University. Inside the same brick building that Toole had passed by every day during his first year at Columbia, the Pulitzer Board reviewed the submissions for fiction writing. After deliberations, the announcement came. In April of 1981 John Kennedy Toole was awarded the Pulitzer Prize for *A Confederacy of Dunces*. It was only the second time the board had awarded a posthumous prize and the first to a writer who was previously unknown. And to date *Confederacy* is the only novel published at a university press to be awarded a Pulitzer.

While reviewers despaired over some aesthetic issues, and some cynics suspected the story of Toole's death a grand hoax to boost sales, in winning the Pulitzer Prize he gained official recognition for the literary merit of his work. Thereafter, a tide of interest in finding out more about this author and his mother swelled from the media. Newspapers and journals ran exposés on Thelma Toole. She was invited to dinners and conferences. She was interviewed on *Canada A. M.*, a national television show broadcast from Toronto. And a few weeks after winning the Pulitzer Prize, she received a request to appear on the *Tomorrow Show* with Tom Snyder in New York. While she had spent her youth dreaming of stardom on the stage and her adulthood preparing her students for performances, claiming only the edge of the spotlight for herself, in her final years Thelma was the star. She rose to the occasion. She was the keeper of her son's story, the hero of the tale. And as she took her place on her throne as the Queen Mother of the literati, people came to her doorstep to pay tribute, offering praise and tokens of gratitude for her accomplishment. She received them graciously.

However, when it came to gifts of flowers, she preferred silk ones. She hated to watch the colors fade, she said. She hated to watch them die.

Chapter 14

Fame

Sitting in his NBC studio in April of 1981, Tom Snyder must have thought the interview with Thelma Toole would be a soft piece compared to his other interviews. Snyder was known for bringing Americans face to face with figures such as John Lennon, Charles Manson, and Iggy Pop. Sitting across from his guests, Snyder would smoke cigarettes as he asked hard-hitting questions. But how hard hitting could he get with a seventy-nine-year-old woman who used a walker and who had relentlessly fought to have her dead son's novel published? Joel Fletcher, who accompanied Thelma to New York, recalled that Snyder didn't know what to make of her. Thelma commanded a surprising presence in the interview. She told the story of her son's life, the book's publication, and she talked about her Irish lineage. Nearing the end of the interview, she gave her signature line that she used to conclude most of her public appearances. "I walk in the world for my son," she said. "I'm humble because I was a vessel to bring a scholarly genius—he was a scholarly genius and a literary genius." Snyder replied, "Well, I'll tell you something, his mom ain't too shabby either." She looked back at Snyder. "I ain't something the cat dragged in, am I?" she said. "You sure ain't," Snyder agreed.

In the great play of life, Thelma reached her pinnacle in her final act. She had her moment of fame in the national media. As reporters sought information on her son, they were also taken by Thelma's unique personality, characterized at times in unflattering terms. When Dalt Wonk did a two-part series on Toole, he ended it with a rather embarrassing, although humorous, depiction of Thelma the socialite, being lifted by a crane onto a boat to meet the consul of Venezuela. And when *People* magazine ran an article by Mary Vespa, who quoted John Broussard calling Thelma a "megalomaniac" and suggesting that Toole "was getting back at Mrs. Toole in the book," it created a dividing line between those who saw Thelma as more of a villain than a hero. Granted, many of Toole's friends in Lafayette never had a rosy impression of Thelma. After all, in 1964 Broussard had listened to his friend in his cups confess his awful situation living with his parents. And four years after that confession, Toole committed suicide. But many people were quick to come to Thelma's defense; several were her previous students. Nola Schneider wrote to *People*, declaring,

> As one of her many students I can say that she is now, and always has been, an intelligent and elegant lady. With regard to the thoughtless and unfounded megalomaniac reference by Mr. Broussard, I pray that at 79 years of age, I will have "delusions of grandeur" rather than "delusions of doom."

And as the public continued to see Thelma as both entertaining and overblown, her students felt compelled to show their appreciation for her instruction and guidance. Even Marion Toole Hosli, aware of the dreadful sentiments Thelma had expressed about the Toole family, wrote her a letter thanking her for the time she had spent with her as a young girl. After congratulating Thelma on her accomplishment in getting the book published, she writes,

> Aunt Thelma, I have something I have wanted to tell you for a long time but never did.
>
> As you know, I don't have many happy memories of my younger years. The few I do have were, and still are, the hours I spent with you at the piano, the quiet thinking times, the poems and teachings of the more beautiful things in life. Most of all, I remember the love I felt

knowing that someone cared enough for me to take an
interest in me! I have never said "Thank you." Please
forgive me.

Clearly Thelma touched the lives of many people. But now edging
into her eighties she had a stage like she had never had before. The
trumpets of her success blared, although she always gave credit to her
son, the genius.

But as if publication and the Pulitzer were not enough vindication,
in her triumph, her derision of Robert Gottlieb became vicious. In a
1981 interview she claimed that she never read the Gottlieb letters until
her son had passed away, because, she said, "I never pried into his life."
And yet Nick Polites specifically recalled her tirades on Gottlieb after
one of his letters had arrived. When asked if those letters would be
made public she explained at the advice of her lawyer that she could
not do anything with them without Gottlieb's permission, which was
both true and convenient. Readers had no other sources to go by other
than her side of the story. She claimed that the last letter Gottlieb had
sent to Toole devastated her son with the line "It could be improved
upon, but it wouldn't sell." In fact, Gottlieb's last letter left the door
open to Toole, even inviting him to submit another manuscript if he
ever decided to work on another novel. But every hero needs a foe.
And in this saga she unabashedly declared of Gottlieb, "He is the villain!" Gottlieb responded to Thelma's assertions by simply stating he
was sorry for her loss, happy the book was published, but saw no connection between Toole's suicide and their correspondence, which
ended years before he took his life. Still, Thelma continued her invective against him. In September of 1980, she made her most scathing attack on him in *Horizon Magazine* when she exclaimed, "He's a
creature . . . a Jewish creature. . . . Not a man. . . . Not a human being."
Her words were reprinted in an article in the *New York Times* in 1981.

Granted, there was an undercurrent of anti-Semitic discourse surrounding the novel at the time. It was suggested, although not coming
from Toole directly, that Gottlieb never accepted the novel on the basis
of its representation of Jews, particularly Myrna Minkoff and the Levys,
characters he felt did not work in the novel. While teaching at Hunter

College, Toole had witnessed the intense sensitivity toward anything that might be construed as anti-Semitic. It would not be surprising if Toole felt the Jewish characters were misinterpreted by Gottlieb. Furthermore, in the early 1960s, many of the publishing houses in New York were privately owned by Jewish families. There remained, according to Michael Korda, who served as editor and editor-in-chief at Simon and Schuster, a slight sense of division between the houses founded by Jewish entrepreneurs and those without Jewish founders, although this seems to have colored competitiveness between houses more so than interactions with writers. Thelma harbored suspicions of a Jewish plot to suppress the genius gentile voice of her son. She responded with clearly anti-Semitic language. It may have been a moment of indiscretion on her part. But in a letter to the author of the article in *Horizon*, Thelma conveys her pleasure with the piece and requests a subscription to the magazine, thereby suggesting she was not misquoted, misrepresented, or the least bit remorseful.

While Gottlieb is a renowned editor, having guided into print works by Toni Morrison, John Cheever, and Ray Bradbury, he is also a human being. In Korda's remembrances of him, he appears as a brilliant and dedicated editor who cut through the clout of the editor's role and could see the greater vision of the work at hand. That doesn't mean he did not make mistakes or turn down authors who went on to have success elsewhere. But for all the criticism he offered writers, which is by definition part of his job, it is evident, especially in his letters to Toole, he recognized the emotional investment writers had in their work.

For the words Thelma repeatedly said, both her anti-Semitic sentiments and her outright claim that Gottlieb drove her son to suicide, he could have sued her for slander. But the fallout of litigation would only worsen the matter. Regardless of the result, Gottlieb would end up even more of a villain had he appeared to be abusing an elderly mother who had suffered the tragedy of her son's suicide. So Gottlieb left Thelma on her stage to gesture, to point, to bite her thumb at him—a man who had never met her son, had never officially rejected his manuscript, and who could be blamed only for seeing talent in a young writer whose work he felt needed refining.

Thelma had a clear answer to the question of her son's suicide, but when interviewers asked more pressing questions about his demise, she usually steered the conversation back to her script, by way of some memory of his childhood. Eventually, the national media turned its head toward other topics, but New Orleans upheld her as a local celebrity. She was named Queen Mother of a Mardi Gras krewe in 1982, a high honor for a New Orleanian. Southeastern Louisiana University awarded her an honorary doctorate degree. Someone from NASA sent her a piece of a spacecraft. And she appeared all over the city in what became one-woman variety shows of interview, lecture, dramatic interpretations, and "musical highlights."

During her talks, she always gave her "genius son" credit. And as a tribute to his creation, she performed wonderful renditions of his characters, from Irene Reilly to Burma Jones. Barely ambulatory, standing at her walker, her voice, facial expressions, and hands would come alive with the characters of *Confederacy*. She also reserved some of the spotlight for herself. She never failed to mention her training in the dramatic arts and her "culture" that she "gave freely" to her son. At most events in her honor, she would perform songs, from jazz numbers to Disney sing-a-longs, dedicating them to people close to her. Her voice, and at times the piano, was out of tune, and she seemed to have lost her sense of rhythm. Still, audience members were entertained, mostly by her vibrant spirit.

Occasionally she claimed that she despised fame. And surely in her loneliest moments when she longed for her son, fame offered little comfort. But from her interviews and performances it is clear she relished the attention. And she was eager at the prospect of a movie rendition of the novel when Hollywood took an interest in *Confederacy*. Before it won the Pulitzer, LSU sent the galleys to Scott Kramer, a young Hollywood producer who expressed immediate interest. With so much media attention it was bound to be a blockbuster hit. LSU and Thelma sold the film rights to Twentieth Century-Fox. But if Thelma found the publication world bewildering, Hollywood was a veritable Rubik's cube. Within a few years the rights bounced between various production companies. And with each transaction came some layer of complication. Originally named producer, Kramer remained a consistent advocate for the film. In 1982 he got so far as to begin casting. John Belushi was a possible choice for Ignatius, but he died soon thereafter of a drug overdose. Despite setbacks, Kramer maintained his dedication to the project, and Thelma had faith in his vision. Alas, attempts to make the film continued long after Thelma died, resulting in a great deal of speculation with eager producers, directors, and actors.

Thelma recognized that her son's ambition was literary in nature, but she desperately wanted to be cast in the film. She confessed she would make a fabulous Irene Reilly. And from her dramatic interpretations of the book, she would have been delightful in that role. In 1982 the film rights were sold to Bumbershoot Productions. Despising the name of the company, which means "umbrella," and learning of where the company was based, Thelma declared, "Nothing artistic can come from Fort Worth, Texas." When the film company came to New Orleans in 1983 and neglected to call her, she wrote to the producers with indignation. It is a letter that expresses in print her boldness:

```
The trite expression "Let me introduce myself" is
not apropos, because we are affiliated with a
masterpiece novel and Pulitzer Prize winner to be
made into an epic picture.

I am Thelma Ducoing Toole, mother of the scholarly
and literary genius, John Kennedy Toole.


It was surprisingly unpleasant that you did not contact
me when you visited New Orleans for publicity and
fundraising. You must remember that I am "Owner of
the Book" by inheritance and the valiant search I made
for ten years seeking publication. With the espousal of
Dr. Walker Percy we succeeded triumphantly. You did not
tender the courtesy and respect due.


Based on sixteen years of Speech and Dramatic Art
training and fifty years of highly professional teaching,
I am requesting to be made consultant to the director. I
know and love New Orleans. I can be of inestimable value.


It is with eagerness that I await your reply.
```

It must have seemed she was losing some grasp on her son's creation. People and companies traded movie rights to the novel, which technically LSU controlled, and she had no part in those discussions. Her sense of superiority so evident in letters like the one above hardly laid the groundwork for collaboration. But she did not appear interested in collaboration. She reveled in adoration. Near the end of her life, she developed an amplified sense of superiority, inflated, no doubt, by the accolades of her son's work.

Few people would deny a mother who had suffered such a great loss a moment in the sun. Still, in the midst of Thelma's fame, as Toole scholar Jane Bethune has noted, "Somehow Ken gets lost." In a promotional photo of her during this time period, she sits at her baby grand piano; a black curtain with "THELMA" in giant white letters hangs behind her. Like a celebrity at an awards show, she basked in the limelight, sometimes forgetting herself, although she was always sure to end her speech with the obligatory credit to her son. It seemed to some of her longtime friends that she created a persona, or perhaps let some inhibitions of modesty go, speaking boldly and earnestly.

And yet, despite her fame and the gains in income from royalty checks, she did not change her lifestyle in any major way. She continued to live with her brother on Elysian Fields in the small house that had no air-conditioning. She still wore her white gloves and a pillbox hat whenever she left home. In her early eighties, she now preferred the company of others to material wealth. And with time and money, she was generous. She sympathetically replied to letters from writers blighted by New York publishers and mothers inspired by her resilience. One writer sent her copies of the threatening letters that he wrote to Gottlieb. He took up a crusade against him with an aim to vindicate Toole. Some of her correspondents turned bizarre. Through a series of letters to Thelma one man became convinced that Toole's writings gave some insight into the fate of the world. He also came to the conclusion that he could perform miracles and sent his ninety-five-page explanation of this claim to both Thelma and the Pope. But most admirers simply wanted to reach out to her. They wanted to know more about her son. And she often extended an open invitation to her home.

When people stopped by to see her, she regularly gave candies and cups; rarely did anyone go away empty handed. When the novel was published, she sent flowers, gifts from D. H. Holmes, and signed first editions. On some occasions, especially before the royalty checks started coming in, she would gift relics of her son, items like fingernail clippers and his bed sheets. She attempted to give Walker Percy and Rhoda Faust a set of silverware. One afternoon when she saw Angela Gregory, the artist who befriended her son as they walked to and from Dominican in the last years of his life, Thelma gave her a porcelain plate, which is now held in the New Orleans Historical Collection. And in the summer of 1978, before LSU had made an offer, she sent one of the first typescripts of *Confederacy* with handwritten corrections to her son's best friend, Cary Laird.

Most of her gifts were tokens of appreciation to those who helped her. But some of them came with unstated expectations of reciprocal thanks and continued loyalty. To get around town, she depended on a coterie of friends, some old acquaintances of her son and others who had been involved in the publication of the novel. She enjoyed the company and usually treated them with kindness. And while she vehemently denied the assertion that she had "delusions of grandeur," she developed a kind of fantasy quality to her life. One afternoon she called up Walker Percy and asked him to come to her home without his wife as she intended to knight him. Likely the knighting ceremony of her chosen ones to attend her as the Queen Mother for the Mardi Gras krewe, the request may have made sense in New Orleans. Across Lake Pontchartrain in Covington, it struck Percy and his wife as odd and sure to be an uncomfortable event. While many people indulged the fantasies of an aged woman near the end of her life, she was quick to lash out at those closest to her if she felt they did not give her the respect she was due. At a promotional event at the Maple Street Bookstore, she saw Percy talking to someone in the back of the room as she sang a song in his honor. She later reprimanded him for his rude conduct, saying, "You are no gentleman, sir!" And when Joel Fletcher told her he was unable to escort her to an engagement, she seemed to forget the times he travelled with her to New York, Canada, and to events throughout New Orleans. She banished him from her court. Of course, her rash behavior concealed a desperate desire to have people around her. When one of her regular visitors, a professor at University of New Orleans and a person whose company she enjoyed very much, simply stopped calling, she was baffled and hurt.

But as long as the popularity of *Confederacy* remained strong, she maintained her audience. And she knew that the success of the novel ensured publication of her son's first novel *The Neon Bible*. She intended to orchestrate the release of the second novel once the dust settled from *Confederacy*. In April of 1981, days after she received word about the Pulitzer, she made some movements toward its publication. Her lawyers sought confirmation that no one currently owned rights to the book. The manuscript had no claims on it in the Library of Congress, but she knew from her experience with *Confederacy* that the application of Louisiana law would grant the surviving Tooles fifty percent of the royalties. And while she often appeared unconcerned over money, the thought of the Tooles profiting from the work of her genius son was inconceivable to her. Certainly, under the laws of most other states, property would not be divided so strangely, but Louisiana was always distinct from the rest of country, for better or worse.

So as Thelma basked in the glow of *Confederacy*, she maneuvered to circumvent Louisiana law. And when she couldn't do that, she sought to change the law. In February of 1983 Thelma wrote to the governor of Louisiana, David Treen, referring to herself as "the writer Thelma Toole." At the time she was working on a prequel to *Confederacy* focused on the parochial schooling of Irene Reilly. She informed the governor of the preceding arrangements in the case of *Confederacy* and that she had invited the four surviving Toole heirs to her home in order to "sign an honorable waiver" and give up rights to *The Neon Bible*. But "no one attended." She goes on to state,

My husband's four relatives are ordinary working people, with no sound education, no vestige of culture and interminable quarreling in their family circles. They are basically and truly unfit to represent my son, and share the fruits of his highly gifted creative ability.

I have formed "A Coalition for the Advocacy of Protecting The Neon Bible from Unjust Claimants" by contacting several attorneys and one judge to whom I taught Speech and Dramatic Art years ago.

On March 4, 1983, the executive counsel to the governor, Cyrus Greco, replied to Thelma, advising her to contact Senator Sydney Nelson who was at "the forefront of legislation revising the laws on heirship." Counselor Greco goes on to admit he read *Confederacy* and commended Thelma for getting it published "since it has brought pleasure to many, many persons."

Thelma also gained the advocacy of U.S. representative Lindy Boggs to press the governor to allow Thelma to address the Louisiana House of Representatives. But here the progress of her activism hit a political brick wall. The summer of 1983 passed without any word from governing powers. It seemed evident that the matter would not be taken up.

In October the Tooles signed a letter agreeing that *The Neon Bible* should be published but requested that Thelma offer details as to the finances of the endeavor. They recognized they had unknowingly signed away tens of thousands of dollars when they waived their rights to *Confederacy*. And with her repeated tirades against them, they were not obliged to be so acquiescent with this book. They had no intention of stopping its publication, but they wanted what was considered their share under Louisiana law. Thelma was horrified by their audacity. In a scathing letter to the Tooles that she instructed her lawyer to read to them, she placed a curse on the entire Toole family. "I have suffered alone," she declares, "therefore I should gain alone." Defying her tempestuous rants, they would not hand over the rights. Each side had a claim of fifty percent, but with Thelma having registered the copyrights of the book, she was confident, "No Toole can ever desecrate it by making a claim."

Time passed, and it seemed the issue had been dropped. *The Neon Bible* would never see publication. But in 1984, Rhoda Faust reclaimed her position, asserting that Thelma had years earlier promised her rights to publish *The Neon Bible*. In July, Thelma's estate lawyer, John Hantel, sent a letter informing Faust's lawyer that Thelma was not inclined to publish the novel, and that she had never entered into any contract, neither verbal nor written, with Faust. A battle was once again brewing over the book, but this time, Thelma was too weak to weather the fight.

She suffered health problems before the publication of *Confederacy*. The remarkable success likely added years to her life. But fame could not rid her body of the tumor growing on her kidney. She refused dialysis. And in late August of 1984, Thelma Toole died in her home on Elysian Fields.

Her son had only three people present at his services, but well over fifty attendants signed the guest book for Thelma's funeral. Even the people she had marginalized from her court returned to pay their respects. Unlike the day-after death notices of her son and her husband, Thelma's memorial services were announced in the *Times Picayune*. After mistakenly stating the funeral "private," the paper printed a correction. It was to be a "public ceremony." On a hot summer day, her body was placed in the Ducoing tomb, where her son had been buried years earlier. Her husband had been laid to rest several miles away in St. Vincent de Paul Cemetery. As in life, John Dewey Toole remained alienated in death, while mother and son were reunited, both their names engraved on the same stone with the surname Ducoing proudly displayed above the gray marble sepulcher.

While Thelma finally rested in peace, the affairs of her estate remained in conflict. In her will she had signed over the rights to *The Neon Bible* to Kenneth Holditch, a friend and professor at University of New Orleans who was one of the students in Walker Percy's class in 1976 and one of the first New Orleanians to praise *Confederacy*. She made him promise that he would block publication of *The Neon Bible* if the Tooles maintained their position as benefactors. What should have been a relatively easy estate to settle was now complicated by a legal battle for the unpublished novel that Toole had deemed a failure in 1954.

Rhoda Faust filed suit against the estate to grant her the rights to publish the book or compensate her for damages, as she depended on Thelma's promise of *The Neon Bible* to get her publishing house started. The judge dismissed Faust's case, and the Tooles immediately filed suit against the estate to force Holditch to release the novel for publication. They argued that under Louisiana law the novel was considered shared property and fifty percent of it belonged to the Tooles. Keeping his promise to Thelma, Holditch fought against the publication, although he came under increasing criticism from readers who were hungry for more of Toole's writing. Two years later a Louisiana judge resolved the dispute with a directive to either publish it or put it up for auction. Holditch was backed into a corner, wanting to honor Thelma's wishes, but realizing a public auction was far more risky to the future of the book. So it was submitted to several publishers. Many, including Louisiana State University Press, declined. But Grove Press, which held the rights to the paperback edition of *Confederacy* saw an opportunity. In 1989, Grove Press published *The Neon Bible*; Holditch authored the introduction; and the Tooles maintained their position as benefactors.

Thelma once claimed that, when published, *The Neon Bible* would "set the world on fire. It would make young people stop doing drugs." But it was not met with the same fervor of *Confederacy*. In many ways it was a surprising let down. With few moments of humor, the Southern gothic tale clearly emulates Flannery O'Connor. Reviewers acknowledged that Toole's early work showed remarkable talent for a sixteen-year-old. And eventually the film industry came sniffing around looking to buy movie rights. The adaptation of *The Neon Bible* was released in 1995, and it flopped. The director and screenplay writer, Terence Davies, admitted the film "doesn't work." He described it as a "transitional piece" for his development as a director. His interest in perspective and cinematic tableaus take clear precedence over pace of the plot or character development. Having served the purpose of Davies, the film left the novel perhaps in its rightful place as a work of juvenilia, a classification with which Toole would have likely agreed.

Undoubtedly, Thelma would be incensed to discover in the end the book was published and turned into a film, while the Tooles received royalties. Considering Thelma never sought riches, her vehement dedication to preventing the Tooles from establishing rights to *The Neon Bible* is puzzling. She had at one time taken Marion Toole Hosli under her wing, teaching her how to play the piano and recite poetry, but her loathing for the Tooles ran so deep she could not overcome it. The intricacies of family feuds aside, Toole's legacy was better served by what Thelma accomplished more so than what she tried to prevent.

We have *A Confederacy of Dunces* today because of her tenacity and dedication. She shepherded an invaluable contribution to American literature into print. And her theatrics certainly prevented the story of the publication from shrinking away. Yet, in designing her son's legacy, Thelma remains a complicated figure. She was keenly aware of her ability to influence how the public viewed her son and how history would remember him. In many ways she did much good. She diligently worked in the last few years of her life to ensure her son's place in literary history. She established the John Kennedy Toole scholarship fund at Tulane, starting it with a $100,000 donation along with the royalties from *Confederacy*. And with a current worth of more than $1 million, the Toole scholarship continues to enable students "with financial need and literary talent" to attend Tulane. She intended to gift the Ducoing home on Elysian Fields to Tulane with the agreement they would turn it into a museum on the life of her son, although because her brother still owned the house, it was never technically hers to donate. She compiled her son's papers, all the letters, school essays, photographs, memorabilia, and miscellany—a great deal of material—and started to write a biography of him using these documents. She abandoned the biography and then aimed to edit and compile some of his academic writings into a collection she would title *The Scholarly Papers of John Kennedy Toole*. But neither of these projects exceeded a few drafted pages. In 1983 she approached LSU to see if they would like to house her collection of papers, and they declined. So she left them to seven men who had stood by her near the end of her days. Shortly after her death, the executor of the estate, John Geiser, maneuvered to persuade all the heirs to donate their shares of the papers to Tulane to form the Toole Papers in the Special Collections at Howard Tilton Memorial Library.

Her efforts in collecting and keeping materials related to his life and the willingness of the heirs to donate them created an important resource to researchers. But her presence is still felt in this collection. The surviving documents provide details into his mind and the events of his life, but there are major pieces missing, letters that did not survive time, or perhaps Thelma's own edited version of her son's life. Suspicion of such gaps are thrown into relief when one ponders the possible contents of the suicide note that Thelma destroyed but yet discovers her dental bridge carefully preserved in an archival folder. Whether out of a mother's love or a desire to recast her son in a particular image, Thelma shaped his story. But in the end time forced her to let go, leaving many questions about his life wide open to interpretation.

Chapter 15

Toward the Heavens

With the voices of Toole and his mother silent, his legacy became
susceptible to the conjectures surrounding his death. Thelma may
have felt she was protecting her son's memory by circumventing questions about his suicide or his social life, focusing almost exclusively on his
"scholarly genius." But this ultimately led to speculation in the absence of
clear information. In some ways Toole's life and death are so indelibly
linked to his works, readers are primed to use them as windows into his
life. Statements like the one made by film critic Georgia Brown of the
Village Voice who described *The Neon Bible* as "the autobiographical
novel of a sixteen year old American Southerner, John Kennedy Toole"
typify this tendency to read his works as a veiled testimony of his life.

This trend has led to grave missteps in biographical and literary interpretations of Toole. The suggestion that Toole was latently homosexual has proliferated into readings of his novel. In 2007 Michael Hardin
applied the lens of queer theory to both of Toole's novels, appearing to
validate the interpretation that Ignatius Reilly from *Confederacy* and
David from *The Neon Bible* are reflections of Toole's conflicted sexuality.
Hardin combs the texts for homoerotic coding, going so far as to suggest Ignatius sucking the jelly out of donuts as "an explicit homoerotic
allusion." Hardin then argues that *Confederacy* "becomes darker, even
tragic, when read as indicative of a closeted sexuality." But whose sexuality? While Hardin focuses on Ignatius at the beginning of his essay, he
laments that "the extra-textual clues to issues such as [Toole's] sexuality
have been destroyed," as if to suggest his suicide note contained clues to

his sexual identity. He then subtly asserts that these clues may still reside hidden in the two novels, thereby the "queer performance" of the novels is actually an implicit declaration of Toole's own sexuality.

Similar suppositions thread through popular discussion of Toole's life and work as well. For example, in 2004, Raymond-Jean Frontain, professor of English at the University of Central Arkansas, makes a direct claim about Toole's sexuality in an entry in *GLBTQ: The World's Largest Encyclopedia of Gay, Lesbian, Bisexual, Transgender, and Queer Culture*. He writes of the author,

> Despite his sympathy for the socially marginalized and his animosity towards the powers that enforce conformity, Toole was never comfortable with his own homosexuality and in his writing presents sexual non-conformity in highly ambivalent and conflicted ways.

It is unclear when Toole ever expressed "animosity towards the powers that enforce conformity." Certainly he didn't do so when he climbed the ranks in the army or as he lectured in a coat and tie, mocking the loose rebelliousness of the late 1960s. But what is more disconcerting in this passage is that Frontain could have made his point about Toole's works as depicting homosexuality without suggestion of Toole's own sexual preference. Such assertions do nothing more than drag a dead man out of the proverbial closet. If in the case of Toole "homosexuality" was something more than a label, if he had claimed that identity in any way, then it might make a difference in interpreting his life and his work. Without his own admission or substantial evidence to support the point, such suggestions remain conjecture.

And yet, perhaps such spicy speculation about Toole's supposed secrets add to his mystery. Perhaps in some backward way it propels his legacy. Readers have long filled the unknowns of an artist's life with inferences derived from his works. And these claims through the digestion of popular discourse solidify into "truths." After all, for more than 160 years readers have concluded that Edgar Allan Poe was an opium addict, an alcoholic, and manic-depressive, citing the content of his works as clear evidence. Of course, in the case of Poe (and perhaps Toole as well) such lore was crystalized by a damaging biography, the first to be written after his death, which purported the ill-contrived assumptions.

Clearly the question of Toole's legacy is a far more complicated one than Thelma likely ever imagined. Sensationalism aside, his name will survive on the lasting merits of his literary work. Commercial success alone does not secure a place in the American literary canon. Plenty of best-sellers have been long forgotten by the reading public. Soon after the publication of *Confederacy,* scholars grappled with the novel. Several early critics responding to the book attempted to classify or explicate it in critical terms. Scholars generally tried to find ways to decode it, as if they were to answer Gottlieb's commentary on the books pointlessness. Some discussed Toole's religion, others discussed the tensions between worldviews in the novel, and others spoke to its function as a satire. In September of 1981, Robert Coles consolidated many of those initial thoughts in a lecture where he claimed Ignatius represented the Catholic Church. His approach elevated the discourse surrounding the novel. But his analysis weakens as he struggles and stretches to find religious symbolism at every turn. Some scholars have tried to define *Confederacy* as a specifically Southern novel. From a regional perspective, it certainly speaks to New Orleanians. The dialect of the characters is unique to the city. And the eccentricity of the characters often strikes a chord with New Orleans readers. And yet, Toole's novel has exceeded the confines of regional literature. Translated editions of the novel sell in bookstores all over the world.

It might very well be that the likenesses between characters in *Confederacy* and those from British, Spanish, and French literature enable international audiences to connect with a novel unique to New Orleans. The British reader certainly understands the wise and indulgent clown from Shakespeare's Falstaff. When the Spaniard picks up the translated version of the novel, there is something familiar. She has followed Don Quixote through his delusions of grandeur and now does the same with Ignatius Reilly. The French have certainly witnessed the grotesque play out in their national literature, starting with Rabelais's *Gargantua and Pantagruel*. And to some translators, Toole's control over his language eases the transition between languages and cultures. When the Italian translation of *Confederacy* by Luciana Bianciardi won the prestigious *Premio Monselice*, Bianciradri wrote to Thelma giving Toole most of the credit, "The novel is 'universal' in itself so that all I needed was to keep silent, and at the right moment, to lend it my language's idioms."

The ease with which European readers access the novel should come as no surprise. As a scholar fluent in Spanish and studied in French, Toole had intimate knowledge of his European literary predecessors. And the tradition and psychology of Carnival so infused in European traditions enables a natural familiarity with the parade of characters. Most importantly to him, he offered an authentic depiction of New Orleans. But in drawing from his vast knowledge of classical and contemporary literature, he created a novel that garners readers from New Orleans to Rome. Toole's novel is no more confined by region than Dickens is restricted to London or Cervantes to Spain.

Recently, scholars have taken note of the book's expanse and have discarded the approach of applying a limited lens of identity or region to Toole's work. They recognize that *Confederacy* has effectively eluded rigorous definition or confined placement within the canon, and yet it shows no signs of waning from its popularity. Scholars such as Robert Rudnicki and H. Vernon Leighton explore the variety of influences on Toole, not as a way to define the novel, but rather as a way to open up both the book and his process of creation, in essence to speak to Toole's multiplicity of views. Rudnicki asserts, "*A Confederacy of Dunces* is . . . a novel of 'influences' and indeed one about the process of influence and artistic development itself." In fact there is so much interweaving of his literary predecessors there is a sense that scholars have yet to fully tap the literary influences present in the novel.

Admittedly, many readers dislike the book, often finding Ignatius insufferable. Some critics maintain that it could use a good editor. But there are those who continue to find both enjoyment and depth in the novel. Scholars continue to look for threads and clues, keeping the book in conversation. It has made its way to high school classrooms and college courses. And it seems the pathway for its continued success is clear.

But one enduring aspect of Toole's legacy is that ultimately those who claim they have found the key, those who have supposedly decoded the underlying message of the novel, end up in Toole's crosshairs, for they become an Ignatius Reilly of sorts, attempting to narrow the focus of interpretation on a world that just doesn't make sense most of the time, a world too complicated to be reduced to a pattern or underlying principle. Perhaps that was the point that Toole wanted to make in that rambling, confessional letter he sent to Gottlieb in 1965. In some parallel universe wherein Toole maintained his faculties and responded to the criticism that the book "isn't about anything," one could imagine him replying with his trademark half-smile, "Of course it's not, Mr. Gottlieb. It's about everything."

Ultimately, the classics of literature transcend the politic of an age. That which endures pushes through the shifts of society, unbound by time, speaking to something perpetual in the human experience. It is the creation of that lasting harmony that drives us back to the classics, to keep looking for something we didn't see before or remind ourselves of what it means to be human. In March of 1969 Toole must have felt he had lost touch with that harmony. But the man destroyed was not who his friends and family knew. They knew an artist in his prime observing the subtleties of the human character and knowing full well, at one point in time, he was creating his literary masterpiece.

This self-awareness, this confidence is evident in a picture of him in the Caribbean in the early 1960s; he leans on the sill of a glassless window frame; he stares into the distance with the slightest smile. It seems he knows something that we do not, as if we will someday behold his work. And then, in another picture, there is only the view from the window; the clouds have moved across the sky, but Toole is gone. He left this earth long before he could realize he had achieved that vision glimmering in his eyes. He accomplished what many writers only dream of. In his small room in Puerto Rico in 1963 he climbed to the top of the world and left behind the victorious and infectious laughter that overcomes mortality. It took nearly twenty years for the rest of us to hear it. But it remains today, echoing through cafes, libraries, and living rooms, wherever a reader opens up the first page of his novel and begins the riotous romp on Canal Street. With each chuckle and chortle, with each tear wiped from the cheeks of laughing readers, the shadow of his death shrinks as the celebration of his life continues.

And through the humor and tragedy of his story, through the brilliance of it all, he reached the heights that he once beheld just before he began writing his first novel at the age of sixteen. One night in 1954 on the side of a country road in Mississippi, he looked up in awe at the cosmos as if searching for his own undying place in the Southern sky. His friend that stood next to him that night would never forget how John Kennedy Toole gasped "at the beauty of the millions of stars." And while it may have cost him his life, he has now "taken his place among them."

Acknowledgments

This book culminates a five-year journey of research and writing, which began when Toole's friend Joel Fletcher and his partner, John Copenhaver, opened their home to me on a cold winter day in 2005. Ever since, they have offered me a wealth of resources, insight, and encouragement. I am forever indebted to them.

Through Fletcher, I met filmmakers Joe Sanford, Charles Richard, and Bobbie Westerfield in February of 2009, as they started production of the documentary *John Kennedy Toole: The Omega Point*. Sanford and I struck an immediate friendship, which became a remarkable, creative relationship. Through sharing our findings and our musings, the biography and the documentary grew in tandem. They are separate projects, but they were largely shaped by our collaboration.

I am grateful to the entire staff at the Special Collections Library at Tulane University, especially Bruce Boyd Raeburn, Lee Miller, Susanna Powers, Eira Tansey, Sean Benjamin, Ann Case, and Lori Schexnayder. Without their stewardship to the John Kennedy Toole Papers, a biography of Toole would be impossible.

Other archives proved helpful as well. Bruce Turner at the Special Collections Library at the University of Louisiana at Lafayette gave me access to documents relating to Toole's time at the school. Also at ULL, James Wilson sent me unpublished information on Toole he had found in the estate of Patricia Rickels. The library at Hunter College and Columbia University provided materials detailing the climate of those institutions in the late 1950s and early '60s.

In addition to archival materials, much of the information gathered from the various stages of Toole's life came from interviews. His childhood friend John Geiser graciously gave me a tour of Uptown New Orleans as we chatted about his memories of the author. I appreciate Harold Toole, Emilie Dietrich Griffin, Rhoda Faust, Clayelle Dalferes, Jane Stickney Gwyn, Jane Pic Adams, Charlotte Powers, Sydney Poger,

Ellen Friedman, Mary Morgan, George Deaux, and John Hantel for the time they dedicated to answering my questions. Dawn Held at Lusher Charter School gave me access to Fortier newspapers and yearbooks. And Tyler Alpern provided information on Frances Faye. I am also delighted to have met Lynda Martin who recounted the many wonderful stories of Toole and her brother, Cary Laird, who passed away in 2008. Cary's partner, Myrna Swyers, also, retold the hilarious stories that Cary used to tell and contributed pictures of the influential Laird-Toole trip to Mississippi. I hope in some way this book serves as a testimony to the friendship between Toole and Laird.

It is quite possible that *A Confederacy of Dunces* would have never been written if it were not for Toole's experience in Puerto Rico. Dave Kubach, Tony Moore, Walter Carreiro, James Alsup, and Harry Edinger willingly shared their memories of Sergeant Toole as well as life in the army in Puerto Rico in the early 1960s.

Jo Ann Cruz and Karen Anklam of Loyola University set up several important interviews as well. I will always cherish the Saturday morning spent with Bunt Percy and Mary Pratt Percy Lobdell, casually chatting about their memories of Walker Percy, Flannery O'Connor, and Eudora Welty. By way of Anklam, I enjoyed an afternoon with Sister Dorothy Dawes, who once taught with Toole at St. Mary's Dominican College, followed by a tour of the old Dominican building. To the alumnae of Dominican, especially Joan Bowen, Elise Diament, Barbara Howard, Candace de Russy, and Pam Guerin—I have carried your heartfelt sentiments for Professor Toole throughout the writing of this book.

I am especially grateful to Robert Gottlieb who gave me permission to publish portions of his letters and offered his perspective on the issue of Toole and the accusations Thelma Toole made against him.

While I was many years too late to interview Bobby Byrne, fortunately Carmine Palumbo did so in 1995. And he graciously shared with me his recorded interview of a true New Orleans character.

Of course, this book would have been nothing more than an idea without my agent, William Clark; my editor, Ben Schafer; and the staff at Da Capo. The talents of Lori Hobkirk at the Book Factory, Cynthia Young at Sagecraft, copy editor Beth Fraser, and proofreader Sandy Chapman guided the book into print. The Popular Culture Association and American Culture Association provided an early source of support, kindly awarding me a grant making possible my first research trip to New Orleans. And Matt Wunder contributed editorial feedback on one of the first drafts.

Furthermore, I thank Germanna Community College, especially David Sam and my colleagues Diane Critchfield, Michael Zitz Beckham, and the library staff, who encouraged me throughout this whole process.

Unfortunately, some people passed away during the writing of this book. Patricia Rickels and Nick Polites shared with me their priceless insights and I regret they never saw this biography in print.

I thank my mother and father who taught me to live life as a voyage of infinite possibilities.

And most of all I thank my wife (my first editor) for her unwavering support and my two children who weathered well my long durations of silence as I hacked away at the manuscript.

To all of those who I have mentioned and failed to mention here, I hope that these pages serve as the highest sign of my appreciation.

Notes

Introduction

xii   Notably, Anthony Burgess . . . : Anthony Burgess, "Modern Novels: The 9 Best," *New York Times Book Review*, February 5, 1984: 1, 33.

xii   In the foreword . . . : Walker Percy, "Foreword," in *A Confederacy of Dunces*, by John Kennedy Toole, vii–ix (New York: Grove, 1980).

xii   Percy writes . . . : Ibid.

xiii   Dear Mr. Allsup . . . : Thelma Ducoing Toole letter to John Allsup, July 8, 1981, Box 12, Folder 5, the John Kennedy Toole Papers, Manuscripts Collection 740, Louisiana Research Collection, Tulane University (hereafter cited as Toole Papers).

xiii   While Nevils and Hardy . . . : In a footnote, the publisher admitted to publishing the letters without Robert Gottlieb's permission and thanked him for not suing. René Pol Nevils and Deborah George Hardy, *Ignatius Rising: The Life of John Kennedy Toole* (Baton Rouge: Louisiana State University Press, 2001).

xiv   Toole's friend Joel . . . : Joel L. Fletcher, *Ken and Thelma: The Story of A Confederacy of Dunces* (Gretna: Pelican Publishing, 2005).

xiv   But as Fletcher . . . : Ibid.

xiv   In *Ken and Thelma* . . . : Ibid.

xiv   While she proclaims . . . : Thelma Ducoing Toole, "A Mother's Rememberence: I Walk in the World for My Son," in *The Flora Levy Lecture in the Humanities Volume II: Gravity and Grace in the Novel A Confederacy of Dunces*, by Robert Coles (Lafayette: University of Southwestern Louisiana Press, 1981), 10–13.

xv   Reminiscing over the . . . : Errol Laborde, "Remembering a Pulitzer Winner," *New Orleans*, December 1981: 74–77.

Chapter 1: Roots

1   On a Sunday . . . : John Kennedy Toole letter to Robert Gottlieb, March 5, 1965. Joel L. Fletcher Papers, Manuscripts Collection 995, Louisiana Research Collection, Howard-Tilton Memorial Library, Tulane University (hereafter cited as Fletcher Papers).

1   For years he . . . : John Kennedy Toole letter to parents. May 15, 1963. Box 1, Folder 8, Toole Papers.

263

1 The novel he . . . : *I Walk in the World for My Son: An Interview with Thelma Ducoing Toole*, a film directed by Kenneth Holditch, Michael J. Adler, Barbara B. Coleman, and David A. Dillon, and featuring Thelma D. Toole, 1983.

1 He deemed the . . . : John Kennedy Toole letter to parents. May 15, 1963. Box 1, Folder 8. Toole Papers.

1 And his summer . . . : John Kennedy Toole letter to Joel Fletcher, July 9, 1961. Toole Papers.

1 His station in . . . : John Kennedy Toole letter to Robert Gottlieb, March 5, 1965. Fletcher Papers.

1 Distanced and unburdened . . . : Ibid.

1 He recalled a . . . : Ibid.

2 Pent up energies . . . : Ibid.

2 As his friend Joel Fletcher . . . : *John Kennedy Toole: The Omega Point*, directed by Joe Sanford and featuring Joel Fletcher, 2010.

2 Toole's earliest ancestor . . . : "Baby Book," Box 5, Folder 16, Toole Papers.

2 Ducoing gained local fame . . . : Henry C. Castellanos, *New Orleans as It Was* (Gretna: Pelican Publishing, 1990).

3 Toole's mother proudly . . . : "Baby Book," Box 5, Folder 16, Toole Papers.

3 Both a romanticized . . . : William C. Davis, *The Pirates Lafitte: The Treacherous World of the Corsairs of the Gulf* (Orlando: Harcourt, 2005).

3 Toole's honored ancestor [. . .] insurance fraud . . . : John Proffatt, "Millandon vs. New Orleans Ins. Co," in *The American Decisions: Cases of General Value and Authority Volume XIII* (Rochester: Bancroft-Whitney, 1910), 358–360.

3 Toole's honored ancestor [. . .] founding . . . : William C. Davis, *The Pirates Lafitte: The Treacherous World of the Corsairs of the Gulf* (Orlando: Harcourt, 2005).

3 Perhaps stretching the truth . . . : David Kubach interview by the author, May 18, 2011.

3 In addition to his French ancestor . . . : Mary Orfila was the daughter of Frank Orfila. Frank Orfila of New Orleans is listed as "commission merchant" in the 1880 U.S. Census.

3 Initially seen as a source . . . : Joseph Lee and Marion R. Casey, *Making the Irish American: History and Heritage of the Irish in the United States* (New York: NYU, 2006).

3 And they made a lasting impact . . . : "The Irish in New Orleans," New Orleans online, accessed December 12, 2011, at http://www.neworleansonline.com/neworleans/multicultural/multiculturalhistory/irish.html.

3   But eventually, as families merged . . . : Federal Writers' Project of the Works Progress Administration, *New Orleans City Guide* (New Orleans: Garret County Press, 1938).

4   Toole's mother, Thelma . . . : "Receipt from Paul A. Ducoing," Box 13, Folder 11, Toole Papers.

4   Later in life . . . : *I Walk in the World for My Son: An Interview with Thelma Ducoing Toole*, a film directed by Kenneth Holditch, Michael J. Adler, Barbara B. Coleman, and David A. Dillon, and featuring Thelma D. Toole, 1983.

4   A proud Creole . . . : Fletcher, *Ken and Thelma*.

4   Unfortunately, her father . . . : Ibid.

4   Only later in life . . . : Ibid.

4   In 1920 she graduated . . . : "TD's Diploma," Box 13, Folder 13, Toole Papers.

4   And in that same year . . . : "Southern Music Co. Diploma," Box 13, Folder 12, Toole Papers.

4   For a time she entertained . . . : *I Walk in the World for My Son*, film.

4   She decided to stay . . . : Ibid.

4   She remembered him in his early days . . . : Laborde, "Remembering a Pulitzer Winner."

5   Born in 1899 . . . : "Birth Certificate," Box 11, Folder 8, Toole Papers.

5   When he was eight years old . . . : *I Walk in the World for My Son*, film.

5   At the newly opened . . . : Laborde, "Remembering a Pulitzer Winner."

5   In 1917 he took . . . : "Birth Scholarship Certificate," Box 11, Folder 8, Toole Papers.

5   He served in the army . . . : "Memorial certificate from Richard Nixon" Box 11 Folder 9. Toole Papers.

5   Holding a position . . . : *I Walk in the World for My Son*, film.

5   So with their grandest dreams . . . : "Copy of marriage certificate" Box 11, Folder 10, Toole Papers.

5   They moved to a house . . . : Fletcher, *Ken and Thelma*.

5   The New Orleans public schools . . . : Ibid.

5   Forced to give up her job . . . : Ibid.

5   Around the time they were married . . . : *Soards' New Orleans Directory 1926* (New Orleans: L. Soards, 1926). Directory lists John Toole as "dept. mgr. of Gulf Oldsmobile."

5   They moved to . . . : *Soards' New Orleans Directory 1931* and *1932* (New Orleans: L. Soards, 1931, 1932). Directory lists their address as 2623 Nashville Avenue.

6 John lost his job . . . : Fletcher, *Ken and Thelma*.

6 In 1932, much to Thelma's . . . : *Soards' New Orleans Directory 1933* (New Orleans: L. Soards, 1933). Directory lists John Toole's address as 2280 St. Claude Ave—same address as John Toole's mother.

6 John and Thelma . . . unable to conceive . . . : Lynda Laird Martin interview by the author, May 5, 2011.

6 As their son would later tell . . . : Ibid.

6 John secured a new salesman job . . . : Entry for John and Thelma Toole. *Polk's New Orleans City Directory 1938.* (New Orleans: R. L. Polk & Company, 1938).

6 And on Friday . . . : "Record of Birth," Box 3, Folder 14, Toole Papers.

6 After the successful . . . : *I Walk in the World for My Son*, film.

7 Remembering the awkward . . . : Ibid.

7 And outside the hospital . . . : "Phases of the Moon: 1901–2000," National Aeronautics and Space Administration, accessed on June 1, 2011, at http://eclipse.gsfc.nasa.gov/phase/phases1901.html; and "The Weather," *Times Picayune.* Friday, December 17, 1937: 1.

7 Like any Friday night . . . : Federal Writers' Project of the Works Progress Administration, *New Orleans City Guide* (New Orleans: Garret County Press, 1938).

Chapter 2: Early Days in Uptown

9 In 1930 Herbert Hoover visualized . . . : Anthony J. Stanonis, *Creating the Big Easy: New Orleans and the Emergence of Modern Tourism* (Athens: University of Greorgia Press, 1918–1945).

9 Surely he had doubts . . . : Douglas Brinkley, *The Great Deluge: Hurricane Katrina, New Orleans and the Mississippi Gulf Coast* (New York: Harper Collins, 2007).

9 By 1938 Mardi Gras . . . : Stanonis, *Creating the Big Easy.*

10 The rundown French Quarter . . . : Ibid.

10 Strip clubs began setting up . . . : Ibid.

10 And in February 1938 . . . : Ibid.

10 A year later, the battlefield . . . : Ibid.

10 Bobby Byrne, a friend of Toole's . . . : Robert Byrne interview by Carmine Palumbo, 1995.

10 And downtown people . . . : Ibid.

10 She always maintained . . . : Film footage of the Levy Lecture Series, University of Southwestern Louisiana (now UL Lafayette), Sept. 18, 1981.

10   While she observed . . . : Ibid.

10   "We had wicker . . . : *I Walk in the World for My Son*, film.

11   They celebrated a . . . : Laborde, "Remembering a Pulitzer Winner."

11   A few weeks . . . : "Baby Book," Box 5, Folder 16, Toole Papers.

11   In the late . . . : "Infant Photos," Box 5, Folder 10, Toole Papers.

11   He could have . . . : *I Walk in the World for My Son*, film.

11   Before selling an . . . : Lynda Laird Martin interview by the author, May 5, 2011.

11   If a family . . . : Ibid.

12   His nephew, Harold . . . : Harold Toole, Jr., interview by the author, March 2, 2009.

12   Harold recalls . . . : Ibid.

12   Perhaps eager for . . . : Fletcher, *Ken and Thelma.*

12   In a heated . . . : "Speech written by TDT" Box 13, Folder 16. Toole Papers.

12   Before he was . . . : "Infant Photos," Box 5, Folder 10, Toole Papers.

12   On his first trip . . . : "Baby Book," Box 5, Folder 16, Toole Papers.

12   At the age . . . : Ibid.

12   And when he . . . : *I Walk in the World for My Son*, film.

13   Thelma wouldn't allow . . . : Harold Toole, Jr., interview by the author, May 9, 2009.

13   But Thelma once . . . : *I Walk in the World for My Son*, film.

13   After his birth . . . : Ibid.

13   On the days . . . : Ibid.

13   On her days . . . : Ibid.

13   She was the . . . : Ibid.

13   And, after a . . . : Ibid.

13   And even as . . . : Ibid.

13   What he didn't know . . . : Ibid.

13   He attended his . . . "Baby Book," Box 5, Folder 16, Toole Papers.

13   And at the . . . : Ibid.

14   He once described . . . : Ibid.

14   And one night . . . : Ibid.

14   Entering kindergarten at . . . : Ibid.

14   After one month . . . : Thelma Ducoing Toole, "A Mother's Rememberence."

14   In preparation for . . . : *I Walk in the World for My Son*, film.

14   And he had . . . : Thelma Ducoing Toole, "A Mother's Rememberence."

14   But the psychologist . . . : Film footage of the Levy Lecture Series.

14   "I'll tell you" . . . : Thelma varied in the ways she told this story. At times she claimed that the psychologist told her that Toole lost interest and observed her. At other times Thelma said she supplied the psychologist the reason for her son's loss of interest in the test.

14   His mother often . . . : "Baby Book," Box 5, Folder 16, Toole Papers.

15   He was "a" . . . : Thelma Ducoing Toole, "A Mother's Rememberence."

15   The nurses at . . . : Laborde, "Remembering a Pulitzer Winner."

15   She even thought . . . : "Baby Book," Box 5, Folder 16, Toole Papers.

15   "He had the" . . . : *I Walk in the World for My Son*, film.

15   "I want to" . . . : *Ibid.*

15   Thelma celebrated how . . . : "Baby Book," Box 5, Folder 16, Toole Papers.

15   "Those children thought . . . : Film footage of the Levy Lecture Series.

16   Jane Stickney Gwyn . . . : Jane Stickney Gwynn interview by the author, October 2010.

16   As Thelma reported . . . : Rhoda Faust interview by the author, June 10, 2011.

16   On the first . . . : John Geiser interview by the author, June 2008.

16   One day Toole . . . : Ibid.

17   As evident in . . . : "Sheet Music for Piano," Box 4, Folder 12, Toole Papers.

17   Pictures of him . . . : Oversize Folder 2, Toole Papers.

17   But Thelma maintained . . . : Laborde, "Remembering a Pulitzer Winner."

17   "He was an" . . . : *I Walk in the World for My Son*, film.

17   His baby book . . . : "Baby Book" Box 5, Folder 16, Toole Papers.

17   When he came . . . : Film footage of the Levy Lecture Series.

17   When he was . . . : Ibid.

18   When in character . . . : Ibid.

18   He took this . . . : "Achievement Scrap Book," Box 22, Vol. 1, Toole Papers.

18   In *Mystery at* . . . : Ibid.

18   And in a . . . : Ibid.

18   Members of the . . . : John Hantel interview by the author, April 13, 2011.

18   However, in Thelma's . . . : *I Walk in the World for My Son*, film.

19   There were many photos . . . : "Scrapbook with photographs," Box 22, Vol. 2, Toole Papers.

19   He appeared on . . . : "Achievement Scrap Book," Box 22, Vol. 1, Toole Papers.

19   From September 1948 . . . : Ibid.

19   One of her . . . : Hantel interview by the author, April 13, 2011.

19   Jane Stickney Gwyn . . . : Stickney Gwyn interview by the author, June 2008.

20   One of his . . . : Film footage of the Levy Lecture Series.

20   She recalled her . . . : "Childhood Photos," Box 5, Folder 11, Toole Papers.

21   In the fall . . . : "Achievement Scrap Book," Box 22, Vol. 1, Toole Papers.

21   In November of . . . : Ibid.

Chapter 3: Fortier

24   Eventually, in 1969 . . . : Adam Fairclough, *Race & Democracy: The Civil Rights Struggle in Louisiana 1915–1972* (Athens: University of Georgia Press, 1999).

24   He rarely studied . . . : Laborde, "Remembering a Pulitzer Winner."

24   So impressed with . . . : Film footage of the Levy Lecture Series.

24   Indeed, Toole maintained . . . : "Honor Roll," *Silver and Blue,* 1950–1954.

24   As his mother . . . : Film footage of the Levy Lecture Series.

25   Much like Toole . . . : Myrna Swyers interview by the author, April 13, 2011.

25   Both incredibly bright . . . : "Honor Roll," *Silver and Blue,* 1950–1954.

25   The two friends . . . : Martin interview by the author May 5, 2011.

25   They were both . . . : Ibid.

25   In 1955 he . . . : "Miscellaneous Letters," Box 1, Folder 13, Toole Papers.

25   Bosley Crowther . . . : Bosley Crowther, "The Screen: Summer Bachelor's Itch," *New York Times,* June 4, 1955: 9.

25   While Toole and Laird . . . : Ibid.

25   Whenever Toole visited . . . : Martin interview by the author, May 5, 2011.

25   One of their . . . : Swyers interview by the author, April 13, 2011.

26   Laird would often say . . . : Ibid.

26   They talked about . . . : Martin interview by the author, May 5, 2011.

26   And the Latin . . . : Ibid.

26   Whatever the tragedy . . . : Ibid.

26   Downtown, there was . . . : Ibid.

26   From the Irish . . . : Ibid.

26   And roaming throughout . . . : Ibid.

26   They attended a . . . : Ibid.

26   And one day . . . : Ibid.

27   On the other . . . : Ibid.

28   He feared intruders . . . : Patricia Rickels interview by the author, February 10, 2009.

28   Once he felt . . . : Martin interview by the author, May 5, 2011.

28   One day, as . . . : Ibid.

28   "Someone is going" . . . : Ibid.

28   When Lynda, Laird's . . . : Ibid.

29   Toole later confided . . . : Rickels interview by the author, February 10, 2009.

29   The first time . . . : "Cat Nips," *Silver and Blue*, October 3, 1952: 2.

29   "Social Whirl" focused . . . : "Social Whirl," *Silver and Blue*, October 3, 1952: 2.

29   It was a movement . . . : Rick Coleman, *Blue Monday: Fats Domino and the Lost Dawn of Rock 'N' Roll* (Boston: Da Capo, 2007).

30   An undisputed innovator . . . : Ibid.

30   Organizations such as . . . : Ibid.

30   Cary Laird asked . . . : Martin interview by the author, May 5, 2011.

30   And to Toole's . . . : Ibid.

30   Evenings out for . . . : Jane Pic Adams interview by the author, November 2010.

30   In January of . . . : "Cat Nips," *Silver and Blue,* January 29, 1954: 2.

31   Her mother, unaware . . . : Martin interview by the author, May 5, 2011.

31   Toole told Laird . . . : Ibid.

31   In regard to . . . : Ibid.

31   While she maintained . . . : Film footage of the Levy Lecture Series.

31   According to his . . . : Martin interview by the author, May 5, 2011.

31   In "Television, Tomorrow's Entertainment" . . . : John Kennedy Toole, "Television, Tomorrow's Entertainment," Box 1, Folder 20, Toole Papers.

32   In a short . . . : John Kennedy Toole, "The Louisiana Purchase," Box 1, Folder 20, Toole Papers.

32   In an essay . . . : John Kennedy Toole, "Democracy Is What You Make of It," Box 1, Folder 20, Toole Papers.

33   In 1951 he . . . : "Tarpon's Harrison Wins World's Ring Toss Championship," *Ess and Bee*, January 26, 1951: 2.

33   In the John Kennedy Toole . . . : John Kennedy Toole, "Going Up," Toole Papers.

34   By 1953 the . . . : *Polk's New Orleans City Directory 1952–1953* (New Orleans: R. L. Polk & Co., 1953).

34   Thelma later explained . . . : Dalt Wonk, "John Kennedy Toole's Odyssey Among the Dunces," *Dixie*, October 25, 1981: 6–17.

34   In Toole's senior year . . . : Martin interview by the author. (May 5, 2011).

34   In 1954 he . . . : Ibid.

34   Toole rode on . . . : Ibid.

34   He commented that . . . : Ibid.

34   The weekend visit . . . : Ibid.

35   The parade of . . . : Film footage of the Levy Lecture Series.

35   Although, she maintained . . . : *Ibid.*

35   He "gasped at" . . . : Martin, "Letter from Lynda," Box 12, Folder 3, Toole Papers.

35   Back in the . . . : Swyers interview by the author, April 13, 2011.

35   He started muttering . . . : Ibid.

36   In this short novel . . . : John Kennedy Toole, *The Neon Bible* (New York: Grove Press, 1989).

36   While Toole never . . . : *I Walk in the World for My Son*, film.

36   His mother recalled . . . : Ibid.

36   Before coming to . . . : William Martin, *A Prophet with Honor: The Billy Graham Story* (New York: William Morrow and Company, 1991).

36   In Los Angeles . . . : "Billy Graham 1949 LA Crusade Newsreel," accessed December 12, 2011, at http://www.youtube.com/watch?v=CUDKehwFWjg.

36   And several years . . . : Martin. *A Prophet with Honor*.

37   But mixed with . . . : *I Walk in the World for My Son*, film.

37   David, the narrator . . . : Toole, *The Neon Bible*.

38   Kerry Luft, senior . . . : Blurb from cover of *The Neon Bible*.

38   She prided herself . . . : *I Walk in the World for My Son*, film.

38   When David explains . . . : Toole, *The Neon Bible*.

38   She explained years later . . . : *I Walk in the World for My Son*, film.

39   He was elected . . . : Flora McIver and Rose Gerald, "Fortier Well Represented at Pelican State; Seven Boys, Three Girls Voted into Offices," *Silver and Blue*, October 9, 1953: 2.

39   In October of . . . : "Achievement Scrap Book," Box 22, Vol. 1, Toole Papers.

39   He took fifth . . . : "Chamber of Commerce News Bulletin," May 28, 1954. Box 4, Folder 10, Toole Papers.

39   And on December . . . : "Fortier Tarps on Television," *Silver and Blue*, December 22, 1953: 1.

39   A month later . . . : "Senior Spotlight," *Silver and Blue*, January 29, 1954: 2.

39   He was one . . . : John Kennedy Toole, "Tarpons Receive Award; See Historic Shrines," *Silver and Blue*, May 28, 1954: 3.

39   These students represented . . . : "24 Fortier Students Leave for Valley Forge Awards," *New Orleans States Item*, May 8, 1954. There seems to be some confusion as to how many students went on this trip. The body of this article states the number of students was twenty. However, Toole lists the number as thirty-one in an article he wrote for *Silver and Blue*.

39   Boarding a train . . . : Toole, "Tarpons Receive Award; See Historic Shrines."

39   They watched the . . . : Ibid.

39   At Valley Forge . . . : Ibid.

39   And like true . . . : Ibid.

40   In an article . . . : Ibid.

40   In a promotional . . . : "Scrapbook of N.Y.-Phil.-D.C. trip," Box 1, Folder 18, Toole Papers.

40   Joel Zelden, a . . . : Janet Zeldon interview by the author, October 10, 2010.

40   Jane Pic Adams . . . : Adams interview by the author, November 2010.

40   His classmates voted . . . : *The Tarpon* (New Orleans: Alcee Fortier High School, 1954).

41   His mother claimed . . . : Wonk, "John Kennedy Toole's Odyssey Among the Dunces."

41   Determined in his . . . : "Senior Spotlight," *Silver and Blue*, January 29, 1954: 2.

41   As the university . . . : Clarence L. Mohr and Joseph E. Gordon, *Tulane: The Emergence of a Modern University, 1945–1980* (Baton Rouge: Louisiana State University Press, 2001).

41   They also came . . . : Ibid.

Chapter 4: Tulane

43   Before Toole started . . . : Wonk, "John Kennedy Toole's Odyssey Among the Dunces."

43   He found a . . . : Ibid.

44   In his first . . . : John Mmahat interview by the author, December 7, 2010.

44   He submitted his . . . : Ibid.

44   More than fifty years . . . : Ibid.

44   Mmahat looked at . . . : Ibid.

44   One day after . . . : *I Walk in the World for My Son*, film.

44   In a 1984 . . . : Ibid.

44   On the back . . . : John Kennedy Toole, "Indecency in Chaucer," Box 2, Folder 2, Toole Papers.

45   Toole sent him . . . : Alvin Foote letter to John Kennedy Toole, February 26, 1957. Box 1, Folder 13, Toole Papers.

45   We turn out . . . : Ibid.

46   I would enjoy . . . : Ibid.

46   Just as Ignatius . . . his mother tried to follow . . . : Film footage of the Levy Lecture Series.

47   Having declared his . . . : Stephen Andry postcard to John Kennedy Toole, August 24, 1955. "Scrapbook of N.Y.-Phil-D.C. trip," Box 1, Folder 18, Toole Papers.

47   He plodded through . . . fair and mild weather . . . : "Weather," *New York Times*, September 5, 1955: 1.

47   Almost every night . . . : Ibid.

47   Despite the long . . . : "Scrapbook of N.Y.-Phil-D.C. trip," Box 1, Folder 18, Toole Papers.

47   In a snapshot . . . : Ibid.

48   Our government tells . . . : John Kennedy Toole, Toole exam by Dr. Ballard, March 12, 1955. Box 2, Folder 11, Toole Papers.

48   With no regular . . . : Byrne interview by Palumbo, 1995.

48   Even Bobby Byrne . . . : Ibid.

48   Fraternity brothers would . . . : Mmahat interview by the author., December 7, 2010.

49   In the fall . . . : "Delta Tau Delta," in *Jambalaya* (New Orleans: Tulane University, 1956), 288.

49   In the caption . . . : Ibid.

49   In another photo . . . : News clippings. Box 10, Folder 10, Toole Papers.

49   And for the . . . : "Receipt from Delta Tau Delta," Box 3, Folder 3, the Toole Papers.

49   In the fall . . . : John Kennedy Toole, "The Development of the Babbit-American," Box 2, Folder 2, Toole Papers.

50   Boethius scholar and . . . : Byrne interview by Palumbo, 1995.

50   "Fortune and Nature" . . . : John Kennedy Toole, Final Exam Lumiansky, Box 2, Folder 11, Toole Papers.

50   "The wheel of" . . . : John Kennedy Toole, Box 2, Folder 2, the Toole Papers.

50   *De Casibus Virorum* . . . : Toole, *A Confederacy of Dunces*.

50   He owned a . . . : John Kennedy Toole personal library list, Box 5, Folder 5, Toole Papers.

51   Others, like Mortimer . . . : Mortimer J. Adler, "God and the Professors," in *Pragmatism and American Culture*, by Gail Kennedy (Boston: D.C. Heath and Company, 1950), 67–76.

51   In another assignment he . . . : John Kennedy Toole, "The Development of the Babbit-American."

51   A debate between . . . : Toole, *A Confederacy of Dunces*.

52   This exploration culminated . . . : John Kennedy Toole, "Untitled: Puritanism and Hawthorne." Box 2, Folder 2, Toole Papers.

52   He observes, "Man" . . . : Ibid.

52   Since he positions . . . : Ibid.

53   He owned a . . . : JKT personal library list.

53   A poet awakes . . . : Don Marquis, *Archy and Mehitabel* (New York: Doubleday, 1955).

53   Addressing Cold War . . . : John Kennedy Toole, *The Tulane Hullabaloo*, October 5, 1956.

54   Toole presented the . . . : John Kennedy Toole, *The Tulane Hullabaloo*, February 22, 1957.

54   In one comic . . . : John Kennedy Toole, *The Tulane Hullabaloo*, October 19, 1956.

54   In the background . . . : John Kennedy Toole, *The Tulane Hullabaloo*, November 9, 1956.

54   The next week . . . : John Kennedy Toole, *The Tulane Hullabaloo*, November 16, 1956.

54   Two weeks later . . . : John Kennedy Toole, *The Tulane Hullabaloo*, December 14, 1956.

54   As Mmahat recalls . . . : Mmahat interview by the author, December 7, 2010.

54   On the first . . . : John Kennedy Toole, "Portraits," in *Carnival Magazine*, Vol 1, No. IX, 1956.

55   As he wrote . . . : Toole, "The Development of the Babbit-American."

55   For example, Patrolman . . . : Toole, *A Confederacy of Dunces*.

55   The real-life . . . : Ibid.

55   The 2002 Grove . . . : Toole, *A Confederacy of Dunces*.

56   He poses among . . . : "Glendy Burke," in *Jambalaya*, 100 (New Orleans: Tulane, 1957).

56   In one of . . . : Nicholas Polites interview by the author, February 14, 2009.

56 Professor Richard Fogle . . . : Richard Fogle letter to Mary Dichmann, June 12, 1959, English Department Records, University Archives, University of Louisiana at Lafayette.

56 He socialized with . . . : David Prescott letter to John Kennedy Toole, October 25, 1958, Box 1, Folder 13, Toole Papers.

56 The professor complimented . . . : Fogle letter to Dichmann, June 12, 1959.

56 In his essay . . . : Toole, "Untitled: Puritanism and Hawthorne." Box 2, Folder 2, Toole Papers.

57 In the essay . . . : John Kennedy Toole, "The Women in Lyly's Plays: An Honor's Essay," Box 2, Folder 15, Toole Papers.

57 His mother deemed . . . : Wonk, "John Kennedy Toole's Odyssey Among the Dunces."

58 She mused years . . . : Emilie Griffin, "Style and Zest: Remembering John Kennedy Toole," *Image*, Fall 1999, accessed June 14, 2011, at http://imagejournal.org/page/journal/articles/issue-24/griffin-confessions.

58 On the winter . . . : Stickney Gwynn interview by the author, October 2010.

58 After the service . . . : Ibid.

58 And according to . . . : Wonk, "John Kennedy Toole's Odyssey Among the Dunces."

58 Mmahat recalled the . . . : Mmahat interview by the author, December 7, 2010.

58 Eventually they started . . . : Wonk, "John Kennedy Toole's Odyssey Among the Dunces."

58 They enjoyed sipping . . . : Ibid.

59 His friend Cary . . . : Martin interview by the author, May 5, 2011.

59 And in 1958 . . . : Incidentally, Anthony Quinn was the director of *The Buccaneer* (1958). In 1981 Thelma Toole would meet Quinn in the green room of the *Tomorrow Show* in New York City.

59 On one of . . . : John Kennedy Toole, "Coleridge on Dramatic Illusion," Box 2, Folder 2, Toole Papers.

59 He was inducted . . . : "Phi Beta Kappa," Box 2, Folder 19, Toole Papers.

60 According to Thelma . . . : *I Walk in the World for My Son*, film.

60 In late March . . . : "Letter from Jaques Barzun," March 14, 1958, Box 3, Folder 5, Toole Papers.

60 While his friend . . . : Martin interview by the author, May 5, 2011.

60 Although, unlike Ignatius . . . : "Payroll stub from Haspel Brothers," Box 4, Folder 9, Toole Papers.

61 In several pictures . . . : "Adult Photos," Box 5, Folder 14, Toole Papers.

Chapter 5: Columbia University

63   Originally named King's . . . : *A Brief History of Columbia* (New York: Columbia University, 2011), accessed June 10, 2010, at http://www.columbia.edu/content/history.html.

64   And during Toole's . . . : *The Graduate Student's Guide: 1958–1959* (New York: Columbia University, 1958).

64   The Woodrow Wilson . . . : Richard C. Boys (national director of Woodrow Wilson National Fellowship Foundation) letter to John Kennedy Toole, April 1, 1958, Box 3, Folder 5, Toole Papers.

64   But according to . . . : *The Graduate Student's Guide: 1958–1959.*

64   Most master of arts . . . : Ibid.

64   Put into perspective . . . : Ibid.

64   These funds would . . . : Ibid.

65   Out of the . . . : In May of 2010 the author visited 1008 Furnald Hall and confirmed the same view over Broadway of a snapshot in the Toole Papers. "Adult Photos," Box 5, Folder 14, Toole Papers.

66   Over the next . . . : "Grades at Columbia," Box 3, Folder 6, Toole Papers.

66   He enrolled in . . . : Sydney Poger interview by the author, October 21, 2010.

66   But never a . . . : Ibid.

66   Students affectionately called . . . : Robert Parker interview by the author, September 29, 2010.

66   Robert Parker, who . . . : Ibid.

66   He maintained that . . . : Poger interview by the author, October 21, 2010.

66   Tindall encouraged students . . . : Ibid.

67   By far the . . . : Wieler letter to Dichmann, June 10, 1959.

67   By 1959 he . . . : Ibid.

67   The English department . . . : *The Graduate Student's Guide: 1958–1959.*

67   Many graduate students . . . : Poger interview by the author, October 21, 2010.

67   There is no . . . : *The Graduate Student's Guide: 1958–1959.*

68   "If it should happen" . . . : Ibid.

68   Another graduate student . . . : Robert Bozanich letter to author, September 8, 2010.

68   Thelma Toole referred . . . : *I Walk in the World for My Son*, film.

68   The clear sense . . . : Poger interview by the author, October 21, 2010.

68   And the "huge" . . . : Bozanich letter to author, September 8, 2010

68   As Dalt Wonk . . . : Wonk, "John Kennedy Toole's Odyssey Among the Dunces."

69   Within the first . . . : David Prescott letter to John Kennedy Toole, October 25, 1958, Box 1, Folder 13, Toole Papers.

69   Prescott responded . . . : Ibid.

69   In a four-page . . . : Ibid.

69   In Toole's novel . . . : Toole, *A Confederacy of Dunces*.

69   The screenplay, as . . . : Ibid.

70   Snapshots from this . . . : "Adult Photos," Box 5, Folder 14, Toole Papers. While the location is not identified on the photos, the author confirmed the location where these pictures were taken by using the architectural sights of the Marblehead Lighthouse and Kresge Auditorium.

70   He was the . . . : Byrne interview by Palumbo, 1995. Byrne coined the phrase "theology and geometry are all wrong" from a line in one of H. P. Lovecraft's stories.

71   In his poem . . . : John Kennedy Toole, "New York: Three Aspects." Box 6, Folder 5, Toole Papers.

71   During the winter . . . : John Kennedy Toole letter to Thelma Toole. Box 6, Folder 4, Toole Papers.

71   The speaker of . . . : John Kennedy Toole, "The Arbiter." Box 6, Folder 4, Toole Papers.

72   "The American Scholar" . . . : John Kennedy Toole letter to Thelma Toole. Box 6, Folder 4, Toole Papers.

72   The poem looks . . . : Toole, "The Arbiter," Box 6, Folder 4, Toole Papers.

73   In fact "The" . . . : Ibid.

73   While in New . . . : Jack Kerouac, *The Subterraneans* (New York: Grove, 1958). Box 5, Folder 17, Toole Papers.

73   His copy, inscribed . . . : Ibid.

73   Once I was . . . : Ibid.

74   On November 6 . . . : Ann Charters, *Kerouac: A Biography* (New York: St. Martin's Press, 1994).

74   Amis earnestly questioned . . . : Ibid.

74   He named influences . . . : Ed Adler, "Friends and Fellaheen," in *Departed Angels*, by Jack Kerouac (Boston: Da Capo Press, 2004), 216.

75   The English department . . . : Diana Trilling, "The Other Night at Columbia: A Report from the Academy," *Partisan Reivew*, Volume 26, 1959: 214–230.

75   However, Diana Trilling . . . : Ibid.

75   As Diana Trilling . . . : Ibid.

75   Instead she found . . . : Ibid.

75   Trilling expresses the . . . : Ibid.

75   During the question . . . : Ibid.

76   In a letter . . . : Allen Ginsberg letter to John Hollander, September 1959, in *Letters of Allen Ginsberg* (Philadelphia: Da Capo, 2008).

76   Fred Kaplan, author . . . : Fred Kaplan, *1959: The Year Everything Changed* (Hoboken: John Wiley & Sons, 2009).

76   It was the . . . : Trilling, "The Other Night at Columbia."

77   "angel headed hipsters" . . . : Allen Ginsberg, *Howl and Other Poems* (San Francisco: City Lights Books, 2006).

77   In March of . . . : "Honor's thesis final draft," Box 2, Folder 14, Toole Papers.

77   Professor Wieler commented . . . : Wieler letter to Dichmann, June 10, 1959. English Department Records, University Archives, University of Louisiana at Lafayette.

78   As the *Graduate* . . . : *The Graduate Student's Guide: 1958–1959.*

78   Toole graduated with . . . : Wieler letter to Dichmann, June 10, 1959. English Department Records, University Archives, University of Louisiana at Lafayette.

78   Wieler tried to . . . : Ibid.

78   In the Woodrow . . . : The Woodrow Wilson National Fellowship Foundation, *Directory of Fellowship Awards for the Academic Years 1945/46–1959/60* (New Jersey: 1960).

78   On June 2 . . . : Lawrence Fellows, "Columbia Gives Degrees to 6,571," *New York Times*, June 3, 1959: 28.

78   Usually the ceremony . . . : Ibid.

78   He reminded them . . . : Ibid.

78   The graduation ceremony . . . : Ibid.

79   He adopted a . . . : Rickels interview by the author, February 10, 2009.

79   Therein, Richard Fogle . . . : Fogle letter to Dichmann, June 12, 1959. English Department Records, University Archives, University of Louisiana at Lafayette.

79   Wieler also wrote . . . : Wieler letter to Dichmann, June 10, 1959. English Department Records, University Archives, University of Louisiana at Lafayette.

79   They would pay . . . : Dichmann letter to Toole, July 8, 1959. English Department Records, University Archives, University of Louisiana at Lafayette.

79   He warned Toole . . . : Paul T. Nolan letter to John Kennedy Toole, June 19, 1959. English Department Records, University Archives, University of Louisiana at Lafayette.

Chapter 6: Cajun Country

81   In his epic . . . : Henry Wadsworth Longfellow, *Evangeline and Other Poems* (Toronto: Dover, 1995).

82   When Toole arrived . . . : Fletcher, *Ken and Thelma*.

82   In early September . . . : *L'Acadien 1959–1960*. Southwestern Louisiana Institute.

82   His landlady, "a" . . . : Fletcher, *Ken and Thelma*.

82   Toole once described . . . : Ibid.

82   On the second floor . . . : Trent Angers, "Author of 'A Confederacy of Dunces' Taught at USL," *Acadiana Profile*, Sept. 4, 1981: 23–26.

83   Originally constructed as . . . : Rickels interview by the author, February 10, 2009.

83   Humidity and termites . . . : Ibid.

83   Occasionally, in the . . . : Ibid.

83   While much of . . . : Joel Fletcher interview by the author, December 23, 2008. This accomplishment was largely due to the foresight of Fletcher's father, the president of the college at the time.

83   Many of them . . . : Rickels interview by the author, February 10, 2009.

83   Many of them came . . . : Ibid.

84   "He was always" . . . : Ibid.

84   In a slow . . . : Ibid.

84   Closing her eyes . . . : Rickels interview by Sanford for the film *John Kennedy Toole: The Omega Point*, February 2009.

84   Toole would later . . . : Angers, "Author of 'A Confederacy of Dunces' Taught at USL."

85   George Deaux, an . . . : George Deaux interview by the author, April 2009.

85   Deaux recalls, "One" . . . : Ibid.

85   Joel Fletcher and . . . : Joel Fletcher interview by the author, October 15, 2011

85   Regardless of the . . . : George Deaux interview by the author, April 2009.

85   Deaux recalls one . . . : Ibid.

85   Bereaved by his . . . : Ibid.

85   He lived in . . . : Rickels interview by the author, February 10, 2009.

85   As an avid . . . : Ibid.

86   As Professor Rickels . . . : Ibid.

86   Byrne often said . . . : Byrne interview by Palumbo, 1995.

86   At one time . . . : Rickels interview by the author, February 10, 2009.

86   "I wasn't going" . . . : Byrne interview by Palumbo, 1995.

86   And yet this . . . : Rickels interview by the author, February 10, 2009.

86   Behind his supercilious . . . : Ibid.

86   He once told . . . : Ibid.

86   "I felt cheated" . . . : Ibid.

87   Byrne's aunt was . . . : Byrne interview by Palumbo, 1995.

87   And his blatant . . . : Ibid.

87   One day Byrne . . . : Fletcher, *Ken and Thelma*.

87   Toole later told . . . : Ibid.

87   When Toole once . . . : Byrne interview by Palumbo, 1995.

87   In an article . . . : Angers, "Author of 'A Confederacy of Dunces' Taught at USL."

87   Bobby Byrne, was . . . : Ibid.

88   Then Broussard noticed . . . : Ibid.

88   In recalling their . . . : Byrne interview by Palumbo, 1995.

88   "Oh my God" . . . : Rickels interview by the author, February 10, 2009.

88   Byrne recognized some . . . : Byrne interview by Palumbo, 1995.

88   Toole even seemed . . . : Toole, *A Confederacy of Dunces*.

89   Rather, he identified . . . : Byrne interview by Palumbo, 1995.

89   In fact, Byrne . . . : Ibid.

89   "He has it" . . . : Ibid.

89   Byrne noticed a . . . : Ibid.

89   Interestingly, in the . . . : Ibid.

89   One night at . . . : Rickels interview by the author, February 10, 2009.

90   His friend Nick . . . : Polites interview by the author, February 14, 2009.

90   Ken used to . . . : Ibid.

90   In the course . . . : Ibid.

91   He dressed in . . . : Rickels interview by the author, February 10, 2009.

91   When Patricia met . . . : *John Kennedy Toole: The Omega Point*, directed by Joe Sanford and featuring Patricia Rickels, 2010.

91   Patricia, having endured . . . : Rickels interview by the author, February 10, 2009.

91   On occasion, with . . . : Ibid.

92   Before leaving Lafayette . . . : Ibid.

92   He told her . . . : Ibid.

92   And he told . . . : Ibid.

92   Toole introduced them . . . : Angers, "Author of 'A Confederacy of Dunces' Taught at USL."

92   But during their stay . . . : Rickels interview by the author, February 10, 2009.

92   In the event . . . : Ibid.

92   But the extreme . . . : Ibid.

92   On the weekends . . . : Ibid.

93   One day as . . . : Ibid.

93   Over modest meals . . . : Ibid.

93   On occasion he . . . : Ibid.

93   His favorite line . . . : Ibid.

93   To his friends' . . . : Ibid.

94   Nearly everyone played . . . : Ibid.

94   "He was a" . . . : Rickels interview by Sanford, February 2009.

94   Of course, with . . . : Angers, "Author of 'A Confederacy of Dunces' Taught at USL."

94   The slim-fitting . . . : Rickels interview by the author, February 10, 2009.

94   At first he . . . : Ibid.

94   Regardless of his . . . : Ibid.

95   Toole positioned himself . . . : Ibid.

95   But on another occasion . . . : Fletcher interview by the author, December 23, 2008.

95   Looking back on . . . : Rickels interview by Sanford, February 2009.

95   She was convinced . . . : Rickels interview by the author, February 10, 2009.

96   Polites entered their . . . : Polites interview by the author, February 14, 2009.

96   Mrs. Toole came . . . : Ibid.

96   For months Toole . . . : Ibid.

96   She played the . . . : Ibid.

96   "When Ken could" . . . : Ibid.

96   "There were a" . . . : Ibid.

97   He "talked to" . . . : Ibid.

97   Near the end . . . : Ibid.

98   In July of . . . : Fletcher, *Ken and Thelma*.

98   "GET IN OUTTA . . . : Ibid.

98   Later that day . . . : Ibid.

98   Elmore Morgan, the . . . : Angers, "Author of 'A Confederacy of Dunces' Taught at USL."

99   And regardless of . . . : Ibid.

99   Joking with Patricia . . . : Ibid.

99   In May of . . . : "John K. Toole: To Washington," *English Department Newsletter*, May 11, 1960: 1. English Department Records, University Archives, University of Louisiana at Lafayette.

99   He would attend . . . : Ibid.

99   According to Patricia . . . : Rickels interview by the author, February 10, 2009.

100   Fortunately, in June . . . : "Mr. Toole to New York," *English Department Newsletter*, June 15, 1960: 5. English Department Records, University Archives, University of Louisiana at Lafayette.

100   The English department . . . : Ibid.

100   He went out . . . : Fletcher, *Ken and Thelma*.

100   Although Nick Polites . . . : Polites interview by the author, February 14, 2009.

100   One weekend in: Martin interview by the author, May 5, 2011.

Chapter 7: Hunter and Columbia

102   He rented a . . . : John Kennedy Toole letter to Nandy and Uncle Arthur, October 18, 1960. Box 1, Folder 1, Toole Papers.

102   Under the guidance . . . : Unofficial Transcript, Columbia University, Box 1, Folder 1, Toole Papers.

102   And he took . . . : Ibid.

102   "He loved New" . . . : Rickels interview by the author, February 10, 2009.

102   The *New York* . . . : "Hunter Opens Calmly," *New York Times*, September 20, 1960: 30.

103   As Toole reported . . . : Toole letter to Nandy and Uncle Arthur, October 18, 1960.

103   Toole observed how . . . : Ibid.

103   From September to October . . . : Ibid.

103   Upon hearing "The Star-Spangled . . . : "Khrushchev 'Conducts' 'Star-Spangled Banner,'" *New York Times*, October 6, 1960: 16.

103   Desperate attempt to . . . : Benjamin Welles, "Khrushchev Bangs His Shoe on Desk," *New York Times*, October 13, 1960: 1.

103   Initially humored by . . . : Toole letter to Nandy and Uncle Arthur, October 18, 1960.

103   One morning in . . . : Ibid.

104   Toole confesses, "I find" . . . : Ibid.

104   She picked up . . . : Clayelle Dalferes interview by the author, Nov. 22, 2008.

104   On one occasion . . . : Ibid.

104   And one night . . . : Griffin, "Style and Zest: Remembering John Kennedy Toole."

105   Dietrich (now Emilie . . .): Ibid.

105   In a letter . . . : Ibid.

105   With great skill . . . : Ibid.

105   Toole wrote to . . . : Toole letter to Fletcher, February 3, 1961. Printed in Fletcher's *Ken and Thelma*.

106   On one occasion . . . : Eugene Archer, "Playgirl on the Town," *New York Times*, October 9, 1960: X7.

106   The Columbia *Graduate* . . . : *The Graduate Student's Guide: 1958–1959.*

107   He went sledding . . . : "Adult Photos," Box 5, Folder 14, Toole Papers.

107   During this playful . . . : Ibid.

108   He wrote to . . . : Toole letter to Fletcher, February 3, 1961. Printed in Fletcher's *Ken and Thelma*.

108   He confides to . . . : Ibid.

108   In March he . . . : Toole letter to parents, March 1, 1961. Box 1, Folder 1, Toole Papers.

108   On the first . . . : Ellen R. Friedman interview by the author, December 31, 2010.

109   "He began a" . . . : Ibid.

109   "He had a" . . . : Ibid.

109   Dear Ken, . . . : "Letter from Ellen" Box 1 Folder 13. Toole Papers.

110   As Fletcher suggests . . . : Fletcher, *Ken and Thelma*.

110   Thelma Toole understood . . . : Thelma D. Toole interview by University of Louisiana at Lafayette, 1981. Hunter yearbooks from 1960 to 1964 do not list a girl by the name of Myrna Minkoff as a graduate of Hunter College.

110   And Anthony Moore . . . : Anthony Moore interview by the author, January 24, 2009.

111   As he admitted . . . : Toole letter to Fletcher, February 3, 1961. Printed in Fletcher's *Ken and Thelma*.

111   In a letter . . . : Toole letter to parents, March 1, 1961. Box 1, Folder 1, Toole Papers.

111   The professor whose . . . : Ibid.

111   As Particia Rickels . . . : Rickels interview by the author, February 10, 2009.

112   He used to . . . : Dalferes interview by the author, November 22, 2008.

112   Nick Polites notes . . . : Polites interview by the author, February 14, 2009.

112   He admits to . . . : Toole letter to Fletcher, February 3, 1961. Printed in Fletcher's *Ken and Thelma: The Story of A Confederacy of Dunces*.

112   In the 1961 . . . : *The Wistarion: 1960–1961* (New York: Hunter College, 1961).

113   Polites remembers . . . : Polites interview by the author, February 14, 2009.

113   Emilie Griffin remembers . . . : Griffin, "Style and Zest: Remembering John Kennedy Toole."

113   It was a . . . : Letter from Emilie Russell Dietrich. Box 1, Folder 14, Toole Papers.

113   Griffin identified Toole . . . : Griffin, "Style and Zest: Remembering John Kennedy Toole."

113   Dalferes tells of . . . : Dalferes interview by the author, November 22, 2008.

114   He was a . . . : Polites interview by the author, February 14, 2009.

114   In June of . . . : Louella Parsons. *New York Journal American*. June 29, 1959.

114   "I know a" . . . : Frances Faye. "Frances and Her Friends." *Caught in the Act* GNP Crescendo Records, 1959.

114   As the *Washington* . . . : Dorthy Kilgallen, "Bobby Has Eye on Sandy's Career," *Washington Post, Times Herald*, 1959–1973, Feb. 18, 1961.

115   *Variety* reports of . . . : *Variety*. March 8 1961

115   Polites observes, "It" . . . : Polites interview by the author, February 14, 2009.

115   So impressed with . . . : Fletcher, *Ken and Thelma*.

115   He began drafting . . . : Toole letter to Gottlieb, March 5, 1965. Fletcher Papers.

116   Along these lines . . . : Polites interview by the author, February 14, 2009.

116   Polites recalls . . . : Ibid.

116   In 1960 Purdy . . . : William Grimes, "James Purdy" *New York Times*. March 13, 2009 accessed on June 10, 2011 at http://www.nytimes.com/2009/03/14/books/14purdy.html.

116   Dalferes came to . . . : Dalferes interview by the author, November 22, 2008.

116   He despised long . . . : John Kennedy Toole letter to Patricia Rickels, January 7, 1963. Personal Collection of James D. Wilson.

117   She knew that . . . : Dalferes interview by the author, November 22, 2008.

117   Dalferes claims, "He . . . : Ibid.

117   Perhaps Polites got . . . : Polites interview by the author, February 14, 2009.

117   Toole declined, explaining . . . : Toole letter to Fletcher, July 9, 1961. Printed in Fletcher's *Ken and Thelma*.

118   After her return . . . : Letter from Emilie Russell Dietrich. Box 1, Folder 14, Toole Papers.

118   "I think it" . . . : Ibid.

Chapter 8: The Army and Puerto Rico

119   And according to David . . . : Kubach interview by the author, November 2008.

120   As Joel Fletcher . . . : *John Kennedy Toole: The Omega Point*.

120   The barracks were . . . : Fort Buchanan photos from the personal collection of Walter Carreiro.

120   And Bob Morter . . . : Due to a story related to this individual in Chapter 9, his name has been changed.

120   Toole described them as . . . : Toole letter to parents, September 14, 1962. Box 1, Folder 4, Toole Papers.

121   Candid pictures from . . . : Fort Buchanan photos from the personal collection of Walter Carreiro.

121   Soon after Toole . . . : Kubach interview by the author, November 2008.

121   As Kubach remembers . . . : Ibid.

121   Tony Moore . . . : Anthony Moore interview by the author, January 24, 2009.

121   On another occasion . . . : Ibid.

122   As Kubach remembers . . . : Kubach interview by the author, November 2008.

122   Moore recalls Toole . . . : Moore interview by the author, January 24, 2009.

122   As I was . . . : Toole letter to parents, July 10, 1962. Box 1, Folder 4, Toole Papers.

123   In March of . . . : Ronald Walker, "P. R. Recruits Busy Learning English," *San Juan Star*, March 23, 1962: 1.

123   The leadership at . . . : Letter of Commendation, February 21, 1963. Box 1, Folder 15, Toole Papers.

123   While several instructors . . . : Moore interview by the author, January 24, 2009.

123   As the *San* . . . : Walker, "P. R. Recruits Busy Learning English."

123   They walked on . . . : "Style and Zest," *Remembering John Kennedy Toole.*

124   She recalls seeing . . . : Ibid.

124   It was the . . . : Ibid.

124   In one of . . . : Letter of Commendation.

124   On May 22, . . . : Toole letter to parents, May 22, 1962. Box 1, Folder 2, Toole Papers.

125   The cool sea . . . : Toole letter to parents, June 24, 1962. Box 1, Folder 1, Toole Papers.

125   On June 24 . . . : Ibid.

125   "I don't feel" . . . : Toole letter to parents, July 1, 1962. Box 1, Folder 2, Toole Papers.

125   He spent his . . . : Ibid.

126   On June 24 . . . : Toole letter to parents, June 24, 1962. Box 1, Folder 1, Toole Papers.

126   By July, the . . . : Toole letter to parents, July 1, 1962. Box 1, Folder 2, Toole Papers.

126   "Whatever its drawback" . . . : Ibid.

127   Whatever the long . . . : Toole letter to parents, July 14, 1962. Box 1, Folder 2, Toole Papers.

128   In an undated . . . : Thelma Ducoing Toole letter to John Kennedy Toole, undated. Box 1, Folder 14, Toole Papers.

128   Yesterday, the Fourth . . . : Toole letter to parents, July 5, 1962. Box 1, Folder 2, Toole Papers.

129   In Puerto Rican . . . : Toole letter to parents, May 22, 1962. Box 1, Folder 1, Toole Papers.

130   In fact, he . . . : Toole letter to parents April 10, 1963. Box 1 Folder 7. Toole Papers.

130   In his letter . . . : Letter of Commendation, Toole Papers.

130   In *Waugh in* . . . : Evelyn Waugh, *Waugh in Abyssinia* (Baton Rouge: Louisiana State University Press, 2007).

130   Therein, a white . . . : Evelyn Waugh. *Black Mischief.* (New York: Back Bay Books, 2002).

130   He won the . . . : Toole letter to parents, July 14, 1962. Box 1, Folder 2, Toole Papers.

131   He writes, "Aruba's" . . . : Toole letter to parents, July 25, 1962. Box 1, Folder 2, Toole Papers.

131   In early August . . . : Toole letter to parents, August 4, 1962. Box 1, Folder 3, Toole Papers.

131   "There was a" . . . : Ibid.

133   Toole was promoted . . . : Toole letter to parents, August 14, 1962. Box 1, Folder 3, Toole Papers.

133   Company A saw . . . : Moore interview by the author, January 24, 2009.

133   Our First Sergeant . . . : Toole letter to parents, August 14, 1962. Box 1, Folder 2, Toole Papers.

134   When another Puerto . . . : Ibid.

135   Sgt. Jose Ortiz . . . : Toole letter to parents, September 14, 1962. Box 1, Folder 4, Toole Papers.

135   The closed mess . . . : Toole letter to parents, August 16, 1962. Box 1, Folder 5, Toole Papers.

136   What a mad . . . : Toole letter to parents, August 14, 1962. Box 1, Folder 2, Toole Papers.

136   Our immediate superiors . . . : Toole letter to parents, September 11, 1962. Box 1, Folder 4, Toole Papers.

136   They sanded the . . . : Toole letter to parents, September 14, 1962. Box 1, Folder 2, Toole Papers.

136   They erected makeshift . . . : Moore interview by the author, January 24, 2009.

136   And when the . . . : Ibid.

137   As Anthony Moore . . . : Ibid.

136   Friday night there . . . : Toole letter to parents, November 18, 1962. Box 1, Folder 5, Toole Papers.

138   In the commotion . . . : Ibid.

138   "Actually, it's a" . . . : Toole letter to parents, November 9, 1962. Box 1, Folder 5, Toole Papers.

138   At the end . . . : Toole letter to Fletcher, September 23, 1962. Printed in Fletcher's *Ken and Thelma*.

139   Dear Dad . . . : Toole letter to parents, November 14, 1962. Box 1, Folder 5, Toole Papers.

140   In late October . . . : Toole letter to parents, November 3, 1962. Box 1, Folder 5, Toole Papers.

140   Over my private . . . : Toole letter to Fletcher, September 23, 1962. Printed in Fletcher's *Ken and Thelma*.

141 After a year . . . : Ibid.

142 For most of his . . . : Toole letter to Fletcher, January 26, 1963. Printed in
Fletcher's *Ken and Thelma.*

143 I also paid . . . : Ibid.

143 Dressed in his . . . : Ibid.

144 Polites is still . . . : Ibid.

144 I spent a . . . : Ibid.

145 so enwrapped in . . . : Fletcher, *Ken and Thelma.*

146 In his letter . . . : Ibid.

146 Dear Pat, Rick . . . : Toole letter to Rickels, January 7, 1963. Personal collection
of James D. Wilson.

147 Reporting to Fletcher . . . : Fletcher, *Ken and Thelma.*

Chapter 9: A Writer Emerges

149 Back to the . . . : Toole letter to Fletcher, January 26, 1963. Printed in Fletcher's
Ken and Thelma.

150 A fairly cool . . . : Toole letter to Fletcher, February 9, 1963. Printed in
Fletcher's *Ken and Thelma.*

150 Emilie Dietrich Griffin . . . : "Style and Zest: *Remembering John Kennedy Toole.*

151 Instructors could hear . . . : Kubach interview by the author, November 2008.

151 "In my private" . . . : Toole letter to parents, April 10, 1963. Box 1, Folder 7,
Toole Papers.

152 I am trying . . . : Toole letter to parents, March 23, 1963. Box 1, Folder 7, Toole
Papers.

152 I am writing . . . : Toole letter to parents, April 4, 1963. Box 1, Folder 7, Toole
Papers.

152 Writing feverishly, I . . . : Toole letter to parents, April 10, 1963. Box 1, Folder
7, Toole Papers.

153 "All is still" . . . : Ibid.

153 Unfortunately, PFC Kubach . . . : Toole letter to parents, April 25, 1963. Box 1,
Folder 7, Toole Papers.

153 This letter is . . . : Toole letter to parents, May 8, 1963. Box 1, Folder 8, Toole
Papers.

154 At the moment . . . : Ibid.

154 I can not . . . : Ibid.

155   Years later, looking . . . : Toole letter to Robert Gottlieb, March 5, 1965. Fletcher Papers.

155   On May 15 . . . : Toole letter to parents, May 15, 1963. Box 1, Folder 8, Toole Papers.

156   Heat, wild trainees . . . : Toole letter to parents, May 27, 1963. Box 1, Folder 8, Toole Papers.

156   He donned dark . . . : Fort Buchanan photos from the personal collection of Walter Carreiro.

157   Enclosed is a . . . : Toole letter to parents, May 27, 1963. Box 1, Folder 8, Toole Papers.

157   His writing suffered . . . : Ibid.

157   If only you . . . : Toole letter to parents, June 11, 1963. Box 1, Folder 9, Toole Papers.

157   On one occasion . . . : Ibid.

157   "What a frightening" . . . : Ibid.

158   As Kubach recalls . . . : The name of the instructor has been changed to Bob Morter to protect his identity. Kubach interview by the author, November 2008.

158   While Toole was . . . : Ibid.

158   Kubach maintains that . . . : Ibid.

158   According to Tony . . . : Anthony Moore interview by the author, January 24, 2009.

158   Moore suggests that . . . : Ibid.

159   As Kubach recalls . . . : Kubach interview by the author, November 2008.

159   While I have . . . : Toole letter to parents, June 30, 1963. Box 1, Folder 9, Toole Papers.

159   If I am . . . : Ibid.

160   On the writing . . . : Ibid.

161   The announcement . . . : Toole letter to parents, July 9, 1963. Box 1, Folder 10, Toole Papers.

161   He shipped his . . . : Toole letter to parents, July 27, 1963. Box 1, Folder 10, Toole Papers.

162   The administration . . . : Toole letter to parents, July 31, 1963. Box 1, Folder 10, Toole Papers.

163   The two years . . . : Toole letter to Fletcher, undated. Printed in Fletcher's *Ken and Thelma*.

164   In the afternoon . . . : Toole letter to parents. July 27, 1963. Box 1 Folder 10.
Toole Papers

164   Stepping down from . . . : Ibid.

Chapter 10: Back Home in New Orleans

165   She recalled the . . . : *I Walk in the World for My Son*, film.

166   He cautioned that . . . : Byrne interview by Palumbo, 1995.

166   For now I . . . : Toole letter to Fletcher, undated. Printed in Fletcher's *Ken and
Thelma*.

166   Toole taught in . . . : Pam Guerin interview by the author, May 28, 2011.

166   In 1980 the . . . : St. Mary's Dominican College "Alumnae Association
Bulletin," New Orleans, 1981, 1–3.

167   She recalls that . . . : Guerin interview by the author, May 28, 2011.

167   As they recalled . . . : Joan Trader Bowen interview by the author, August 22,
2011.

167   He "ridiculed *Reader's*" . . . : Ibid.

167   He "made the" . . . : Ibid.

167   And Joan's sister . . . : Ibid.

167   In his courses . . . : Ibid.

168   I tried to . . . : Guerin interview by the author, May 28, 2011.

168   To this day . . . : Dorothy Dawes interview by the author, May 24, 2011.

168   And his mother . . . : Wonk, "John Kennedy Toole's Odyssey Among the
Dunces: Part 2."

168   Whether by chance . . . : Candace de Russy interview by the author, June 7,
2011.

168   He was undeniably . . . : Ibid.

168   One autumn afternoon . . . : de Russy interview by the author, June 27, 2011.

170   He later confessed . . . : Toole letter to Gottlieb, March 5, 1965. Fletcher
Papers.

170   Toole had an . . . : Ibid.

170   And when his . . . : Film footage of the Levy Lecture Series.

170   But in the . . . : Michael Korda, *Another Life: A Memoir of Other People* (New
York: Delta, 2000).

171   In fact, the . . . : Bruce Jay Friedman, *Lucky Bruce: A Literary Memoir*.
(Emeryville: Biblioasis, 2011).

171   She ended that . . . : Jean Ann Jollett letter to Toole, June 9, 1964. Box 1, Folder 11, Toole Papers.

172   He took issue . . . : Gottlieb letter to Toole, June 15, 1964. Fletcher Papers.

172   His comments echoed . . . : Emilie Russ Dietrich letter to Toole. Box 1, Folder 14, Toole Papers.

172   Jollett, a Southerner . . . : Jollett letter to Toole, June 9, 1964. Box 1, Folder, 11, Toole Papers.

172   Dear John . . . : Joe Hines letter to Toole, August 2, 1964. Box 1, Folder 14, Toole Papers.

173   One evening in . . . : Fletcher, *Ken and Thelma*.

173   But he was . . . : Ibid.

173   Still troubled by . . . : Gottlieb letter to Toole, December 14, 1964. Fletcher Papers.

174   They agreed Toole . . . : Ibid.

174   Having typed it . . . : Ibid.

175   One wonders how . . . : Hines letter to Toole, December 6, 1964. Box 1, Folder 14, Toole Papers.

175   Ken came for . . . : J. C. Broussard letter to Fletcher, 1965. Fletcher Papers.

176   Whenever I visited . . . : Polites interview by the author, February 14, 2009.

177   In January of . . . : Toole letter to Gottlieb, March 5, 1965. Fletcher Papers.

177   As he spoke . . . : Ibid.

178   During that conversation . . . : Ibid.

178   By this point . . . : Gottlieb interview by the author, June 3, 2011.

178   He writes to . . . : Toole letter to Gottlieb. March 5, 1965. Fletcher Papers.

178   The book is . . . : Ibid.

179   No doubt this . . . : Ibid.

179   He fully acknowledges . . . : Ibid.

179   One night recently . . . : Ibid.

180   Echoing the editorial . . . : Ibid.

180   He confesses he . . . : Ibid.

180   this book is . . . : Ibid.

181   In fact, George Deaux . . . : George Deaux interview by the author, April 2009.

181   In passing, Deaux . . . : Ibid.

181   Gottlieb's response was . . . : Ibid.

181   When someone like . . . : Gottlieb letter to Toole, March 23, 1965. Fletcher
      Papers.

182   In closing the . . . : Ibid.

182   Toole found Gottlieb's . . . : Toole letter to Robert Gottlieb, March 28, 1965.
      Fletcher Papers.

183   What is most . . . : Ibid.

183   Since both of . . . : Toole letter to Fletcher, May 4, 1965. Printed in Fletcher's
      Ken and Thelma.

184   All of which . . . : Ibid.

184   Although you may . . . : Ibid.

185   "It was the" . . . : Dalferes interview by the author, November 22, 2008.

185   And yet, in . . . : Ibid.

185   Dear Mr. Toole . . . : Gottlieb letter to Toole, January 17, 1966. Box 1, Folder
      11, Toole Papers.

187   In the afternoon . . . : Geiser interview by the author, June 2008.

Chapter 11: Decline and Fall

189   Thelma's uncle, James . . . : Fletcher, *Ken and Thelma.*

189   In December of . . . : Ibid.

190   My brother's nervousness . . . : Arthur Ducoing letter to coroner, Feburary 28,
      1966. From the Toole Papers.

190   But he tried . . . : *John Kennedy Toole: The Omega Point*, film.

190   Kubach had read . . . : Ibid.

190   As Kubach observed . . . : Ibid.

191   However, Pam Guerin . . . : Guerin interview by the author, May 28, 2011.

191   She was described as . . . : Dawes interview by the author, May 24, 2011.

191   On at least . . . : Ibid.

191   Kubach, who had . . . : Kubach interview by the author, May 18, 2011.

192   One day, as . . . : Ibid.

192   He wrote to . . . : John Kennedy Toole postcard to parents, July 20, 1967. Box
      1, Folder 10, Toole Papers.

193   "John never wanted" . . . : Kubach interview by Joseph Sanford for the film *John
      Kennedy Toole: The Omega Point*, 2009.

193   "I suppose I" . . . : *John Kennedy Toole: The Omega Point*, film.

194   Charlotte Powell enjoyed . . . : Charlotte Powell interview by the author
      December 10, 2011.

194   While some guests . . . : Ibid.

194   Powell marveled at . . . : Ibid.

194   In fact, she . . . : Ibid.

194   Enjoying the extra . . . : Laborde, "Remembering a Pulitzer Winner."

195   Polites recalls . . . : Polites interview by the author, February 14, 2009.

195   Polites recounts . . . : Ibid.

195   The student body . . . : Joan Trader Bowen, interview by the author.
      August 22, 2011.

195   One of the . . . : Ibid.

196   As Elise explained . . . : Ibid.

196   He was humorless . . . : Mary Pratt Percy Lobdell interview by the author,
      November 2010.

196   He made snide . . . : Ibid.

196   While the threat . . . : Ibid.

196   As Elise admits . . . : Bowen, interview by the author. August 22, 2011.

196   He confessed he . . . : Byrne interview by Palumbo, 1995.

196   "He was so" . . . : Kubach interview by the author, May 18, 2011.

197   They began frequent . . . : Huling Ussery interview by the author,
      January 31, 2011.

197   When asked about . . . : Ibid.

197   With growing concern . . . : Ibid.

197   The chair decided . . . : Ibid.

197   Thomas Bonner . . . : Thomas Bonner interview by the author, June 25, 2009.

198   Typically he would . . . : Rickels interview by the author, February 10, 2009.

198   "What are you" . . . : Ibid.

198   Indeed, during the . . . : George Deaux, *The Humanization of Eddie Cement*
      (New York: Simon and Schuster, 1964); George Deaux, *Exit* (New York: Simon
      and Schuster, 1966); and George Deaux, *Superworm* (New York: Simon and
      Schuster, 1968).

199   Patricia listened to . . . : Rickels interview by the author, February 10, 2009.

199   Toole owned Deaux's . . . : Toole's personal library list, Box 5, Folder 5, Toole
      Papers.

202   Thomas Lask of . . . : Thomas Lask, "Two on the Lighter Side," *New York
      Times*, May 8, 1968: 45.

202   Thomas Lask observed . . . : Ibid.

202   As Henry Raymont . . . : Henry Raymont, "Book Trade Upset by Changes in Ownership, Size and Staff," *New York Times*, March 4, 1968: 28.

203   When Patricia Rickels . . . : Rickels interview by the author, February 10, 2009.

203   Patricia and Milton . . . : Rickels interview by the author, February 10, 2009.

203   Edgar Allen Poe, "The Conqueror Worm," from *The Unabridged Edgar Allen Poe* (Philadelpia: Courage, 1997).

205   When Ernest Hemingway . . . : Jeffrey Meyers. *Hemingway: A Biography* (New York: Da Capo, 1999).

205   In July of . . . : Mary Welsh Hemingway, *How It Was* (New York: Knopf, 1975).

205   And when Allen . . . : Ginsberg, *Howl and Other Poems*.

205   She had undergone . . . : Connie Ann Kirk, *Sylvia Plath: A Biography* (Westport: Greenwodd, 2004).

205   In February of 1963 . . . : Paul Alexander, *Rough Magic: A Biography of Sylvia Plath* (New York: Viking, 1991).

205   And in 1966 . . . : Arthur Ducoing letter to coroner, Feburary 28, 1966. Box 11, Folder 12, Toole Papers.

Chapter 12: Final Journey

209   In his inaugural . . . : Richard Nixon, "Richard Milhous Nixon: First Inaugural Address," *Bartleby.com*, January 2001, accessed July 13, 2011, at http://www.bartleby.com/124/pres58.html.

209   She suspected he . . . : Rickels interview by Sanford, February 2009.

209   The next day . . . : Ibid.

211   It was March . . . : "Toole," *Times Picayune*, March 27, 1969: 23.

211   At 3:30 the . . . : Ibid.

211   There were only . . . : Wonk, "John Kennedy Toole's Odyssey Among the Dunces: Part 2."

212   The "beloved son" . . . : "Toole," *Times Picayune*.

212   But if he . . . : Rickels interview by Sanford, February 2009.

212   From his receipts . . . : Wonk, "John Kennedy Toole's Odyssey Among the Dunces: Part 2."

212   And Alvin Foote . . . : Foote letter to Toole, February 26, 1957. Box 1, Folder 13, Toole Papers.

212   In a taped . . . : Film footage of the Levy Lecture Series.

213   As she saw . . . : *I Walk in the World for My Son*, film.

214   In fact, when . . . : George Deaux interview by the author, April 2009.

214   "I always found" . . . : Ibid.

214   Biographers René Pol Nevils . . . : René Pol Nevils and Deborah George Hardy, *Ignatius Rising: The Life of John Kennedy Toole* (Baton Rouge: Louisiana State University Press, 2001).

215   On one occasion . . . : Film footage of the Levy Lecture Series.

215   Cary Laird and . . . : Martin interview by the author, May 5, 2011.

215   According to Thelma . . . : Film footage of the Levy Lecture Series.

215   He "didn't like" . . . : Ibid.

215   Guibet was later . . . : Fletcher, *Ken and Thelma*.

215   The myterious "Ellen" . . . : Ellen letter to Toole. Box 1, Folder 13, Toole Papers.

215   "A lot of people" . . . : Rickels interview by Joseph Sanford, February 2009.

215   And one of . . . : Huling Ussery interview by the author, January 31, 2011.

216   One reviewer of . . . : Smiley Anders, "Gone Too Soon: New Book Chronicles Short, Tragic Life of John Kennedy Toole," *The Advocate*, June 17, 2001: 1.

216   When using such . . . : Polites interview by the author, February 14, 2009.

217   He coined the . . . : Edwin Shneidman, *Suicide as Psychache: A Clinical Approach to Self-Destructive Behavior* (Plymouth: Rowman & Littlefield, 1993).

217   In his definition . . . : Ibid.

217   In his papers . . . : The date of this manuscript may be 1967. Charlotte Powell recalled at one of her parties in 1967 guests talking about a woman who had just committed suicide at an apartment building a few doors down the street in the French Quarter. Toole was present at the party and heard the discussion. Just like Toole's character Samuel, the woman slit her wrists in her second floor apartment. John Kennedy Toole, "Disillusionment." Box 6, Folder 2, Toole Papers.

218   Someone was calling . . . : Ibid.

218   The woman realizes . . . : Ibid.

218   The boy watched . . . : Ibid.

219   Cary Laird thought . . . : Martin interview by the author, May 5, 2011.

219   David Kubach wondered . . . : Kubach interview by the author, November 2008.

219   And staring out . . . : Rickels interview by the author, February 10, 2009.

219   She remarks, "What" . . . : Ruth Lafranz Kathmann interview by the author, January 6, 2011.

220   Coincidentally, on the . . . : Mallord, *Love Alone Finds Cold* (New Orleans: Silver Bicycle Press, 1969). The inscription reads, "January 20, 1969. Mr. Toole,

Enjoy my misplaced anti-cedents. In universal oneness with you and Shelley, and being. Mallord."

Chapter 13: Publication

221   Dear Mrs. Toole . . . : Joan Trader letter to Thelma D. Toole, April 12, 1969. Box 11, Folder 12, Toole Papers.

222   Bowen felt that . . . : Joan Trader Bowen interview by the author. August 22, 2011.

222   The college did . . . : Ibid.

222   All of Mr. Toole's . . . : St. Mary's Dominican College yearbook, 1969.

223   In a reply . . . : Letter to John Toole, June 19, 1971. Box 11, Folder 13, Toole Papers.

223   Harold Toole recalls . . . : Harold Toole, Jr., interview by the author, May 9, 2009.

223   On December 28 . . . : John D. Toole, Certificate of Death. Box 11, Folder 9, Toole Papers.

223   In the spring . . . : Box 11, Folder 13, Toole Papers.

224   In March of . . . : Thelma D. Toole letter to Knopf, April 8, 1973. Box 11, Folder 13, Toole Papers.

224   Indignant when they . . . : Thelma D. Toole letter to Knopf, May 16, 1973. Box 11, Folder 13, Toole Papers.

224   She contacted literary . . . : Thelma D. Toole letter to Matson and Matson, May 8, 1973. Box 11, Folder 13, Toole Papers.

224   She informed them . . . : Thelma D. Toole letter to Knopf, May 16, 1973. Box 11, Folder 13, Toole papers.

224   "It has literary" . . . : I Walk in the World for My Son, film.

224   Perhaps feeling rebuffed . . . : Thelma D. Toole letter to Pelican, May 30, 1973. Box 11, Folder 13, Toole Papers.

224   In July she . . . : Thelma D. Toole letter to Harcourt, July 25, 1973. Box 11, Folder 13, Toole Papers.

225   "Each time I" . . . : Film footage of the Levy Lecture Series.

225   When asked why . . . : Ibid.

225   She spent much . . . : Thelma Toole letter to International City Bank and Trust. August 6, 1976. Box 11, Folder 13. Toole Papers.

225   She made an . . . . . . : Thelma D. Toole letter to Third Press. July 16, 1976. Box 11, Folder 13, Toole Papers.

226   One day in . . . : I Walk in the World for My Son, film.

226   She first reached . . . : Percy, "Foreword," in *A Confederacy of Dunces*.

226   She told Arthur . . . : Details of this narrative are taken from the impressions Walker Percy conveyed to his wife, Bunt Percy. Bunt Percy interview by the author, November 4, 2010.

227   "But you are" . . . : Film footage of the Levy Lecture Series.

227   He walked into . . . : Bunt Percy interview by the author, November 4, 2010.

227   Originally from a . . . : Ibid.

228   A few days . . . : Ibid.

228   He prided himself . . . : Ibid.

228   The *Chicago Tribune* . . . : Stephen E. Rubin, "The Saga of a Rejected Novelist," *Chicago Tribune*, June 29, 1980.

229   In March she . . . : Thelma D. Toole letter to *New Orleans Review*, March 21, 1978. Box 11, Folder 15, Toole Papers.

229   He saw an . . . : Faust interview by the author, June 10, 2011.

229   Meanwhile, Percy got . . . : Bunt Percy interview by the author, November 4, 2010.

230   Thelma entertained self-publication . . . : Film footage of the Levy Lecture Series.

230   On April 19 . . . : Les Phillabaum letter to Thelma D. Toole. Box 11, Folder 15, Toole Papers..

231   She claimed the . . . : Thelma D. Toole speech. Box 13, Folder 16, Toole Papers.

231   Thelma sent a . . . : Letter from LSU Press, July 10, 1979. Box 11, Folder 15, Toole Papers.

232   It was upon . . . : Bunt Percy interview by the author, November 4, 2010.

232   "the guardian spirit" . . . : Film footage of the Levy Lecture Series.

232   Before the release . . . : Form for [Arthur Ducoing], February 8, 1978. Box 11, Folder 14, Toole Papers.

232   LSU Press printed . . . : LSU contract. Toole Papers.

233   In March 1980 . . . : "John Kennedy Toole: *A Confederacy of Dunces*," in *Kirkus Reviews*, March 15, 1980.

233   A month later . . . : "*A Confederacy of Dunces*," *Publisher's Weekly*, April 11, 1980: 71.

233   In the summer and fall . . . : Comprehensive collection of reviews. Box 9, Folders 1–3, Toole Papers.

234   In 1980 in . . . : Michael O'Connel, "Observations of an Outcast," *Bloomsbury Review*, November–December 1980.

234   Even the *Chicago* . . . : Shirley Ann Grau, "Slapstick Tragedy from a Writer Rescued by Percy," *Chicago Tribune Book Review*, June 29, 1980.

234   David Shields barely . . . : David Shields, "*Confederacy of Dunces* Called Very Good Book," *Waycross Journal-Herald*, August 6, 1981.

234   Jonathan Yardley . . . : Jonathan Yardley, "A Posthumous Protege Proves Himself Worthy of Direct Comparison," *Washington Star*, July 1980.

235   Anthony Burgess imagined . . . : Anthony Burgess, "Mad Knight of New Orleans," *London Observer*, May 31, 1981.

235   And one reviewer . . . : Marcel Sauvage, "Notes: *A Confederacy of Dunces*," *San Francisco Review of Books*, November–December 1980.

236   Toole made changes . . . : Fletcher interview by the author, December 23, 2008.

236   She instructed LSU . . . : Film footage of the Levy Lecture Series.

236   David Evanier, fiction . . . : David Evanier, "Behemoth," *National Review*, June 26, 1981.

236   Evanier echoes . . . : Mikhail Bakhtin, *Rabelais and His World* (Bloomington: Indiana University Press, 1984).

237   It was one . . . : Edwin McDowell, "Five Nominated for Writing Prize," *New York Times*, February 12, 1981.

237   She was interviewed . . . : Fletcher, *Ken and Thelma*.

237   And a few . . . : Ibid.

237   However, when it . . . : Film footage of the Levy Lecture Series.

Chapter 14: Fame

239   Joel Fletcher, who . . . : Fletcher, *Ken and Thelma*.

239   She told the . . . : Typescript of interview with Tom Snyder. Box 14, Folder 8, Toole Papers.

239   When Dalt Wonk . . . : Wonk, "John Kennedy Toole's Odyssey Among the Dunces: Part 2."

240   And when . . . : Mary Vespa, "A Much Rejected Novel Creates a Literary Sensation Thanks to an Indomitable Mother," *People*, September 1980: 56–57.

240   Nola Schneider wrote . . . : Toole Papers.

240   Aunt Thelma, I . . . : Marion Toole Hosli letter to Thelma D. Toole. Box 11, Folder 19, Toole Papers.

241   In a 1981 . . . : Film footage of the Levy Lecture Series.

241   And yet Nick . . . : Polites interview by the author, February 14, 2009.

241   When asked if . . . : Film footage of the Levy Lecture Series.

241   She claimed that . . . : Ibid.

241 And in this . . . : Vespa, "A Much Rejected Novel Creates a Literary Sensation Thanks to an Indomitable Mother."

242 There remained, according . . . : Korda, *Another Life*.

242 But in a . . . : Sudie Frese letter to Thelma D. Toole. October 1, 1980. Box 11, Folder 20, Toole Papers

243 Southeastern Louisiana University . . . : SLU honorary diploma. Box 11, Folder 20. Toole Papers.

243 Barely ambulatory, standing . . . : Film footage of the Levy Lecture Series.

243 She never failed . . . : Ibid.

243 Occasionally she claimed . . . : Laborde, "Remembering a Pulitzer Winner."

244 She confessed she . . . : Film footage of the Levy Lecture Series.

244 Despising the name . . . : Ibid.

244 The trite expression . . . : Thelma D. Toole letter to Mr. Langdon and Mr. Wolf. January 24, 1983. Box 12, Folder 13. Toole Papers.

245 Still, in the . . . : Jane Bethune interview in *John Kennedy Toole: The Omega Point*.

245 In a promotional photo . . . : Karen Kane, "Anatomy of a Pulitzer Prize," *Texas Houston Chronicle Magazine*, December 2, 1984. Photos by Larry Reese.

245 One writer sent . . . : Gus Levy letter to Robert Gottlieb. Box 12, Folder 4. June 1, 1981. Toole Papers.

245 Through a series . . . : David Rosen letter. Box 13, Folder 6. Toole Papers.

246 She attempted to . . . : Bunt Percy interview by the author, November 4, 2010.

246 And in the . . . : Martin interview by the author, May 5, 2011.

246 One afternoon she . . . : Bunt Percy interview by the author, November 4, 2010.

246 At a promotional . . . : Ibid.

246 And when Joel . . . : Fletcher, *Ken and Thelma*.

247 In February of . . . : Thelma D. Toole letter to David Treen. Box 11, Folder 3, Toole Papers.

248 On March 4 . . . : Cyrus Greco letter to Thelma D. Toole. Box 11, Folder 3. Toole Papers.

248 In October the . . . : Letter from heirs to Thelma D. Toole. October 3, 1983. Box 11, Folder 3. Toole Papers.

248 In July, Thelma's . . . : John L. Hantel letter to Brian M. Bégué. July 5, 1984. Box 11, Folder 3. Toole Papers.

249 And in late . . . : Fletcher, *Ken and Thelma*.

249   Her son had . . . : Wonk, "John Kennedy Toole's Odyssey Among the Dunces: Part 2."

249   In her will . . . : Kenneth Holditch, "Introduction," in *The Neon Bible*, by John Kennedy Toole (New York: Grove Press, 1989), v–xi.

249   Rhoda Faust filed . . . : Susan Feeney, "Suit Adds Chapter to an Early Work by Author of 'Dunces'," *Times Picayune-The States Item*, August 10, 1984: Book A1, 4.

250   And the Tooles . . . : Harold Toole, Jr., interview by the author, March 2, 2009.

250   Thelma once claimed . . . : Film footage of the Levy Lecture Series.

250   The director and . . . : Cath Clarke, *The Directors: Terence Davies*, n.d., accessed on July 12, 2011, at http://www.timeout.com/film/features/show-feature/2761/2/.

251   She established the . . . : Geiser interview by the author, June 2008.

251   And with a . . . : Correspondence from Tulane anonymously given to author. January 1, 2010.

251   She intended to . . . : Hantel interview by the author, April 13, 2011.

251   Shortly after her . . . : Geiser interview by the author, June 2008.

Chapter 15: Toward the Heavens

253   Statements like the . . . : Georgia Brown, "The Fire Within," review of *The Neon Bible*, *Village Voice*, February 27, 1996: 61.

253   In 2007 Michael . . . : Michael Hardin, "Between Queer Performances," *Southern Literary Journal*, 2007: 58–77.

254   Despite his sympathy . . . : Raymond-Jean Frontain, "John Kennedy Toole," 2004, accessed July 14, 2011, at http://www.glbtq.com/literature/toole_jk,4.html.

255   In September of . . . : Robert Coles, *The Flora Levy Lecture in the Humanities Volume II: Gravity and Grace in the Novel A Confederacy of Dunces* (Lafayette: University of Southwestern Louisiana, 1981).

255   When the Italian . . . : Luciana Bianciardi letter to Thelma D. Toole, May 25, 1984. Toole Papers.

256   H. Vernon Leighton . . . : H. Vernon Leighton. "Evidence of influences on John Kennedy Toole's *A Confederacy of Dunces*, including Geoffrey Chaucer," accessed December 12, 2011 at http://www.winona.edu/library/staff/vl/toole/Leighton_Toole_Chaucer.html.

256 Rudnicki asserts that . . . : Robert Rudnicki, "Euphues and the Anatomy of Influence: John Lyly, Harold Bloom, James Olney, and the Construction of John Kennedy Toole's Ignatius," *Mississippi Quarterly*, 2009: 281–302.

258 His friend that . . . : Lynda Martin letter to Thelma D. Toole. April 21, 1981, Box 12, Folder 3, Toole Papers.

258 And . . . "taken his place among them" . . . : Ibid.

Index

and frustrations and
disappointments as writer, 1,
39, 156, 219
and girls and women, 29, 30–31,
40, 57, 58–59, 68, 74, 91–95,
109–111, 168–169, 186–187, 192,
215, 219
and Haspel Brothers job, 60
in high school, 21, 23–25, 26, 27,
29, 30–32, 33–34, 39–41, 48,
53, 56, 58
and homosexuality, xiii,
96–97, 132, 214–215, 216, 253–
254
humor and wit of, xiv, xv, 16, 25,
26, 40, 43, 52–55, 56, 59, 76,
84, 93, 98, 99, 102, 105, 109,
115, 121–122, 136, 137, 154, 157,
167, 184, 194, 203, 211, 236
at Hunter College (*See* Hunter
College: and Toole)
and impersonations and
mimicking, 17, 21, 25, 27, 59,
89–90, 93, 98, 105, 117, 118,
122, 194, 201
and Kennedy assassination,
170
in kindergarten and grade school,
14–17, 20
and liberalism and political
sensibilities, 113
and literary criticism, 71–73, 77,
78
literary influences on, xi, 162, 256
master's thesis of, 77

mental illness of, xi, xiv–xv, 189–
199, 205, 206, 213, 214, 215,
216, 219, 235
and Mississippi visit (1954),
34–36, 142
and money, 47–48, 60, 64, 77,
78, 94, 99–100, 101, 106, 107,
108, 116, 126–128, 132, 140,
160, 162, 166, 189, 205, 210
and Monroe, 25, 54, 131–132
and Morter suicide attempt,
158–159
and mother's musical talents, 96,
210
and mother's stifling, dominance,
protectiveness, and narcissism,
31, 57, 87, 176–177, 191, 216
narrative voice in letters of, 130,
137
nervous breakdown of, 177–178
and New Orleans' attraction and
fascination, 2, 11, 52, 70, 77,
99, 117, 139, 142, 149, 165, 173,
185, 194
and New York City's attraction,
fascination, and repellency, 40,
47, 52, 56, 60, 63–64, 68–69,
70–71, 73, 76, 77, 78–79, 100,
101, 102, 104–108, 113–114, 116,
117, 184
and observations of people, 1, 2,
11, 14–15, 21, 24–25, 26, 27,
44, 56, 59, 60, 69, 70, 88, 89,
98–99, 113, 121, 122, 133–136,
143–144, 179, 201, 228

CPSIA information can be obtained
at www.ICGtesting.com
Printed in the USA
LVHW031611100521
687012LV00015B/772

9 780306 821912